THE POSSIBILITY OF
COOPERATION

STUDIES IN RATIONALITY
AND SOCIAL CHANGE

Michael Taylor
University of Washington, Seattle

THE POSSIBILITY OF
COOPERATION

CAMBRIDGE
UNIVERSITY PRESS

Published in collaboration with Maison des Sciences de l'Homme, Paris

Published by the Press Syndicate of the University of Cambridge
The Pitt Building, Trumpington Street, Cambridge CB2 1RP
40 West 20th Street, New York, NY 10011, USA
10 Stamford Road, Oakleigh, Victoria 3166, Australia

First published 1987
Reprinted 1992

Printed in the United States of America

ISBN 82 00 18386 6 paperback (Scandinavia only)

British Library cataloguing in publication data
Taylor, Michael, 1942–
The possibility of cooperation—[Rev.ed.]
—(Studies in rationality and social change)
1. Anarchism   2. State, The
3. Prisoners' dilemma game
I. Title   II. Taylor, Michael, 1942-
Anarchy and cooperation   III. Series
320.1'01   HX833

Library of Congress cataloging in publication data
Taylor, Michael
The possibility of cooperation.
(Studies in rationality and social change)
Rev. ed. of: Anarchy and cooperation. c1976.
Bibliography.
Includes index.
1. Anarchism   I. Taylor, Michael
Anarchy and cooperation.   II. Title.   III. Series.
HX833.T38   1987   320.5'7   86-30969

ISBN 0-521-33990-1 paperback

Contents

This book is a revised edition of
the author's *Anarchy and Cooperation*
first published in 1976 by
John Wiley and Sons Ltd
and now out of print

Preface

The Possibility of Cooperation is, I hope, much more than the preceding statement might suggest, 'a new edition of *Anarchy and Cooperation*'. The chapter dealing with the political theories of Hobbes and Hume is the only one to survive intact, though the short chapter on altruism and the rather informal Epilogue contain much of the corresponding chapters of the earlier book. All the rest has been substantially re-cast. Amongst other things, I have devoted much more of the book to the theory of collective action, which in the years since writing *Anarchy and Cooperation* I have come to see as absolutely fundamental to the study of politics and history, and in particular I have devoted more space to the theory of conditional cooperation in supergames and at the same time tried to make the formal treatment of this subject more accessible to the non-mathematical reader than it was before.

Anarchy and Cooperation was constructed as a critique of the liberal theory of the state, according to which the state is necessary because people, being rational, will not voluntarily cooperate to provide themselves with public goods, in particular the basic public goods of social order and defence. At the heart of this critique was a study of the Prisoners' Dilemma supergame, for it had been (as it still is) widely assumed that the problem of public goods provision, or 'the collective action problem' more generally, has the form of a Prisoners' Dilemma. So in the central chapters of *Anarchy and Cooperation* I wanted to question whether the Prisoners' Dilemma game was the correct representation of preferences in public goods interactions and then, assuming that it was, to examine the prospects for voluntary cooperation in this game. At that time there had been little theoretical study of the iterated Prisoners' Dilemma, especially in its N-person form. Yet it

seemed obvious to me that the one-shot game had little to do with
anything of importance in the real world and that most problems of
public goods interaction and of collective action generally had more
than two players. Accordingly, I devoted the central chapter of *Anarchy
and Cooperation* to an analysis of the two-person and N-person
Prisoners' Dilemma supergames (in which the basic games are played an
indefinite number of times).

This purely formal treatment of collective action and the Prisoners'
Dilemma supergame could be – and generally was – read and used
independently of the critique of the liberal theory of the state. In this new
edition, the critique stands, though parts of the old final chapter
('Anarchy') have been rewritten and are offered less confidently in the
Epilogue. (Further doubts about 'anarchy' have also crept into my
Community, Anarchy and Liberty, which is in some respects a companion
piece to this book, and some day I hope to publish a third volume giving
a fuller and more historical account of the state.) But, as before, the
analysis of collective action and the Prisoners' Dilemma supergame can
be read – and assessed – independently of the critique, and this part of the
book has been substantially recast and extended. Chapter 3 of the old
book – the central chapter dealing with the Prisoners' Dilemma
supergame – has been almost completely rewritten: the material has
been re-organized, some of the arguments have been modified and extended, and several new sections have been added. I have endeavoured
to make the analysis more accessible to readers with little training in
mathematics, and in pursuing this end I found that I could derive the
same results – and indeed strengthen and extend them – using far less
algebra. The new treatment is split between two chapters. To the first of
these, dealing with the two-person supergame, I have added amongst
other things a brief section commenting critically on related work by
Robert Axelrod and Russell Hardin published since *Anarchy and
Cooperation* appeared. All the results in this chapter which formerly gave
only necessary conditions for various equilibria now provide conditions
which are both necessary and sufficient. To the second of these chapters,
dealing with the N-person supergame, I have added, partly in response
to a critical point raised by several readers of *Anarchy and Cooperation*, a
section which shows how this game can give rise to a Chicken game (thus
introducing a troublesome indeterminacy into the analysis of the N-
person case).

The brief account of the effects of altruism on behaviour in Prisoners' Dilemma games has also been pruned of some unnecessary algebra. Removing much of the mathematics from this chapter and from the treatment of the Prisoners' Dilemma supergame has made redundant the old chapter 5, which provided an informal summary of the mathematical parts of the book, and I have therefore removed it.

Chapter 2 is almost entirely new. Amongst other things it develops an argument to the effect that in public goods problems individual preferences at any point in time are not necessarily those of a Prisoners' Dilemma; that in fact many interesting public goods problems, both two-person and N-person, are better represented by Assurance and Chicken games; and that where individuals can choose from a *continuous* range of strategies their preferences are quite likely to be those of a Chicken-like game or of a hybrid between a Chicken and an Assurance game. In all of these cases, arguably, *some* cooperation is more likely than in the case of a Prisoners' Dilemma, even when the game is played only once. Chicken emerges from this discussion, and from the account in chapter 4 of the N-person Prisoners' Dilemma supergame, as an important game. A little analysis of this neglected game is offered here, but much more needs to be done.

Much of chapter 1 is also new (i.e., not to be found in *Anarchy and Cooperation*). Partly in order to make the book a little more self-contained, I have given in the opening section a fuller summary of Olson's 'logic of collective action' and in particular his important argument that the larger a group is, the less likely are its members to cooperate voluntarily in the provision of a public good. I agree with those writers who have shown that this 'size' effect is not always present, but I want also to argue that not too much weight should be attached to any of these 'size' arguments – Olson's or his critics' – because the *model* from which they derive, being entirely static, is an unrealistic representation of almost all problems of public goods provision, which are of course typically recurring. In a dynamical formulation, but not of course in a static one, there is the possibility of *conditional* cooperation; and I would argue that the 'size' effect which should be taken most seriously is the increased difficulty of conditional cooperation as group size increases.

Many of the arguments in this book apply not just to problems of public goods provision but to 'collective action problems', a much larger category. So I added to chapter 1 a brief attempt to characterize this category. I have also added a new section which both characterizes the range of possible solutions to collective action problems and examines the particular claims that such problems can be solved by political entrepreneurs, by the establishment of property rights and by norms.

I have made no attempt to provide a comprehensive survey of developments in the study of public goods, collective action and supergames that have occurred since the publication of *Anarchy and Cooperation*. Although I have commented briefly on the most closely related work (such as that of Hardin and Axelrod) and have made a number of excisions and revisions that were prompted by some of these developments, I have not, for example, reviewed either the extensive recent theoretical work of economists and game theorists on supergames or the even more extensive experimental work of psychologists, sociologists and others on iterated Prisoners' Dilemmas. I still believe that, if problems of public goods provision or other collective action problems are to be modelled as iterated games, then the appropriate model is a game iterated an indefinite number of times in which players discount future payoffs. But although most economists seem to share this view, most of the recent *mathematical* work on supergames treats either *finitely* iterated games or infinite supergames *without* discounting. I have, however, provided some references to this work for those wishing to pursue it. As for the vast experimental literature, I remain unpersuaded that its results can tell us much about the real world beyond the experiments. There are two general problems with this literature. First, the experiments are of short duration relative to the time span of the processes in the real world they are supposed to simulate; so discounting plays no role in the experiments, while in the real world it is crucial. Second, the experimental payoffs are generally too small to elicit rational behaviour. It is therefore not surprising that these experiments yield such mixed results, with some studies finding significant free riding and 'size' effects and others not.

Much more promising, in my view, are *historical* studies of collective action. I have not tried to summarize such studies, which are thin on the ground, for the best of them are still in progress and yet to be published, but a good example of the sort of thing I have in mind is John Bowman's forthcoming study of collective action amongst capitalists (based on his doctoral dissertation, 'Economic competition and collective action: the politics of market organization in the bituminous coal industry, 1880–1940', University of Chicago, 1984), which amongst other things uses the theory of conditional cooperation in Prisoners' Dilemma supergames to scrutinize the historical data. Arduous though it is compared with experimental work, this, it seems to me, is the kind of empirical work we need more of.

Anarchy and Cooperation owed much to the kind help of Brian Barry, Alan Carling, Ian Grant and Michael Nicholson, who commented extensively on the manuscript. If I had heeded more of Brian Barry's advice at that time, much of the rewriting that has gone into this new version would not have been necessary. For their help in various ways in the preparation of this edition I should like also to thank Jon Elster, who suggested it; Russell Hardin, who in conversation has helped me to clarify a number of points; Dawn Rossit, who as my research assistant in Seattle in the autumn of 1985 gave me valuable help in connection with the discussion of property rights in chapter 1; and Hugh Ward, who collaborated with me in work on the game of Chicken on which a part of chapter 2 is based. The first edition was written during 1973–74 when I was a Fellow at the Netherlands Institute for Advanced Study, whose staff I would like to thank for their hospitality and help. For freedom to work on this new edition, I am grateful to the University of Essex, and for provision of a research assistant and for general support I would like to thank the chairman of the Department of Political Science at the University of Washington in Seattle.

M.J.T.

1. Introduction: the problem of collective action

The most persuasive justification of the state is founded on the argument that, without it, people would not successfully cooperate in realizing their common interests and in particular would not provide themselves with certain public goods: goods, that is to say, which any member of the public may benefit from, whether or not he or she contributes in any way to their provision. The most appealing version of this justification would confine the argument about voluntary cooperation to what are supposed to be the most fundamental public goods: goods (or services) which are thought to be preconditions of the pursuit and attainment of all other valued ends, including less basic public goods, and are therefore desired by *everyone* within the jurisdiction of the state in question.

The Possibility of Cooperation is a critique of this justification of the state, and the heart of the critique (chapters 2–4 below) is a detailed study of cooperation in the absence of the state and of other kinds of coercion. (The arguments about public goods provision and the theory of cooperation which make up these chapters can be read – and assessed – independently of the critique of the Hobbesian justification of the state.)

Hobbes's *Leviathan* was the first full expression of this way of justifying the state. The public goods with which he was principally concerned were social order – domestic peace and security – and defence against foreign aggression. Without these, very little else that was worth having could be had. Without internal and external security, there would be not only actual violence but such pervasive uncertainty as to undermine the incentive to invest resources in any projects with delayed returns. But although everyone would prefer the condition of peace and security that mutual restraint ensures to the 'war of all against all' that is the result of everyone pursuing his own interests without restraint, no individual has the incentive, in the absence of the state, to restrain himself. It is therefore rational, says Hobbes, for everyone to institute a government with sufficient power to ensure that everybody keeps the peace.[1]

Many writers who came after Hobbes, including some who professed no sympathy with what they took to be Hobbes's ideas, have taken over the core of his case for the state. Most economists who nowadays write about public goods believe that the failure of people to provide themselves voluntarily with these goods constitutes at least a *prima facie* case for state activity, and most of them presume that the state is the *only* means for remedying this failure.[2] (For nearly all the rest, the remedy is to establish or extend private property rights. I'll comment briefly on this view later in the chapter.)

Of course, many people believe that the state can be justified on further grounds and that it has functions other than that of providing public goods. Certainly, modern states do more than provide such goods. However, the justification I wish to criticize here is common to the arguments of nearly all those who believe that the state is necessary. Its persuasiveness lies in the fact that the state, on this view, exists to further *common* interests, to do what *everybody* wants done. Other arguments – for example, that income redistribution is desirable and can be brought about only through the intervention of the state – do not appeal to common interests, not, at any rate, in an obvious or uncontroversial way.

In recent years, this argument about the necessity of the state has found new supporters amongst those concerned with the degradation of the environment, the depletion of non-renewable resources and rapid population growth. According to them, people will not *voluntarily* refrain from discharging untreated wastes into rivers and lakes, from hunting whales and other species threatened with extinction, from having 'too many children', and so on. Only powerful state action, they say, can solve or avert these problems, which are the consequence of failures to provide public goods (and more generally 'non-excludable' goods – about which more later). For many environmentalists, some of these public goods are at least as fundamental as peace and security were for Hobbes. Continued failure to provide them will eventually result in ecological catastrophe. Without them, the life of man will not just be 'solitary, poore, nasty, brutish, and short'; it will be impossible.[3]

There have of course been other responses to the environmental crisis. In particular, some writers, who probably did not think of themselves as anarchists, have come to embrace essentially communitarian anarchist ideas. However, of those who desire on ecological grounds the goal of a social organization along communitarian anarchist lines, there are very few who believe that a transition to such a society can be made without extensive state activity.[4]

As for the members of governments themselves, and indeed of most political parties, especially in industrialized countries, they generally do not recognize that there is or will be an environmental crisis and they believe, not unnaturally, that pollution and resource depletion are problems which can be adequately dealt with by minor modifications within the present institutional framework of whatever country they happen to live in.[5] Generally speaking, the proposed modifications involve an extension of state activity, in the form of state-enforced pollution standards and resource depletion quotas, taxes on industrial pollution, government subsidies and tax credits for the development of pollution control technology, and so on. Most economists who have written on problems of pollution and resource depletion have also confined their discussions to 'solutions' of this sort, or otherwise have recommended the extension of private property rights.

Much of what I shall have to say in this book will in fact apply, not just to the voluntary provision of public goods but to 'collective action problems', a much larger category. The defining characteristic of a collective action problem, as I shall use this expression, is very roughly that rational egoists are unlikely to succeed in cooperating to promote their common interests. (I will clarify this in a later section.) On this account, as we shall see, the category of collective action problems includes many but not all public goods problems. There is, in particular, a very important class of collective action problems which arise in connection with the use of resources to which there is open access – resources, that is, which nobody is prevented from using. These resources need not be public goods, as I will define them shortly. Garrett Hardin's well-known 'tragedy of the commons' concerns resources of this kind.[6]

Hardin asks us to imagine a common, a pasture open to all. The village herdsmen keep animals on the common. Each herdsman is assumed to seek to maximize his own gain. As long as the total number of animals is below the carrying capacity of the common, a herdsman can add an animal to his herd without affecting the amount of grazing of any of the animals, including his own. But beyond this point, the 'tragedy of the commons' is set in motion. Asking himself now whether he should add another animal to his herd, he sees that this entails for him a gain and a loss: on the one hand, he obtains the benefit from this animal's yield (milk, meat or whatever); on the other hand, the yield of each of his animals is reduced because there is now overgrazing. The benefit obtained from the additional animal accrues entirely to the herdsman. The effect of overgrazing, on the other hand, is shared by all the herdsmen; every one of them suffers a slight loss. Thus, says Hardin, the benefit to the herdsman who adds the animal is greater than *his* loss. He therefore adds an animal to the common. For the same reason, he finds that it pays him to add a second animal, and a third, a fourth and so on. The same is true for each of the other herdsmen. The result is that the herdsmen collectively bring about a situation in which each of them derives less benefit from his herd than he did before the carrying capacity of the common was exceeded. The process of adding animals may indeed continue until the ability of the common to support livestock collapses entirely.

For similar reasons, many species of fish and whales are hunted without limit and in some cases brought close to extinction: the oceans are like a great common. For similar reasons, too, lakes and rivers are polluted, since each polluter finds that the costs of treating his wastes before discharging them or of modifying his product are too great in comparison with what he suffers from the decline in the quality of the air or water caused by his effluent.

In all these situations, we can say that it is in every individual's interest not to restrain himself (from adding animals to the common, polluting the lake, etc.) but the result of everyone acting without restraint is a state of affairs in which every individual is less well off than he would be if everybody restrained themselves.

In such situations, we might expect people to make an agreement in which they all promised to restrain themselves. However, in the absence of the state (or some other form of coercion), no individual has any greater incentive to abide by the agreement than he had to restrain himself before the agreement was made.

I shall later question whether grazing commons – such as those which were part of the European open-field systems or those which were once widespread in pastoral economies – do in fact typically have open access. But certainly there are many such resources to be found in other contexts. The recent history of the whale 'fisheries' provides a sad example. During the 1950s and 1960s, unlimited killing of blue and fin-back whales, which are the biggest, brought these two species close to extinction. When stocks of blues and fin-backs became very low, the other large species were hunted without limit. In each case the annual harvest far exceeded the maximum sustainable yield, that is, the maximum number which can be replaced each year through reproduction (and the whale hunters knew this). The profitability of whaling declined, and most of the former whaling countries were obliged one by one to leave the industry (so that, by 1968, there were only two countries, Japan and the USSR, left in the field). It seems fairly certain that if it were not for the diminished profits from hunting a sparse population, the blue whale and other species would in fact have been hunted to extinction. After the Second World War, the International Whaling Commission was set up by the seventeen countries who were then interested in whaling and was charged with regulating harvests and ensuring the survival of threatened species. Until very recently, this Commission, which has no powers of enforcement, has not been very successful. Its members were often unable to agree to impose the quotas recommended by biologists, or else they could agree only to limits in excess of these recommendations; and when the Commission did decide either to limit harvests or to protect a species completely, the agreement was not always observed by every country.[7]

The provision of public and other non-excludable goods

Before embarking on a detailed analysis, we need to define a little more carefully some of the terms that have already been used, and in particular the notions of a 'public good' and a 'collective action problem'.

I shall say that a good or service is a *public good* (or collective good) if it is in some degree indivisible and non-excludable. A good is said to exhibit perfect *indivisibility* or *jointness of supply* (with respect to a given set of individuals, or public) if, once produced, any given unit can be made available to every member of the public, or equivalently if any individual's consumption or use of the good does not reduce the amount available to others.[8] A good is said to exhibit *non-excludability* (with respect to some group) if it is impossible to prevent individual members of the group from consuming it or if such exclusion is 'prohibitively costly' (a notion whose precise definition matters for some purposes but not for mine here).

A perfectly *divisible* good is one that can be divided between individuals. Once any part of it is appropriated by any individual, the same part cannot be made available to others; and once any unit of it is consumed by any individual, the amount available for consumption by others is reduced by the whole of that unit. A loaf of bread and a pot of honey are examples of perfectly divisible goods. A good which is perfectly divisible is called a *private good*. Thus, in order to be public, a good must exhibit some degree of indivisibility or jointness.[9]

A good may be indivisible yet excludable. A road or bridge or park can be provided in this form. Once supplied to one individual, it *can* be made available to others, but it need not be, for it is possible and may not be prohibitively costly to exclude particular individuals. Hence tolls and admission charges can be imposed. Goods like these can be provided in an excludable or non-excludable mode. Indivisibility, then, does not imply non-excludability. Furthermore, divisibility does not entail excludability, although important examples of non-excludable, divisible goods are not easy to come by: economists have suggested such examples as a garden of flowers, whose nectar can be appropriated by individual bees but particular bees cannot be excluded from consumption.

If an individual is not excluded from consumption or use of a public good, it is possible for him to be a *free rider* on the efforts of others, that is, he can consume or use the public good that is provided by others (unless of course everyone else tries to free-ride as well!). Whether or not he will in fact be a free rider is something we have to examine.

Free rider problems (and hence, as we shall see, collective action problems) can arise where there is non-excludability but not indivisibility. In fact non-excludability (or *de facto* non-exclusion) and divisibility (at least in principle) characterize Garrett Hardin's 'commons', or any resource to which there is open access, such as a common fishing ground, a common underground reservoir of oil or water, or the open range on the Great Plains before any property rights were established (including the 'common property' rights that the cattlemen tried to maintain when they formed associations to regulate access and use). I will have a little more to say about such resources in a later section. With some of them, exclusion is possible and economically feasible, but whether or not there is in fact exclusion, consumption or use by one individual reduces the amount available to others and any cutting back on consumption by one individual allows others to consume more.

Most, if not all, public goods interactions are characterized by a certain degree of *rivalness*. It is normally said that a good is *rival* to the extent that the consumption of a unit of the good by one individual decreases the *benefits* to others who consume that same unit. Obviously, in the case of a perfectly divisible good the consumption of a particular unit prevents any other individual from consuming it at all, so that there can be no question of his benefiting from consumption. In this case we might say that the good is perfectly rival. But non-rivalness is not the same thing as indivisibility, as some writers like to say, even though they are usually closely associated. Where there is some degree of divisibility, consumption reduces the *amount* available to others; but where there is some degree of rivalness, consumption reduces the *benefits* to other consumers. An individual's benefit from consumption may not change at all as the amount available for consumption declines, until some threshold of 'crowding' is reached. In fact, although others' consumption usually *lowers* an individual's utility – as is normally the case with congested parks, beaches and roads and with various forms of pollution – some individuals' utilities may *rise* as the number of other consumers increases, at least up to a point; they may, for example, prefer a semi-crowded beach or park to an empty one. This brings out the point that rivalness, unlike indivivisibility, is strictly speaking a property of individuals (or of their utility functions), not of the goods themselves.

Rivalness is clearly important in the analysis of collective action problems. As we would expect – and as we shall see in the next chapter – it plays a crucial role in the analysis of 'size' effects. For just as the alternatives actually available to an individual must change as the number of people in the group increases if there is some degree of divisibility, so the *utilities* of these alternatives must change with group size if there is rivalness.

I said in an earlier section that social order and national defence are public goods. This needs some qualifying and we are now in a position to do so. National defence can in fact be decomposed (on a first rough cut) into deterrence, which is a pure public good because it is both perfectly indivisible and completely non-excludable, and protection from attack, which is imperfectly indivisible and more or less excludable depending on the form it takes. (And of course the production of the means to these ends produces incidental private goods, including income for shareholders and employees of business firms.)[10] The security of persons and their property which I have taken to be constitutive of social order is similarly the product of a variety of goods and services, which range (in a modern society) from purely private goods like locks and private bodyguards through such services as police forces and law courts to deterrence, which, again, can be purely indivisible – as it would be if the fact that attack was deterred on one individual did not diminish the deterrent effect with respect to other individuals.[11]

Under what circumstances, then, will people cooperate to provide a public good or any non-excludable good which the members of a group have a common interest in providing? The now standard answer to this question (which, however, needs to be qualified, as we shall see) is the one provided by Mancur Olson in his well-known study, *The Logic of Collective Action*. Olson's main contention is that 'the larger a group is, the farther it will fall short of providing an optimal supply of any collective good, and the less likely that it will act to obtain even a minimal amount of such a good. In short, the larger the group, the less likely it will further its common interests.'[12]

There are three arguments in support of this conclusion to be found in Olson's book. Before setting them out, we need some definitions. A group is *privileged* if it pays at least one of its members to provide some amount of the public good unilaterally, that is, to bear the full cost of providing it alone. Any group which is not privileged is said to be *latent*. Where the group is privileged, there is, in Olson's view, a 'presumption' that the public good will be provided; but there should be no such presumption in the case of a latent group. Nevertheless, some latent groups (in Olson's account, which is a little muddy at this point) are sufficiently small that through some sort of strategic interaction amongst their members they may succeed in providing some amount of the public good. (They do not have so many members, says Olson, that an individual contribution to the provision of the public good will go unnoticed by other members.) Such groups are called *intermediate*. The remaining latent groups are so large that this sort of strategic interaction, depending as it does on individual contributions being 'noticeable', is impossible and an individual will contribute only if there is a *selective incentive* to do so, that is, the individual receives a (private) benefit if and only if he contributes and/or incurs a (private) cost if and only if he fails to contribute. Thus, for example, trade unions, which are founded primarily to provide for their members certain public goods such as higher wages and better working conditions, have also had to offer prospective members sickness, unemployment and dispute benefits and other positive selective incentives, and to operate a 'closed shop' which bars non-members from employment.

In deciding whether or not to contribute or participate, the individual compares the cost to him of making his contribution and the benefit *to him* of the additional amount of the public good *provided as a result of his contribution*. The final italicized phrase encompasses both the public good which he himself directly produces or which is funded by his contribution *and* whatever additional public good is provided by the contributions that *others* may make as a result of his contribution (because their contributions are in some way contingent on his). This second component of his benefit may not be forthcoming, because the required interdependence is absent. It is this interdependence which for Olson characterizes 'intermediate' groups.

Now we can state the three arguments which Olson offers in support of his argument that larger groups are less likely than smaller groups to provide any (or an optimal) amount of the public good.[13]

(i) The larger the group, the smaller is each individual's net benefit from the public good.

(ii) The larger the group, the less the likelihood that it will be privileged or intermediate.

(iii) The larger the group, the greater the 'organization costs' of providing the public good (including the costs of communication and bargaining amongst group members and perhaps the costs of creating and maintaining a formal organization).

The last of these claims is the most straightforward. It is also no doubt empirically true, for very many cases.

The second claim is a little less straightforward. How much support it gives to the argument that a public good is more likely to be provided in smaller groups depends on the reliability of Olson's 'presumption' that the public good will be provided in privileged groups and on how likely it is that collective action will be successful in intermediate groups. Olson says that the outcome of interaction in intermediate groups is 'indeterminate'. As for the 'presumption', it is perhaps appropriate only where there is just one individual who is willing to provide the public good unilaterally (and even then there should be no presumption that an optimal amount of it will be provided). But if two or more individuals are so willing, then there could be strategic interaction amongst them . . . and the outcome of such interaction is indeterminate.[14] (The game amongst these players may be what is known as a Chicken game, which will be discussed in some detail in the next chapter.) The privileged group is therefore in effect a group within which there is an intermediate group, that is, a group with a subgroup whose members interact strategically.

The privileged group, it seems to me, is a special case of a group *with at least one subgroup whose members collectively find it worthwhile to provide some amount of the public good by themselves*, that is, a subgroup such that, if all its members cooperated to provide the public good, each of them would be better off than they would be if none of the public good was provided. Again, this does not guarantee that any of the public good will be provided, since normally there will be strategic interaction amongst the members of the subgroup, and there will be strategic behaviour of a different kind – which may also obstruct provision of the public good – resulting from the coexistence of *several* such subgroups. A group which is 'privileged' in this generalized sense is also, then, a group within which there is at least one 'intermediate' subgroup.

A final point about claim (ii) is that, as Russell Hardin has observed, there is no necessary connection, and probably a very weak correlation, between the size of a group and whether it is privileged (in Olson's or my generalized sense) or intermediate. Privileged groups can be large; groups as small as two can be intermediate or latent.[15]

It is worth emphasizing here parenthetically that it is dangerous to distinguish intermediate and latent groups, as Olson sometimes did and as so many later authors have done, by reference to whether an individual contribution is 'noticeable' or 'perceptible'. Such talk has led a number of writers astray.[16] Individual contributions can be perfectly 'noticeable' in a group which is not privileged and in which there is no strategic interaction, and which therefore fails (in the absence of selective incentives) to provide any of the public good; the failure arises because each individual's contribution, though 'noticeable', brings too little of the public good to be worth the cost of the contribution.

This leaves the first of Olson's three arguments about the effect of increasing group size. As it stands this claim is undecidable. Before we can assess it, we must know what kind of public good is involved and what is held constant as size varies, for, as Hardin says, it is not possible to increase size while holding *everything* else constant.[17] We should, however, hold as many things as possible constant if we are to isolate a pure *size* effect. Now the individual's net benefit can decrease as group size increases because the costs of providing the public good (excluding the organizational costs) increase or the individual's benefits decrease or both. If it is a pure size effect we are looking for, we should count a cost increase as support for Olson's claim only where such an increase is unavoidable. The individual's benefit, on the other hand, decreases with group size only if there is *imperfect jointness* or some degree of *rivalness* or both. If jointness is less than perfect, that is, there is some 'crowding', then the amount available to an individual decreases as the number of consumers increases. If there is rivalness, then, as size increases, the individual's benefits decrease, whether or not the amount actually available to him decreases. (Normally, rivalness is an effect of imperfect jointness. But the two are analytically distinct, and in practice the effects of rivalness can set in, as group size increases, before the effects of imperfect jointness or literal 'crowding' do.)[18]

Olson's first claim in support of the 'size' effect, then, is not necessarily true. It holds only where costs unavoidably increase with size or where there is imperfect jointness or rivalness or both. Most goods, however, exhibit *some* divisibility, and most public goods interactions exhibit *some* rivalness (which is, recall, a property of individual utility functions rather than directly of the good). That is the theoretical position; in practice, we often want to compare groups which differ not only in size but in so many other particulars that this claim is undecidable because isolating a pure size effect is impossible.

There is a more important reason for not pursuing the issue here. The argument here (following Olson and Hardin) assumes that we can simply subtract costs from benefits. This is generally unrealistic (as Olson himself admits[19]). Preferences should instead be represented by indifference maps. This will be done in chapter 2. Further, Olson's whole analysis is entirely static: the individual is supposed in effect to make just one choice, once and for all, of how much to contribute to the public good. But in the real world, most public goods interactions are dynamical. The choice of whether to contribute and how much to contribute is a recurring one. There is interaction *over time* between different individuals' choices. And the individual's intertemporal preferences (how much he discounts future relative to present benefits) matter. A dynamical analysis is the subject of chapters 3 and 4.

Olson's *model*, then, is rather unrealistic. Accordingly, not too much weight should be attached to conclusions derived from it, including conclusions about the effects of increases in group size. The size effect which I think should be taken most seriously is *the increased difficulty of conditional cooperation* in larger groups. For, as we shall see, in a dynamical analysis the provision of a public good, or collective action more generally, requires that amongst at least some members of the group there is conditional cooperation. Olson is of little help here, since he does not provide (indeed cannot provide, within his static model) an analysis of conditional cooperation or of any other sort of strategic interaction over time.

To round out this brief discussion of Olson's treatment of the problem of collective action, a comment is in order on his assumptions about incentives and individual motivation. Recall that, according to Olson, only a selective incentive will motivate the member of a large latent group (one that is too large to be intermediate) to contribute to the provision of the public good. (If Olson did not think of individual contributions in such groups as being 'imperceptible' or 'infinitesimal', he would perhaps have said: only the *addition* of a selective incentive will make the difference between contribution and non-contribution. For there is no reason why, upon the introduction of selective incentives, the public good benefit to the individual should drop out of his calculation even though it is very small: it is never so small as to be 'infinitesimal'.) In fact, says Olson, the public good lobbying efforts of large groups are *by-products* of organizations which obtain their support by offering selective incentives.[20] But this argument, as several writers have pointed out, though it helps to explain the maintenance of the organization, does not explain its origin.

Now selective incentives can be either positive or negative – providing a benefit to a contributor or imposing a cost on a non-contributor – and they are limited, in Olson's account, to either 'monetary' or 'economic' incentives and 'social' incentives. The *social* incentives essentially derive from the desire for approbation and the dislike of disapprobation, and work through mechanisms like criticism and shaming by friends and associates. Such incentives are effective only in relatively small groups. Hence, a very large group might yet succeed in providing a public good if it has a *federal* structure, for within the local branches or subgroups social incentives can operate to maintain support. (And I would add: if the local branches are small enough for social incentives to be effective, they are probably small enough for conditional cooperation to be sustained, perhaps with the help of the social incentives. More on this in later chapters.)

There are therefore at most four components in the individual's benefit-cost calculations: (i) the benefit to the individual from the increased amount of the public good provided as a result of his contribution; (ii) the cost of his contribution; (iii) the individual's portion of the costs of organization; and (iv) the 'economic' and 'social' benefits and/or costs which operate as selective incentives.

Olson explicitly excludes other types of incentives, including 'psychological' ones, such as 'the sense of guilt, or the destruction of self-esteem, that occurs when a person feels he has forsaken his moral code'.[21] The important reason why (in any explanatory theory) the range of incentives which are assumed to motivate individuals must be limited – though this is not among the reasons Olson gives for *his* restriction – is that without such a limitation a rational choice theory such as Olson's is liable to become tautologous. Three important kinds of motivation which Olson – in common with nearly all other rational choice theorists – excludes are altruistic motivations (to be discussed in chapter 5), expressive motivations and 'intrinsic' motivation by benefits got in the very act of participating in the provision of the public good as opposed to the benefits which successful provision would bring. The last two give rise to non-instrumental action.[22]

The Prisoners' Dilemma

It has been widely asserted that individual preferences in public goods interactions and in collective action problems generally are (or usually are) those of a Prisoners' Dilemma game.[23] This game is defined as follows.

Suppose that there are just two individuals (or *players*) and that each of them may choose between two courses of action (or *strategies*). The players are labelled 1 and 2 and the strategies C and D. The two players must choose strategies simultaneously, or, equivalently, each player must choose a strategy in ignorance of the other player's choice. A pair of strategies, one for each player, is called a *strategy vector*. Associated with each strategy vector is a *payoff* for each player. The payoffs can be arranged in the form of a *payoff matrix*. The payoff matrix for the two-person Prisoners' Dilemma which will be studied in this book is:

		player 2	
		C	D
player 1	C	x, x	z, y
	D	y, z	w, w

where $y > x > w > z$. Throughout the book, the usual convention is adopted that rows are chosen by player 1, columns by player 2, and that the first entry in each cell of the matrix is the payoff to player 1 and the second entry is 2's payoff.

Notice first that, since we have assumed $y > x$ and $w > z$, each player obtains a higher payoff if he chooses D than if he chooses C, *no matter what strategy the other player chooses*. Thus, it is in each player's interest to choose D, no matter what he expects the other player to do. D is said to *dominate* C for each player.

However, notice now that, if each player chooses his dominant strategy, the outcome of the game is that each player obtains a payoff w, whereas there is another outcome (C, C), which yields a higher payoff to both players, since we have assumed $x > w$.

Let us say that an outcome (Q) is Pareto-optimal if there is no other outcome which is not less preferred than Q by any player and is strictly preferred to Q by at least one player. An outcome which is not Pareto-optimal is said to be Pareto-inferior. Thus, in the two-person Prisoners' Dilemma, the outcome (D, D) is Pareto-inferior.

If the players could communicate and make agreements, they would presumably both agree to choose strategy C. But this would not resolve the 'dilemma', since neither has an incentive to keep the agreement: whether or not he thinks the other player will keep his part of the agreement, it pays him to defect from the agreement and choose D.

C and D are the conventional labels for the two strategies in the Prisoners' Dilemma. They stand for Cooperate and Defect. I use them throughout this book, though they are not entirely appropriate: one player may 'Cooperate' (choose C) by himself, and he may 'Defect' (choose D) even though no agreement has been made from which to defect. In this book, Cooperation and Defection (with capital initials) will always refer to strategies in a Prisoners' Dilemma (or, in chapter 2, in some other game).

If communication between the players is impossible or prohibited, or if communication may take place but agreements are not binding on the players, then the game is said to be *non-cooperative*. The Prisoners' Dilemma is defined to be a non-cooperative game. If it were not, there would be no 'dilemma': the players would obtain (C, C) as the outcome, rather than the Pareto-inferior outcome (D, D). In the situations of interest in this book, communication is generally possible but the players are not constrained to keep any agreements that may be made. It is the possibility of Cooperation (to achieve the outcome (C, C)) in the *absence* of such constraint that will be of interest.

As a generalization of this two-person game, an N-person Prisoners' Dilemma can be defined as follows. Each of the N players has two strategies, C and D, available to him. For each player, D dominates C, that is, each player obtains a higher payoff if he chooses D than if he chooses C, no matter what strategies the other players choose. However, every player prefers the outcome $(C, C, \ldots, C)$ at which everybody Cooperates to the outcome $(D, D, \ldots, D)$ at which everybody Defects. Thus, as in the two-person game, every player has a dominant strategy but if every player uses his dominant strategy the outcome is Pareto-inferior.

Two-person and N-person Prisoners' Dilemmas can both be defined in the more general case when any finite number of strategies is available to each player. The generalization, which could be made in several ways, must at least have the characteristic that the predicted outcome is Pareto-inferior. In particular, it could again be stipulated that every player has a strategy which dominates each of the others, and if every player uses his dominant strategy the outcome is Pareto-inferior. I shall not elaborate on this here, as my discussion in this book will mainly be confined to the two-strategy games, though in chapter 2 I shall also consider games in which each individual can choose to contribute a continuously variable amount within some range.

Let us go back now to the 'tragedy of the commons'. In Garrett Hardin's account, each individual has in effect a dominant strategy: to add an animal to his herd on the common, to discharge his sewage untreated, to kill as many whales as possible and so on. Each of these corresponds to strategy D. The alternative, strategy C, is to refrain from doing these things. Hardin assumes, in effect, that D yields the highest payoff to each individual, no matter what strategies the other individuals choose (that is, no matter how many of them Cooperate); and he assumes that every individual prefers the mutual Cooperation outcome $(C, C, \ldots, C)$ to the mutual Defection outcome $(D, D, \ldots, D)$. In other words, individual preferences are assumed to be those of an N-person Prisoners' Dilemma.

Russell Hardin has argued explicitly that public goods interaction in sufficiently large groups – in fact 'the collective action problem' more generally – can be represented by the N-person Prisoners' Dilemma.[24] His analysis is as follows. Suppose that each of N individuals has the choice (and only the choice) between contributing and not contributing one unit of the cost of producing a non-excludable good (one unit of a *numeraire* private good) and that every unit contributed produces an amount of the public good with benefit r. Suppose that each individual's utility is nr/N if he does not contribute and $nr/N - 1$ if he does, where n is the total number of units contributed. (Notice that this means that the public good exhibits some rivalness: each individual's utility declines with increasing N, which is the number of individuals who actually consume the good, since nobody is excluded.) Then, if m *other* individuals contribute, an individual's utility is mr/N if he does not contribute and $(m + 1)r/N - 1$ if he does. Thus, the first of these utilities exceeds the second if and only if $N > r$, which is independent of m. In other words, no matter how many other individuals contribute, it does not pay anyone to contribute as long as the size of the public (N) exceeds the ratio of benefits to costs (r). When $N > r$, the game is an N-person Prisoners' Dilemma (as defined above): each individual has a dominant strategy, and the outcome which results when everyone chooses his dominant strategy is for everyone less preferable than another outcome.

But when $N < r$, the dominant strategy for every individual is to contribute and the resulting outcome is the only Pareto-optimal position.

This argument, if correct, would apply also to the public goods with which Hobbes was chiefly concerned, namely domestic peace and security and national defence. I shall indeed show (in chapter 6) that Hobbes assumed men's preferences in the absence of the state to be those of a Prisoners' Dilemma game. The remainder of Hobbes's theory can then be summarized, somewhat crudely, as follows: (a) in the absence of any coercion, it is in each individual's interest to choose strategy D; the outcome of the game is therefore mutual Defection; but every individual prefers the mutual Cooperation outcome; (b) the only way to ensure that the preferred outcome is obtained is to establish a government with sufficient power to ensure that it is in every man's interest to choose C.

This is the argument which I wish to criticize in this book. But there is one element of the argument which I shall not quarrel with, namely, the analysis of the Prisoners' Dilemma given above. If individual preferences in the provision of a public good are in fact those of a Prisoners' Dilemma, then it is quite correct to conclude that the players will not voluntarily Cooperate. To avoid any misunderstanding, I emphasize that the conclusion is correct no matter what the entries in the payoff matrix (which is assumed to be a Prisoners' Dilemma) actually represent, just as long as it is assumed that each player is concerned only to maximize his own payoff. Of course, the payoffs may not reflect *all* the incentives affecting the individuals in the situation in question. The conclusion still follows logically; but it is possible to argue that the payoff matrix is a poor description of the relevant real world situation and that in reality the players *do* Cooperate, because the omitted incentives are more important than those reflected in the payoff matrix.

In the next three chapters, the payoffs are assumed *not* to reflect, *inter alia*, (i) incentives due to external coercion, including that applied or threatened by the state or any other external agency or by other members of the group (apart from the tacit threats and offers which may be thought to be embedded in conditional Cooperation – about which more later); (ii) altruistic motivation; and (iii) any 'internal sanctions' like guilt, loss of self-respect and so on, which may result from failure to conform to a norm, live up to one's own ideals, perform one's duties, or whatever. In chapter 5 I shall begin with a matrix of payoffs which again do not reflect these three classes of incentives, but then I shall consider the effects of assuming that individuals are altruistic (that is, they take account of other players' payoffs as well as their own in choosing strategies).

The expression 'voluntary Cooperation', used occasionally throughout the book, refers to Cooperation chosen only on the basis of the matrix of payoffs (or utilities, where the individual is in some way altruistic); thus, voluntary Cooperation is Cooperation which, amongst other things, is *not* the result of external coercion, including that applied or threatened by the state.

The problem of collective action

I shall argue in the next chapter that, in many interesting problems of public goods provision, individual preferences at any point in time are *not* those of a Prisoners' Dilemma. Many other preference structures can arise. These include Chicken and Assurance games, whose two-person payoff matrices are shown below.

	C	D			C	D
C	3, 3	2, 4		C	4, 4	1, 2
D	4, 2	1, 1		D	2, 1	3, 3
	Chicken				*Assurance*	

Surely, then, we should not equate 'the problem of collective action' with the Prisoners' Dilemma, as many writers have done – even though *some* of these alternative representations of public goods interaction (most notably the Assurance game) do not seem to present 'problems' in the sense which I think most people intend by use of the expression 'collective action problems'. What then do we mean by this expression?

Jon Elster gives a 'strong definition' of the collective action problem, which identifies it with the Prisoners' Dilemma, and a 'weak definition' which requires that (i) universal cooperation is preferred to universal non-cooperation by every individual (as in the Prisoners' Dilemma) and (ii) cooperation is 'individually unstable' and 'individually inaccessible'.[25] There is individual instability if each individual has an incentive to defect from universal cooperation, and there is individual inaccessibility if no individual has an incentive to move unilaterally from universal non-cooperation. But then he points out that there are cases in which cooperation is either individually unstable or individually inaccessible but not both – for example Chicken and Assurance games – but which nevertheless present collective action problems (though 'less serious' ones in the case of Assurance games).

The definition which I think gathers up all the cases that Elster and others are actually concerned with is that a collective action problem exists where rational individual action can lead to a strictly Pareto-inferior outcome, that is, an outcome which is strictly less preferred by every individual than at least one other outcome. The problem with this definition – an unavoidable problem, it seems to me, if one wants to give a general definition that covers *all* the cases one intuitively thinks of as collective action problems – is that it's not clear in some situations what rationality prescribes (even if we rule out, as I am assuming we should do here, notions of rationality not considered by game theorists). This is true of Chicken games. Any outcome of a Chicken game, including the Pareto-inferior mutual Defection outcome, can be rationalized. Hence, rational action *can* plausibly lead to a Pareto-inferior outcome, so that on my account it is a collective action problem.

Whether Assurance games are collective action problems again depends on what one takes rationality to prescribe. I shall take the view that, if a game has multiple equilibria (as the Assurance game does) but one of them is strictly preferred to all the others by everyone, then the Pareto-preferred one will be the outcome. On this view, rational action in an Assurance game does *not* lead to a Pareto-inferior outcome, so that this game is not a collective action problem.

Since preferences in some public goods interactions are those of an Assurance game, not all such interactions are collective action problems.

In the case of the (one-shot) Prisoners' Dilemma, rational action unequivocally leads to a Pareto-inferior outcome, so on my account all situations representable as Prisoners' Dilemmas are collective action problems. So are many other games (some of which will be encountered in the next chapter). Of course, not all of these games (including the Prisoners' Dilemma and Chicken games) correspond to public goods interactions.

Elster has said that politics is 'the study of ways of transcending the Prisoners' Dilemma'.[26] In the light of this discussion of 'the collective action problem' (and in anticipation of the discussion of alternatives to the Prisoners' Dilemma in the next chapter), I think we should be a little more expansive and say that politics is the study of ways of solving collective action problems.

Time and the lone exploiter

It's worth noting parenthetically that the degradation of a 'common' may *not* be the result of failure to solve a collective action problem. It may occur even where the common has only one user and he acts rationally.

The 'tragedy of the commons', on Garrett Hardin's account, arises because, at any point in time, each individual finds it in his interest to exploit the common (choose strategy D) no matter what the others do. The 'tragedy' does *not* arise, as some people have written, because each man reasons that '*since* the others are going to ruin the common anyway, I may as well exploit it too'. (In fact, if the others do *not* exploit the common, if they restrain themselves and choose strategy C, then each individual will find it even more profitable to exploit it than if they do.) It cannot be said, then, that the common would not be ruined if only *one* individual had access to it; that if a lake and all its lakeside factories were owned by one man, he would treat his wastes before discharging them into the lake; that if one man had an exclusive right to kill whales, he would see that they did not become extinct.

But surely, it may be said, the sole hunter of whales would not kill them all off, for his whole future livelihood, or at least all his future profits, depends on their survival. Unfortunately, this may not be the case.

Consider a common which one man has exclusive rights to exploit without restraint, and suppose now that at some point in time he is contemplating his whole future course of action with respect to this common. Let us suppose that he divides the future into equal time periods (months, years or whatever) and that in each time period he will receive a payoff. The sequence of payoffs he will receive depends on the course of action he chooses (for example, how many whales he kills in each period). Clearly, what he chooses to do will depend on the *present* value to him of future payoffs. At one extreme he may place no value whatever on any payoff except the one in the time period immediately before him. In this case, the prospect of zero payoffs from some point in the future onwards (as a result of the extinction of the whales, for example) does not trouble him at all. He will act in each time period so as to maximize his payoff in the current time period, and the result may be the ruin of the common.

It is generally assumed that future payoffs are exponentially *discounted* to obtain their present values. In the case when future time is divided into discrete periods, this means that the present value of a payoff X_t to be made t time periods from the present is $X_t a^t$, where a is a number such that $0 < a < 1$ and $1 - a$ is called the *discount rate*. The higher the discount rate, the lower the present value of future payoffs. If, for example, the individual's discount rate is 0.1 (that is, $a = 0.9$), then a payoff worth 100 units if received now would have a present value of 90 if it were to be received one period hence, 81 if it were to be received two periods hence and so on.

Intuitively, we should expect that if the discount rate is sufficiently high, then an exploiter who is seeking to maximize present value may eventually and quite 'rationally' ruin the common, even in the absence of other exploiters. The simple mathematics of this are set out by Colin Clark in his study of the exploitation of renewable resources (which, it should be remembered, include atmospheric, soil and water resources as well as such things as whales, fish and bison).[27] In the case when the resource of the common is a biological population, the discount rate which is sufficiently high to result in the extinction of the population will depend above all on the reproductive capacity of the population. (In Clark's model, this is *all* it depends on.)

The ruin of the common by a single individual, though it may be unfortunate, is not a 'tragedy' in Hardin's sense. (In the 'tragedy of the commons', the tragedy resides in the fact that 'rational' action on the part of each individual brings about a state of affairs which nobody wants.) Nor would it be a 'tragedy' if several individuals with similar preferences, including a shared high discount rate, ruined the common together, for this outcome would not be Pareto-inferior for them.

Solutions? Community, states, entrepreneurs, property rights and norms

There are, broadly speaking, two sorts of solution to collective action problems, which I will call 'spontaneous' or 'internal' solutions and 'external' solutions. *Internal* solutions neither involve nor presuppose changes in the 'game', that is, in the *possibilities* open to the individuals (which are in part determined by the 'transformation function', specifying how much of the public good can be produced with a given contribution), the individuals' preferences (or more generally *attitudes*), and their *beliefs* (including expectations). *External* solutions, on the other hand, work by changing the game, that is, changing people's possibilities, attitudes or beliefs. The changes do not necessarily originate outside the group of individuals who have the collective action problem. Since individual action is the product directly of the individual's possibilities, attitudes and beliefs, these two exhaust the possible sorts of solution.

It could be said that in the case where an internal 'solution' is forthcoming, there was no 'problem' there to solve. For example, if the 'problem' is correctly modelled as a dynamic game which, though it consists let us say of an iterated Prisoners' Dilemma, is not itself a Prisoners' Dilemma and as a consequence the outcome produced by rational egoists (without any external assistance or other interference) would be mutual cooperation throughout the game, then it could be said that preferences (*including intertemporal preferences*), etc., are such that there is no collective action *problem*. This would be a perfectly reasonable use of the word problem, but I shall not adopt it here. In fact, I shall take the view that the internal solution is the *basic* one, in two connected senses. It is, first, the only one which is complete in itself. All the external solutions presuppose the prior and/or concurrent solution of other problems, usually (always?) of collective action problems. Many of them, for example, involve the use of threats and offers of sanctions, and the creation and maintenance of the sanction system entail the prior or concurrent solution of collective action problems. (Why, for example, should the rational egoist pay his portion of the taxes that the state requires to maintain its police forces, etc., or why should the individual member of a community go to the trouble of punishing a free rider when he could be a free rider on the sanctioning efforts of others?) The internal solution is basic in a second sense: until we know whether a solution of this kind is possible and what form it will take, we cannot say what work, if any, remains to be done by other putative solutions. Thus, understanding the prospects for and obstacles in the way of an internal solution helps us to see what sorts of external solution are necessary and are likely to emerge in a given context.

External solutions can themselves be divided into two broad categories, which for short I will call centralized and decentralized; or, better, they can be arrayed along a continuum running from perfectly centralized to perfectly decentralized. Combinations of them are possible – normal, in fact. A solution is *decentralized* to the extent that the initiative for the changes in possibilities, attitudes or beliefs that constitute an external solution is dispersed amongst the members of the group; or, the greater the proportion of the group's members involved in solving the collective action problem (e.g. applying sanctions to free riders), the more decentralized the solution. Contrariwise, a solution is *centralized* to the extent that such involvement is concentrated in the hands of only a few members of the group.

Centralized solutions are typified, of course, by *the state*, while decentralized solutions characterize *community*. I have devoted another book to the ways in which a community can provide itself with public goods without the help of the state and will not reproduce the arguments here.[28] By a community I mean a group of people (i) who have beliefs and values in common, (ii) whose relations are direct and many-sided and (iii) who practise generalized as well as merely balanced reciprocity. The members of such a group of people, or all of its active adult members, can wield with great effectiveness a range of positive and negative sanctions, including the sanctions of approval and disapproval – the latter especially *via* gossip, ridicule and shaming. Decentralized solutions can sometimes be effective where there is little community, but the size of the group would still have to be relatively small (as it must be in a community).

External solutions are not necessarily restricted to the use of threats and offers of positive and negative sanctions. These, it is true, work not by altering an individual's preferences among outcomes (properly defined) but by altering his expectations about the actions to be taken by others (and hence the expected utility associated with alternative courses of action). But there are other ways in which an individual's expectations about others' behaviour can be altered and other ways in which he can be got to contribute to a public good, without the use of threats and offers or of force, whether centralized or decentralized. These include persuasion – providing information and arguments about the alternatives, about the consequences of adopting the various courses of action, about others' attitudes and beliefs and so on. Such methods are characteristic of the political entrepreneur, an external solution (relatively centralized, though usually closely combined with decentralized mechanisms) which I shall discuss shortly.

My main concern in this book is with the internal solution – with the possibility of spontaneous cooperation – as an alternative to the state. But before turning to this, I want to comment briefly, first, on the role of the political entrepreneur in the solution of collective action problems, and secondly, on the claims made by a number of writers that certain collective action problems can be solved by establishing private property rights and by norms.

Political entrepreneurs

In what sense do political entrepreneurs or leaders 'solve' collective action problems? In general, to solve or remove a collective action problem he or she must of course change individual preferences (or more generally attitudes), or change beliefs (including expectations) or inject resources (very probably knowledge, or new technology, like guns) into the group so as to make its members' efforts more productive.

Merely offering his services (working to obtain the public good) in exchange for support (subscriptions, food and shelter, or whatever) does not in itself constitute a distinctive solution to the problem. For, in the first place, the entrepreneur's services are themselves a public good, so that supporting him also gives rise to a collective action problem. This includes the case of the politician who in seeking electoral support offers his constituents legislative or other changes they favour. The collective action problem his potential supporters had in obtaining the public goods which such changes would have brought them is replaced by the collective action problem of getting him elected. And secondly, if the entrepreneur gains support by offering selective incentives, as well as by promising to work for the public good, then the solution is precisely the one proposed by Olson himself, in his 'by-product' theory.[29]

In many interesting cases the political entrepreneur may require little or no support from the members of the group whose collective action problem is at issue, because he is supported by (i.e., brings resources from) some external source. He might, for example, in his efforts to solve a *local* collective action problem, be supported by a pre-existing organization (the Communist Party, say, or the Catholic Church). This makes it easier to explain why the local problem is solved (for the members of the local group do not have to produce a 'surplus' to pay or feed the entrepreneur), but it leaves unexplained (a) the production of the resources brought in by the political entrepreneur, which will usually entail that a prior collective action problem – for example the creation and maintenance of an organization – has been solved; and (b) how, even though the (local) group does not have to support the entrepreneur, it now manages to solve a collective action problem that it could not solve without him. If the only difference the entrepreneur makes is the addition of selective incentives to their benefits, then, once again, we do not have a distinctive solution.

But the political entrepreneur is not just 'an innovator with selective incentives',[30] or someone who simply concentrates or centralizes resources. What is perhaps more characteristic of political entrepreneurship is its role in changing beliefs – beliefs about the public good itself, about what others have done and are likely to do and about others' beliefs. Above all, we must remember that most collective action must involve some form of conditional cooperation, for at a minimum an individual would not cooperate if *nobody* else did. And as we shall see (in chapters 3 and 4) conditional cooperation is a very precarious business. It requires amongst other things that the conditional cooperators have information about others' behaviour. The required monitoring can be done by the political entrepreneur.

The entrepreneur can also try to persuade people that their contributions make a big enough difference, either directly or indirectly through their effect on others' behaviour. The second of these might be achieved by persuading people that others' efforts are contingent on theirs.

An organization whose aim is to provide public goods for a very large group might be able to expand its membership and achieve its aims by having its cadres work to solve, through any or all of these entrepreneurial methods, smaller-scale collective action problems for much smaller subgroups. A nationwide movement, for example, may be built upon the success of its cadres in solving local collective action problems and bringing tangible benefits quickly. Samuel Popkin has given an excellent account of activities of this sort in Vietnam, showing how four politico-religious movements (the Catholic Church, the Cao Dai, the Hoa Hao and the Communist Party) won support by having their cadres help the villages, both by providing selective incentives and by facilitating cooperation in the provision of public goods.[31] These private and public goods – with varying degrees of indivisibility and excludability – included the provision of educational opportunities; the creation of insurance and welfare systems; agricultural improvements; the establishment of stock-farm cooperatives; improvements in water storage and irrigation facilities; the creation of local courts to arbitrate disputes; and protection against French courts, marauding notables and local landlords.

Property rights

Many economists, and nearly all those of the 'property rights' school, believe that the solution to free rider problems in public goods provision, and in particular those which would lead to the over-exploitation of a 'common property resource', lies in the establishment of private property rights. Without such rights, the argument goes, every individual has an incentive to intensify his use of the resource because (as we saw in discussing Garrett Hardin's 'tragedy of the commons') although, with each increment in use, every unit of his (and everybody else's) input becomes slightly less productive, this is up to a point outweighed by the marginal return from the increased input. Intensifying use of the resource is continued up to the point where all the 'rent' (income or other return) from the resource has been dissipated. Likewise, the benefits arising from any improvement or renewal or other investment he might make in the resource would be shared by all the users while the costs would be borne by the individual alone. There will therefore be overuse and underinvestment. With the establishment of private property rights, however, the external effects of each individual's actions are 'internalized': *all* the costs of an increase in use of the resource are borne by the individual, as are all the benefits of investing in its conservation or improvement.

The argument that the 'tragedy of the commons' is the fate of common property resources, and that overuse or underinvestment will be avoided only if common property rights are displaced by private property rights, seems to be positively mocked by the facts. The commons of the European open field system, far from being tragically degraded, were generally maintained in good health during the whole of their lifetimes of many hundreds of years. There is a detailed study of a Swiss alpine village (not, of course, operating an open field system) whose members have for more than five hundred years possessed and used in common various resources, including mountain-side pastures, side by side with privately owned land and other resources and during all this time the productivity of the common land has been maintained and much effort has been invested in its improvement.[32] Contrast with this the treatment, especially in recent decades, of much privately owned land by its very owners: the destruction of vast tracts of rain forest for the sake of a few profitable years of ranching; or the set of practices which together are causing the loss of topsoil from cultivated land through wind and water erosion on such a scale that, according to a recent report, there will be a third less topsoil per person by the end of the century.[33] In parts of Africa, and elsewhere in the world, overexploitation of grazing lands has been caused not by common property arrangements *per se* but by their destruction or disruption.[34] There are, as we saw earlier, perfectly good reasons why the rational private owner or user of a resource might knowingly destroy it; in particular, he might place a very low value on benefits to be derived from the resource in the distant as opposed to the immediate future.

Where do the property rights economists go wrong?[35] In the first place, many of them do not distinguish common property in a resource from *open access* to it. 'Communal rights', say Alchian and Demsetz, '... means that the use of a scarce resource is determined on a first-come, first-serve basis and persists for as long as a person continues to use the resource'.[36] This is wrong, or at least an abuse of language. If there is open access, then nobody is excluded from using the resource and there is no regulation of the activities of those who do use it. But if there is common ownership or collective control of the resource, then the members of the collectivity, whatever it is, can regulate its use. This is what happened in the European open field system, where the villagers rigorously excluded outsiders from use of the various commons they owned or possessed collectively, and carefully regulated insiders' use, typically by allotting to individuals 'stints' in proportion to their (privately owned) arable holdings and punishing people for infringements. The alpine community described by Netting similarly practised strict external and internal regulation of its commons. So too have countless 'primitive' collectivities and peasant villages all over the world.

It is to resources with open access, not to 'common property resources', that the property rights economists' argument about overexploitation and underinvestment applies. It is not a matter of establishing the right sort of property rights, of moving from collective to private property rights. It is rather a matter (at this stage of the argument at least) of establishing property rights where there were none; for property entails exclusion, so that where there is open access to a resource, there is no property in it.[37]

The property rights economists tend to see only two or three possibilities: open access and private property, to which is sometimes added state ownership. But almost any group of individuals can own or possess property collectively. Historical and contemporary examples are: a family; a wider kin group, such as a matrilineage; all those in a village who also possess land privately; a band; an ethnic group. Where the property rights economists do notice common property rights, they then argue that the costs of negotiating agreements regulating use and, if agreements are forthcoming, the costs of policing them, will be very great, and in this respect, common property rights compare unfavourably with private property rights.[38] But there is no necessary reason why transaction costs of all kinds should in total be greater in the case of common property rights than in the case of private property rights – and in the case of the open field system it was in fact the other way round, essentially because of economies of scale in pastoral production.[39]

Finally, the property rights economists, having generally failed to notice common property (as opposed to open access) and to study how individual rights in it are guaranteed, tend to assume that property rights must be enforced by the state.[40] But there can also be decentralized enforcement or maintenance of property rights – both private and common. (The sense of 'decentralized' intended here is the same as that used in the general remarks made earlier on the solution of collective action problems.) If a collectivity itself is to enforce its members' private property rights or their rights to use the common property, then it must of course be able to wield effective sanctions – unless the property rights are respected as a result of 'spontaneous' conditional cooperation. If the collectivity is a community, then, as we have seen, conditions are conducive to conditional cooperation, and if this fails the community's members have at their disposal a range of effective sanctions. The joint owners of the commons in European open field villages, for example, were communities in the required sense.

Enough has now been said, I think, to show that, insofar as the solution of collective action problems is concerned, nothing new is added by the introduction of property rights *per se*. An individual has property in something only if others forbear from using it, and the forbearance is the result of the threat or offer of *sanctions*, centralized or decentralized (or of conditional cooperation – unless this be reckoned also to involve threats and offers). It is the threats and offers of sanctions (and/or conditional cooperation) that is solving the collective action problem, if it is solved at all. Furthermore, as I remarked in an earlier section, the use of some of these sanctions presupposes the solution to prior collective action problems (for example, the formation and maintenance of a state!).

Norms

There is, finally the suggestion that norms solve collective action problems. I will comment on this very briefly, for my reaction to it is similar to my view of the suggestion that the introduction of private property rights solves collective action problems, and both follow from the general remarks about solutions to these problems made in an earlier section (though I shall not argue, as some have done, that property rights *are* norms). The view that norms solve collective action problems – or more precisely that they solve, amongst other things, the problems inherent in 'generalized PD-structured situations' and coordination problems – has been expounded by Edna Ullman-Margalit.[41] I shall take it that a norm is generally conformed to and is such that non-conformity, when observed, is generally punished. It is unclear whether this is what Ullman-Margalit means by a norm, but in any case it is fairly clear from her discussion of 'PD norms' that it is only 'a norm, *backed by sanctions*' or 'a norm . . . *supported by sufficiently severe sanctions*' that is capable of solving Prisoners' Dilemma problems.[42] So norms alone – mere prescriptions for action that people generally conform to – do *not* solve these problems.

If a norm is generally observed simply because it pays the individual to do so (in the absence of sanctions), then there is no (collective action or other) 'problem' to be solved in the first place. This would be the case if the norm had been 'internalized'. I take this expression to indicate that conformity to the norm does not require the application of external sanctions, inducements or any other considerations; as a result of the norm being internalized, the individual *prefers* to conform (without the threat of punishment) or at least has some sort of motivational disposition to do so. But then, as I say, we would not say that there was a Prisoners' Dilemma or collective action 'problem' to be solved: the individual preferences would not be those of a Prisoners' Dilemma or would not be such as to lead to a collective action problem. Of course, we might nevertheless wish to explain how the norm came to be internalized or how people came to have such preferences.

If, on the other hand, a norm is generally observed because non-conformity, when noticed, is generally punished, then it is the sanctions that are doing the real work of solving the Prisoners' Dilemma or collective action problem. The sanction system can of course be centralized or decentralized, in the way discussed in an earlier section. And again, it remains to be explained how the system of sanctions itself came into being and is maintained. To this problem, the general point made earlier about sanction systems applies: the maintenance of a system of sanctions itself constitutes or presupposes the solution of another collective action problem. Punishing someone who does not conform to a norm – punishing someone for being a free rider on the efforts of others to provide a public good, for example – is itself a public good for the group in question, and everyone would prefer others to do this unpleasant job. Thus, the 'solution' of collective action problems by norms presupposes the prior or concurrent solution of another collective action problem. And as my earlier remarks make clear, this would still be the case if the sanctions were wielded by the state or by a political entrepreneur.

Plan of the rest of the book

My purpose in this book is to examine the possibility of voluntary cooperation in the provision of public goods and in the solution of other collective action problems, and in doing so – and in other ways – to raise questions about what I take to be the most persuasive justification of the state. The detailed study of voluntary cooperation which follows (chapters 2, 3 and 4) can be read – and evaluated – independently of the critique of the liberal theory of the state. Both as a study of cooperation and as a study of the state and its alternatives, it is obviously far from complete; another part of the story is tackled in my *Community, Anarchy and Liberty*, which is complementary to this book.

As a critique of the liberal justification of the state, the argument will be in three stages. First, I argue in chapter 2 that in public goods interactions the individual preferences at any point in time are not necessarily those of a Prisoners' Dilemma game. This is true, I shall argue, of both two-person and N-person games and of cases where strategy sets are continuous as well as those where individuals have only two strategies available to them. It will emerge that important classes of public goods provision problems are better represented by Assurance and especially Chicken games, and in the continuous case by hybrids of these two. In all these games, arguably, if the game is played only once, *some* cooperation is more likely to be forthcoming than in cases for which the Prisoners' Dilemma is the appropriate model.

In the next two chapters (3 and 4), however, I shall assume the worst: that preferences at any point in time are those of a Prisoners' Dilemma game. But I then go on to show that if *time* is introduced and the problem is treated more dynamically, under certain circumstances voluntary Cooperation is rational for each player, even assuming that he seeks to maximize only his own payoff.

My argument here will be cased in terms of the Prisoners' Dilemma *supergame*. This is the game consisting of an indefinite number of iterations of one of the Prisoners' Dilemma games (two-person and N-person) which were defined earlier. In each *constituent game* (as the repeated game is now called), players choose strategies simultaneously, as before, but they know the strategies chosen by all other players in previous games. Each player discounts future payoffs; his discount rate does not change with time, but discount rates may differ between players. The constituent game is assumed not to change with time. (It would be desirable to relax this last assumption in a more general treatment, and permit the payoff matrix to change with time. See the final section of chapter 4 below.)

The really important difference between the one-shot game and the supergame is that players' strategies can be made interdependent in the latter but not, of course, in the former, since players must choose strategies simultaneously or in ignorance of each other's choices. In the supergame, a player can, for example, decide to Cooperate in each constituent game *if and only if* the other player(s) Cooperated in the previous constituent game. It is on this possibility, the possibility of using *conditional* strategies, that the voluntary Cooperation of all the players turns.

Finally, in chapter 7, I shall raise doubts about the way in which this justification of the state is approached. It is an essential and fundamental feature of the theory I am criticizing that it takes individual preferences as given and fixed. In particular, it is assumed that the state itself has no effect on these preferences. This rules out *ab initio* the possibility, amongst many others, that the state may exacerbate an already existing collective action problem or create such a problem where none existed before: that the state may affect, in other words, the very conditions which are supposed to make it necessary. If preferences may change, especially as a result of the activities of the state itself, it is not at all clear what is *meant* by the desirability of the state.

Criticisms of this sort can of course be levelled against any theory which is founded on assumptions about fixed individual preferences (as most of economic theory and some polotical theory is); but they are especially important, it seems to me, when the theory purports to justify an institution (like the state) and when the theory is to apply to a very long period of time (as a theory used to justify the state or to explain its origin must do).

I have said that the arguments which are the object of my criticisms in this book have been set out most explicitly by Thomas Hobbes. I shall therefore give (in chapter 6) an exposition of his political theory. My chief reason for devoting to this exposition a rather long chapter later in the book, rather than a short summary at the start of the book where it would otherwise belong, and for making what would otherwise be an unpardonable addition to the considerable critical literature on Hobbes, is that I think it is illuminating to look at these theories in terms of some of the ideas presented in the earlier chapters on the Prisoners' Dilemma and its supergame. I have asserted rather baldly in this informal Introduction that Hobbes's theory is about non-Cooperation in Prisoners' Dilemma games (other writers have made similar assertions, equating Hobbes's theory with, for example, Hardin's analysis of the 'tragedy of the commons'); but the story is more complicated and more interesting than this and deserves a fuller account.

I shall also consider, more briefly, David Hume's political theory. For although it is very similar to Hobbes's theory (despite Hume's objections to what he took to be a fundamental element of Hobbes's theory, the idea of the social contract) and although it is generally less rigorous than Hobbes's version (in *Leviathan*), it does partly supply a deficiency in

Hobbes's treatment, namely that it is too static. Hobbes in effect treats only a one-shot Prisoners' Dilemma game, whereas Hume's treatment is more dynamic, with the discounting of future benefits playing an important role. Also, in Hume, but not in Hobbes, there is explicit recognition of the effects of size, a partial anticipation of Olson's 'logic of collective action'.

Some of the ideas I am interested in here appeared much earlier than *Leviathan* (above all in the *Book of Lord Shang* and the works of Han Fei Tzu which were written in China in the fourth and third centuries BC), but it was Hobbes and Hume who gave the first full, explicit statements of the argument. And in later political theorists the argument is not always explicit, does not stand out boldly and is less precise and less coherent.

In *Leviathan*, Hobbes seems to assume that each man seeks to maximize not merely his own payoff, but also his 'eminence', the difference between his own and other people's payoffs. Hume, on the other hand, assumes that most people are chiefly concerned with their own payoffs but are also possessed of a limited amount of 'benevolence'. In both cases, individuals take *some* account of other individuals' payoffs; I call this 'altruism'. The effects of various sorts of altruism on the outcomes of Prisoners' Dilemma games are treated briefly in chapter 5. Some of the material in that chapter will be of use in the discussion of Hobbes and Hume and also in the final chapter.

2. The Prisoners' Dilemma, Chicken and other games in the provision of public goods[1]

It has often been said – and indeed is still being said – that 'the problem of collective action and the Prisoner's Dilemma are essentially the same'[2] (at least where the group is large or where it is not privileged) *and* that the Prisoners' Dilemma game is the appropriate model of public goods provision. Neither of these is the case. The argument against the first claim – which has been made by a number of writers, most explicitly perhaps by Russell Hardin[3] – was begun in the last chapter. Against the second claim I argue in this chapter that the Prisoners' Dilemma is *not* the only applicable game in the study of public goods provision. Since many (though not all) important collective action problems arise in connection with the provision of public goods, this chapter, in attacking the second claim, will also attack the first.

More specifically, I shall argue that in public goods interaction the individuals' preferences *at any point in time* are not necessarily those of a Prisoners' Dilemma. I shall argue this, first, in the case where the individuals choose between just two strategies, Cooperate (or contribute to the provision of the public good) and Defect (not contribute), and then in the case where each individual can choose to contribute a *continuously* variable amount within some range (or choose from a large number of discrete amounts which may be approximated by a continuous variable). We shall see in particular that important classes of public goods provision problems are better represented by the game of Chicken, both in the two-strategy, two-person case and in the two-strategy, N-person case to which Chicken can be generalized, and that structures of preferences can also be 'Chicken-like' in the case when the strategy sets are continuous.

I emphasize that this chapter does not begin to consider the *dynamics* of choice in public goods interaction; it is concerned only with individual preferences at one point in time and with choices in one-shot games.[4] Genuinely dynamical considerations enter into the analysis in the next chapter, which considers *repeated* plays of the Prisoners' Dilemma, or 'supergames'. These supergames are themselves typically *not* Prisoners' Dilemmas. So this chapter and the next two will establish (amongst other things) that preferences in public goods interaction at a point in time are often not those of a Prisoners' Dilemma and that, even if they are, the 'dynamic' or intertemporal preferences of the resulting supergame are usually not.

Alternatives to the Prisoners' Dilemma

If a 2×2 game is to be a Prisoners' Dilemma, then amongst other things each player must (a) prefer non-Cooperation if the other player does *not* Cooperate, and (b) prefer non-Cooperation if the other player *does* Cooperate. In other words: (a') neither individual finds it profitable to provide any of the public good by himself; and (b') the value to a player of the amount of the public good provided by the other player alone (i.e., the value of being a free rider) exceeds the value to him of the total amount of the public good provided by joint Cooperation *less* his costs of Cooperation. Of course a player could not even form these preferences if it were not *possible* for each player to provide some of the public good *alone*. For many important public goods, I shall argue, either or both of the conditions (a') and (b') fail, and sometimes even this precondition for forming the preferences in question may fail.

If (a') fails for at least one of the players – if one of them has an incentive to provide some amount of the public good even if he alone has to pay the full costs – then we have what Olson calls a 'privileged' group. In this case there is, according to Olson, a 'presumption' that the public good will be provided by the players. If only one of the players is willing to act unilaterally in this way, this presumption is reasonable. But if both

	C	D
C	3, 3	1, 4
D	4, 1	2, 2

Figure 1   The 2×2 Prisoners' Dilemma

are so willing, so that the group is 'doubly privileged', then there should be no such presumption, unless each player is willing to contribute *regardless* of what the other player does, that is, if C is a dominant strategy for each player. If, however, each player is willing to provide some of the public good unilaterally *but not if the other player will provide it* – that is, if condition (a′) fails but all the other assumptions of the Prisoners' Dilemma game are retained – then we have a game of *Chicken*, and in a game of Chicken it is not at all obvious what the outcome will be, as we shall see.

	C	D
C	3, 3	2, 4
D	4, 2	1, 1

Figure 2   The 2 × 2 Chicken Game

This structure of preferences is more appropriate than the Prisoners' Dilemma game as a model of certain widespread reciprocity practices involving the production of public goods and, especially in its *N*-person generalization which we shall look at shortly, of a variety of situations involving ecological or environmental public goods. Consider, for example, two neighbouring cultivators whose crops depend upon proper maintenance of dykes and ditches for flood control or irrigation. There is a minimum amount of work which must be done; *either individual alone can do it all*, but each prefers the other to do all the work. The consequences of *nobody* doing the work are so disastrous that either of them would do the work if the other did not. The structure of preferences here is that of the game of Chicken.

Not all reciprocity or mutual aid practices resemble games of Chicken. If the product of the reciprocal assistance is not itself a public good, the game is more likely to be a Prisoners' Dilemma. Consider, for example, our two neighbouring cultivators, each of whom can choose to give or withhold assistance to the other at crucial times, such as when they need to get a harvest in quickly. With help, each gets enough done to enjoy a satisfactory winter; without help, a miserable winter of near-starvation ensues. Then (*if* we isolate this game from any wider or continuing relations between the two individuals) each player would prefer to have the other help him without having to return the favour (i.e., to be a unilateral Defector) rather than mutual assistance (since helping the other is costly); and each would prefer mutual Defection to being a unilateral Cooperator, since in either case he would have no help (in getting his harvest in, etc.). Mutual Cooperation is nevertheless preferred by both players to mutual Defection. This game is therefore once again a Prisoners' Dilemma. It is, in fact, just an instance of *exchange*, in which each party has a choice between yielding up his good or service (*C*) and holding on to it (*D*). The asymmetric outcomes, where one player yields and the other does not, would normally be said to involve stealing. In anarchy, games of exchange/stealing are generally Prisoners' Dilemmas.[5]

For a second example of public goods interaction resembling a Chicken game, consider the case of two large factories which discharge effluent into a small lake. Each producer can choose between polluting (*D*) and refraining from polluting (*C*). The lake can absorb waste from one factory and still remain usable, but the wastes from both factories carry it over a critical threshold. The resulting ecological catastrophe is so bad that each producer, though he finds a free ride on the restraint of the other producer preferable to mutual Cooperation, would prefer to refrain unilaterally if the other producer pollutes (the cost of refraining deducted from the benefits derived from this unilateral restraint being less than the (dis)utility of the catastrophe).

We have here a case of a public good which is not provided in smoothly increasing amounts as the level of contributions increases. Ecological systems such as lakes, rivers, the atmosphere, fisheries and so on can normally be exploited up to some critical level while largely maintaining their integrity and retaining much of their use value. If exploitation rates go beyond that critical level, use value falls catastrophically. With fisheries, for example, once the population has fallen below that necessary to maintain a viable breeding stock the species will rapidly cease to be commercially exploitable. Although the use value of the 'common' may decline somewhat as rates of exploitation approach the critical level, it falls catastrophically beyond that level.

A similar sort of discontinuity is found with many public goods of the 'public works' variety, such as road and rail links and bridges, which cannot be usefully provided in *any* amounts but only in more or less massive 'lumps' or *tranches*. In some cases *no* amount of the public good can be provided until total contributions exceed some threshold. If, in the 2×2 game, a single individual's contribution is insufficient to provide any of the public good, or provides only a very little of it, then each player will prefer D if the other player chooses D, but may prefer to contribute if the other contributes too. In this case, we have a variant of a third type of game, the game of *Assurance*.

	C	D
C	4, 4	1, 2
D	2, 1	3, 3

Figure 3   The 2×2 Assurance Game

Consider again a reciprocity practice which produces a public good: the maintenance of dykes and ditches for irrigation or flood control by two neighbouring cultivators. We saw earlier that if one of them *alone* could do all the necessary work (though of course preferring that the other did it all) and *would* do if the other did not (to avoid disaster), the resulting game is one of Chicken. Now suppose that neither individual can alone produce any of the public good: if the benefit of the public good to each of them is 4 and the cost of contributing is 2, we have the First Variant of the Assurance game shown in Figure 4. If one individual alone can produce *some* of the public good (with a benefit to each of 1, say) but not enough to justify his costs (2, again), then we get the Second Variant of the Assurance game. For another example of this case, consider two members of a community sharing a vegetable patch: one individual's weeding does not keep pace with the growth of weeds, though it enables *some* crop to be grown; if both weed, the crop will be good.

We see, then, that the games of Chicken and Assurance, as well as the

	C	D
C	2, 2	−2, 0
D	0, −2	0, 0

First Variant

	C	D
C	2, 2	−1, 1
D	1, −1	0, 0

Second Variant

Figure 4   Two variants of the Assurance Game

Prisoners' Dilemma, can be relevant to the problem of collective action to provide public goods. This conclusion will be reinforced when we come to consider the N-person generalizations of these games and allow for the individual's choice of contributions to vary continuously.

When individual preferences are those of an Assurance game, there is unlikely to be a problem of collective action to provide the public good, as there is when the game is a PD. The 2×2 Assurance game, in its standard form or in either of the variants, has two equilibria (C, C) and (D, D), but since both players prefer (C, C) to (D, D), neither will expect the latter to be the outcome, so the unique Pareto-optimal outcome (C, C) will result.

But there is an interesting collective action problem in a Chicken game. The important feature of this game is that there are two equilibria and in each of these one player Cooperates while the other has a 'free ride' on the public good provided out of his contribution, so that it will pay each player to attempt to be the first to bind himself irrevocably to non-Cooperation, if this is feasible. *This pre-commitment strategy 'forces' the other player into Cooperation.* However, where each player is able to bind himself in this way both may realize the dangers of simultaneous binding and may forgo this for the fully Cooperative outcome. This is, unfortunately, unstable (at least in the single play game) so that one can expect any Cooperation to be fragile. I shall discuss the possibility of Cooperation in Chicken games at length below.

	C	D
C	3, 3	1, 4
D	4, 2	2, 1

Figure 5   PD for Row, Chicken for Column

If Chicken and Assurance as well as Prisoners' Dilemma games can characterize public goods interaction, then there is no reason why *hybrids* of these games should not also arise. Consider for example the game, whose payoff matrix is shown in Figure 5, in which the Row-chooser's preferences are those of a Prisoners' Dilemma while the Column-chooser's preferences are those of a Chicken game. Preferences might take this form because Column (i) values the public good much more highly than Row does, or can provide some amount of it at lower cost or is better able to contribute to it than Row, or again because he suffers much more than Row if none of the public good is provided at all and hence is willing to provide some of the public good if Row provides none, but (ii) does not value the public good so highly, or does not value large amounts of it sufficiently highly that he would be prepared to contribute *more* of it if Row provided some. The outcome of this game, unlike that of the pure Chicken game, is not at all problematic. Row will of course choose his dominant strategy D and this will make it rational for Column to choose C, so that the outcome is (D, C). This is the only equilibrium and it is the only Pareto-optimal strategy pair.

An N-person game of Chicken

Few interesting games in the real world (outside of international relations) have only two players. So the N-person generalizations of the games considered in the last section are of greater interest than the two-person versions. An N-person generalization of the Prisoners' Dilemma was discussed briefly in chapter 1. If this game is played only once, there is no more to be said about it: universal Defection will be the outcome. When the game is repeated, it's another story altogether, as we will see in chapter 4 (where we will also see that the N-person Prisoners' Dilemma supergame can be a Chicken game). The natural way to generalize the Assurance game is to stipulate that (i) universal Cooperation is preferred by each player to universal Defection, and (ii) an individual will prefer C to D if at least a certain number of other players Cooperate but otherwise will prefer D to C, so that the only equilibria are universal Cooperation and universal Defection, and any 'intermediate' strategy vector (in which some players Cooperate and some Defect) will not be an equilibrium because each player will want to change strategy either to C or to D. Again, the analysis of this game is unproblematic: universal Cooperation will be the outcome, since of the two equilibria it is preferred by every player to the other.

The most interesting of these (one-shot) games is Chicken. Its generalization to any (finite) number of players is less straightforward. It seems to me that the central feature of the 2×2 game which should be retained in any such generalization is the existence of an incentive for each player to attempt to bind himself irrevocably to non-Cooperation

Table 1

	If both the others Cooperate	If one Cooperates, the other Defects	If both the others Defect
G1: I prefer	D to C	C to D	C to D
G2: I prefer	D to C	D to C	C to D
G3: I prefer	D to C	C to D	D to C
PD: I prefer	D to C	D to C	D to C

(or at least to convince the others he is certain not to Cooperate), an incentive deriving from his expectation that such a commitment will compel some or all of the other players to choose Cooperation (on which he is then able to free-ride). So we define an N-person Chicken to be any game having this property, with the qualification that the pre-commitment incentive exists before the *costs* of commitment are taken into account. (Pre-commitment is sometimes costly and may be so costly as to remove the incentive.) It is of course assumed that each player prefers universal Cooperation to universal non-Cooperation and that each player's most preferred outcome is that he choose D while all others choose C (this is his most profitable free ride). As it stands the definition does not fully determine the permissible structures of preference. A three-person case illustrates this. We know that each player prefers D to C if both of the other players choose C. There are then four possible preference structures. One of these is a PD (the only one in which D dominates C) and the remaining three are labelled G1, G2 and G3. These four games are shown in table 1, which gives the preferences between C and D of any one of the players (called 'I') in each of the three possible contingencies (it being assumed that the game is symmetric, so that the preference structures shown are invariant under any permutation of the players). Each player is assumed also to prefer (C, C, C) to (D, D, D).

Now in the 2×2 Chicken game, each player prefers to Defect if the other Cooperates but prefers to Cooperate if the other Defects. A natural N-person generalization of this is to stipulate that each player prefers to Defect if 'enough' others Cooperate, and to Cooperate if 'too many' others Defect. This requirement is met in the 3-person game by G1 and G2 above; and more generally, for any number of players, the preferences of any player must switch direction from 'D to C' to 'C to D' only once as the number of players choosing D increases. (This corresponds to a rightward movement in a row of table 1 above.) Now in the three games shown above, the last two columns can also be viewed as the game between the first two players when the third (a Defecting column-player in table 1) has already committed himself to non-Cooperation. These two columns can now be headed by 'C' and 'D'. Let us assume that in all these 2×2 subgames (C, C) is preferred by each player to (D, D). In G1, then, the new row-player will choose C (since he prefers C to D whether the column-player chooses C or D). So will the new column-player, who has identical preferences. Thus, if one player pre-commits himself to D, the others are certain to choose Cooperation. The incentive for each player to pre-commit is therefore strong.

In G2, the 2×2 subgame remaining when one player has pre-committed himself to D is a Chicken game. Since, as we shall see, there is no obviously, unequivocally rational strategy to pursue in a Chicken game, a row-player who commits himself to D cannot be certain that this will compel the remaining players to Cooperate. But since there is a reasonable likelihood that they will, so that there is *some* positive incentive to pre-commit oneself to D, I shall allow that G2 is also a case of Chicken.

In G3 the 2×2 subgame remaining when one player has pre-committed himself to D is a game of Assurance, so the player contemplating pre-commitment can be virtually certain that this will compel mutual Cooperation amongst the others. In fact, for each player in G3 D is better than C if no others Cooperate or if two others Cooperate, but if one other Cooperates, C is the best strategy. So each player is in two possible Cooperative coalitions and will be tempted to try to 'force' the other two into Cooperation by pre-committing himself to non-Cooperation. According to our central criterion, then, G3 qualifies as an N-person Chicken game. But notice that G3 does not have the feature, mentioned above and possessed by G1 and G2, that each player prefers to Defect if 'enough' others Cooperate and to Cooperate if 'too many' others Defect. Games possessing this feature also have the property that each player has an incentive to pre-commit himself to non-Cooperation, but the converse is not true, as G3 shows. It is the existence of this pre-commitment incentive (if the cost of pre-commitment is ignored) which I believe to be the distinguishing feature of the 2×2 game of Chicken; accordingly I prefer the broader definition of the N-person game which admits any game having this feature.

It is clear, then, that in the N-person Chicken, as in the N-person Prisoners' Dilemma, rational individual action can lead to the unintended consequence of a Pareto-inferior outcome. For in the rush to be among the first to make a commitment to non-Cooperation (and thereby secure a free ride on the Cooperation of others), the number so binding themselves may exceed the maximum number of players able to commit themselves without inducing non-provision of the public good. Nevertheless, the prospects for Cooperation are a little more promising in Chicken games than they are in the Prisoners' Dilemma. I return to this later. Before doing so, let us again consider, in the light of this account of the N-person game, a few examples showing the relevance of the Chicken game to practical problems of public goods provision.

Mutual aid, fisheries, and voting in committees

All three variants of the three-person Chicken game, G1, G2 and G3, can characterize reciprocity and environmental situations of the sort already mentioned. Consider again the example of the irrigation and flood control system. Suppose now that it is a public good for three cultivators, any one of whom is able profitably to do the necessary work, the additional benefit (from the increased provision of the public good) to any other player who assists the first being less than the costs of such a contribution. Again, each prefers the others to do the work, but the consequences of nobody doing the work are so disastrous that each would do the work if nobody else did it. The preferences here are those of the Chicken game G2. If the job can be done profitably by one player alone, but can be done so much better by two players that it pays a player to contribute if another player is already doing so, then the preferences are those of G1. If the job cannot be done by any one of the players alone but can be done by two of them with profit to each, then the preferences are those of G3.

For an environmental example, consider a fishery, which can profitably be exploited up to some critical level beyond which there is catastrophic collapse. There are no plausible further assumptions in this case which would yield the game G3. But suppose that the fishery can tolerate one or two users, while three would surpass the critical level. Fishing being costly, if two are already fishing the third would prefer to refrain. Then (with other appropriate assumptions) the game is G2. Each player should want to be one of the pair which can 'force' the third into refraining from fishing. If at least two players must refrain from fishing to prevent collapse, and the much reduced catch which a player would get if either one or two others were fishing yields less benefit than the fishing would cost, then the game is G1. Each player should want to be the sole player who can enjoy a free ride on the remaining two by pre-committing himself to fishing and 'forcing' the others (who are then in an Assurance game) into restraint.

This is of course a highly stylized model of a fishery, and if we were to examine a real world 'fishery' we would find a much messier picture. In the case of whaling, for example, I think it can be plausibly argued that, although the 'game' once resembled a Prisoners' Dilemma, for the period from about 1947, when the International Whaling Commission was formed, Chicken would be a better approximation.[6] In the recent period, which saw the elimination of all the major whaling nations except Japan and the USSR (as well as the commercial extinction of the Blue Whale and other commercially important species), the behaviour of Japan and the USSR can be interpreted as attempts to demonstrate their commitment to non-Cooperation with a view to forcing other whaling nations to withdraw from the market, that is, to force them into Cooperation.

My final illustration of a public goods problem to which the game of Chicken is appropriate is less speculative. It concerns the rationality of the act of voting, which involves a perfectly lumpy public good.

Suppose that two options, A and B, come up before a committee operating under simple majority rule. Attendance and voting is optional. There is a group of players who both prefer A and know that they collectively constitute a majority of the players. For this group *obtaining* A is a pure *lumpy* public good (even if A itself *is not* a public good). Assume for simplicity that all players outside the group (who prefer B) turn up. So long as just enough of the A-supporters to form a bare majority turn up, the public good is provided; if less than this number turn up, none of the good is provided. There is no advantage in additional members over and above the bare majority turning up. So long as we can assume that the advantages of A over B are greater than the cost of voting for members of the majority group, the situation is modelled rather well by Chicken. Each member of the group will attempt to be among the first to find convincing reasons for being unable to attend the committee. There are three possible outcomes: either a group just sufficient to get A through is 'forced' into attending; or if the group members are risk averse and the issue is vital they might all turn up, realizing the danger that A will not be passed; or insufficient of them attend to get A through and the public good is lost. In the first and second situations voting is perfectly rational for those who do attend (on expected payoff grounds in the second case).

For obvious reasons this argument makes more sense where numbers are small (as in committees) than where they are very large (as in constituencies).

Pre-commitment as a risky decision and the prospects for cooperation in Chicken games

If for whatever reasons it happens that the players in a game of Chicken are not all identically placed, so that some are unable to commit themselves to non-Cooperation or can commit themselves only at prohibitive cost or are unable to commit themselves as early as others, then it may turn out that one of the stable profitable subgroups is 'forced' into Cooperation and some of the public good is provided. Otherwise there is, as we have seen, a danger that all the players will bind themselves irrevocably to non-Cooperation, or that in the case of a lumpy good so many will bind themselves that the good cannot be provided at all. Recognizing this, risk-averse players might in fact forgo commitment and Cooperate.

It can be argued that forgoing binding in this way is consistent with some well-known principles of decision-making under uncertainty. The pre-game is quite likely to be characterized by uncertainties about the other players' attitudes towards risk and whether they were irrevocably bound to non-Cooperation. Under uncertainty, players might choose to maximize the minimum payoff they could get (the maximin strategy) or choose the strategy which minimizes the difference between the best and worst payoffs obtainable from each strategy (the minimax regret strategy). Adoption of the maximin strategy by all players leads to the Cooperative outcome in Chicken. Use of the minimax regret principle can lead to Cooperative or non-Cooperative choices, depending on the payoff differences. There are, however, well-known doubts about the use of either of these principles, particularly in variable-sum games.

Suppose that each player is not totally uncertain about other players'

Table 2. *Outcomes and i's payoffs*

		Less than $s-1$ others Cooperate	$s-1$ others Cooperate	More than $s-1$ others Cooperate
i's strategy	C	public good not provided $-c$	public good provided $b-c$	public good provided $b-c$
	D	public good not provided 0	public good not provided 0	public good provided b

future behaviour but has rather a subjective probability which he puts on each other player committing himself to non-Cooperation. Consider the case of a perfectly lumpy good, which, I have argued, is often best represented by the game of Chicken, and to simplify the analysis assume that any cooperative coalition of at least s players out of the total of N can provide some amount of the public good while larger coalitions cannot provide any more of it. (This model applies to, *inter alia*, the act of voting on committees which was discussed earlier, and it is therefore not surprising that it bears a formal resemblance to accounts of power, such as that given by Shapley and Shubik, which relate power to the question of whether an individual is pivotal in a committee vote.)

Suppose that a player, i, assigns a probability p to any other player Cooperating, that Cooperation costs him c, and that the lumpy good is worth b to him.[7] Player i faces the set of contingencies shown in table 2, which also gives the payoff to each player for each possible outcome. Denote by $P_{<s-1}$, P_{s-1} and $P_{>s-1}$ the probabilities that fewer than $s-1$, exactly s, and more than $s-1$ other players will contribute. Player i's *expected* payoff if he chooses strategy C is the sum of the three payoffs in the top row of table 2 each multiplied by the probability that the outcome in question will occur, that is, by $P_{<s-1}$, P_{s-1} and $P_{>s-1}$ respectively. His expected payoff if he chooses D is calculated similarly. Then the difference between these two expected payoffs – the expected payoff if he chooses C *less* the expected payoff if he chooses D – is:

$$d = -c.P_{<s-1} + (b-c)P_{s-1} + (b-c-b)P_{>s-1}$$

Since the coefficients of c sum to one, this reduces to

$$d = b.P_{s-1} - c$$

which is of course just i's payoff if the public good is provided multiplied by the probability that i will be pivotal in providing it, *less* the cost to i of contributing. Denoting the number of coalitions of size $s-1$ that can be formed from the $N-1$ other players by $\binom{N-1}{s-1}$ in the usual way, the expected payoff differential is

$$d = b\binom{N-1}{s-1}p^{s-1}(1-p)^{n-s} - c$$

Player i will Cooperate just as long as $d > 0$, which implies that the probability that exactly $s-1$ others Cooperate is greater than the cost/benefit ratio c/b. If for example $N = 10$, $s = 3$ and $p = 0.25$, player i's probability of being pivotal is about 0.14, so that b must be about seven times greater than c or more if i is to decide not to commit himself to non-Cooperation.[8]

If, for given values of N, s, b and c, we plot the expected payoff differential as a function of p, we see that it is a unimodal curve with a maximum at $p = (N-1)/(s-1)$, from which it falls monotonically on both sides, as p decreases or increases, to a minimum of $-c$ when $p = 0$ and $p = 1$. It's clear, then, that d is negative for at least some values of p, whatever the values of N, s, b and c, and may be negative for all values of these parameters. If, for example, $N = 5$, $s = 3$, $c = 2$ and $b = 3$ (i.e., the public good is very costly to produce, or little valued by i relative to the value of i's contribution), then there is *no* value of p which makes d positive and hence i will not Cooperate whatever the subjective probability he places on other players Cooperating. But for some values of N, s, b and c, the expected payoff differential d will be positive over some (intermediate) range of values of p. Outside this range, p is either so small that player i expects that not enough others will Cooperate for his contribution to make the difference, or is so large that i expects so many others to Cooperate that his contribution would be redundant.[9]

This analysis of pre-commitment as a risky decision gives us a further reason for believing that some Cooperation will be forthcoming in Chicken games, and hence that in those public goods interactions for which Chicken is the appropriate model *some* amount of the public good will be provided. But unfortunately it has to be said that this analysis has an unsatisfactory implication. Consider the effect on player i's decision to Cooperate of increases in the size of the group, N, and the size of the smallest coalition which is able to provide the public good, s. For given values of b and c, the behaviour of d as N varies depends on the behaviour of the binomial term $\binom{N-1}{s-1}p^{s-1}(1-p)^{N-s}$. The first part of this, the number of subgroups of size $s-1$ that can be drawn from a group of size $N-1$, *increases* with N. Now suppose that player i assumes that *ceteris paribus* each of the other players is *less* likely to Cooperate as N increases and is *more* likely to Cooperate as s increases. Then the probability that any one of the subgroups of size $s-1$ will occur, $p^{s-1}(1-p)^{N-s}$, *decreases* with increasing N.

It turns out that *in some circumstances* increasing the group size N so increases the *number* of subgroups of size $s-1$ in which i's Cooperation is pivotal that this more than compensates for the smaller *probability* that any such subgroup will form, with the result that i is more likely to Cooperate as N increases. Whether or not this happens depends on *how* p declines with increasing N and on the value of $s-1$ relative to that of Np.[10] In a similar way it can be shown that as s increases, the expected payoff differential d can rise or fall (depending on the same two factors).

The upshot is that, when a player assumes every other player is *less* likely to Cooperate as N (or s) increases, under certain conditions he himself is *more* likely to Cooperate as N (or s) increases. We have reached, in other words, the rather unsatisfactory conclusion that i's behaviour as N and s change may be inconsistent with the way he assumes others will behave. (The model is in this sense analogous to the Cournot analysis I shall examine briefly below.)

We do not, however, encounter this problem if player i makes no assumptions about the effects of increases in N or s on p. For some *given* values of N and s (and of b and c), there will be values of p such that his expected payoff from Cooperation is greater than his expected payoff from Defecting. This conclusion, taken together with the (admittedly rather informal) points made in the first two paragraphs of this section, give us grounds for believing that some Cooperation is more likely to occur in games of Chicken than in Prisoners' Dilemmas, if these games are played only once. This conclusion will be reinforced by the analysis in the next section, where I treat games in which each player's strategy set is continuous. But, I must reiterate, the real-world 'games' we are concerned with are rarely played only once, and we should therefore be more interested in the analysis of dynamic or repeated games. The analysis of the iterated Prisoners' Dilemma is the subject of the next two chapters. Of the dynamics of behaviour in iterated Chicken games almost nothing is known – though an encouraging early result from work in progress shows that, contrary to a belief popular amongst students of international relations, it may *not* be rational to try to acquire a reputation for 'toughness' (by making commitments to non-Cooperation) if the game has more than two players.[11]

Continuous strategy sets

In many (but certainly not all) cases of public goods interaction each individual can choose to contribute a continuously variable amount within some range, or choose from a large number of discrete amounts which may be approximated by a continuous model.

Consider, for example, Russell Hardin's model of collective action, introduced in chapter 1. Each individual can choose only between contributing or not contributing one unit of the cost of producing the good (one unit, let us say, of a *numeraire* private good) and every unit contributed produces an amount of the public good with benefit r. Hardin assumed that the benefit to an individual of the public good produced from n units of contributions is nr/N.

Let us now modify this example by allowing each individual to choose to contribute *any* amount from zero to some personal maximum. Then, if the total contribution of all other individuals is C and his own contribution is c, his utility is $(C+c)r/N-c$, so that his utility is a linear function of c, which increases with increasing c if $N < r$, decreases if $N > r$, and remains at a constant level if $N = r$. Thus, when $N > r$, the game is a Prisoners' Dilemma and each individual's utility is maximized if he chooses to contribute nothing, but when $N < r$ he should contribute the maximum possible.

This simple model is not at all typical of public goods interaction. In particular, each individual's utility is a linear function of the total amount (X, say) of public good produced and of the amount of the private good (Y) which he contributes towards the costs of production. Thus, his *indifference curves*, each one a locus of points (X, Y) between which he is indifferent, are linear. The *transformation function*, specifying the quantity of public good which can be produced with a given input of the private good, is also linear.

More generally, we should expect neither of these two functions to be linear. The indifference curves normally will exhibit convexity; that is, as the amount of either one of the goods increases, an additional unit of it requires a smaller sacrifice of the other good in order to maintain utility at the same level. (See, for example, the indifference curves in figure 6.) Also, the transformation function could assume a variety of forms. Over some range it would probably exhibit diminishing marginal returns, that is, as the amount of public good produced increases, the cost of producing an additional unit increases. In the case of lumpy public goods, it would exhibit discontinuities. Let us go on to consider, then, the more general situation in which the indifference curves have the conventional convexity property.[12]

Consider a public for which some good is perfectly indivisible and non-excludable. Consider some member of the public, player i, who may contribute any amount y_i, between zero and some personal maximum $\overline{Y}_i$, of a *numeraire* private good Y_i ('money'). Denote by X the amount of public good produced, and by X_o the amount produced by all the remaining players, whom I shall henceforth refer to as 'the Others'. (Notice that X is the *amount* of public good, not benefit, as in the discussion of Hardin's case above.) Assume that each individual's preferences can be represented by the usual convex indifference curves. If the transformation function, specifying the quantity of public good which can be produced with a given input (y) of the private good, is linear (i.e., an additional unit of y yields the same additional amount, r say, of X at every level of X) and has no discontinuities, then the situation in which i finds himself is that shown at figure 6. If the amount of the public good produced by the Others is *given* and for the time being fixed, then i can decide what is his best course of action. Suppose, for example, that the amount of public good produced by the Others is X_o^1. (Since the good is perfectly indivisible and nobody is excludable, i also consumes X_o^1). Then if i contributes nothing (produces no additional amount of the public good), he is at the point A. If he devotes *all* of his endowment $\overline{Y}_i$ to the public good, he is at point B. The points on the line AB give the whole range of alternatives available to him, *given* the Others' level of production. He will therefore choose the point P_1 at which his utility is maximized – *if* he assumes that the Others' choices will not in turn be influenced by his choice. Similarly, P_o is his optimal response if the Others' production of the good is zero, P_2 if it is X_o^2, and so on. Clearly, the greater the public good return on a unit outlay of the private good, the more of the public good i will choose to produce for a given production by the Others.

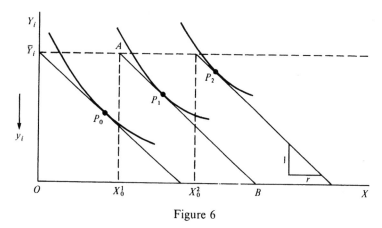

Figure 6

It can be seen that, in this example, the more Others contribute, the *less* will the individual in question contribute. In this respect i's preferences are like those of a Chicken game.

But transformation functions are unlikely to be linear. In many cases they will exhibit diminishing marginal returns, as in figure 7; or the amount of public good which can be provided will at first increase only slowly with increasing contributions, then much faster, then fall off with diminishing marginal returns, as in figure 8. (The shape of the transformation function facing i changes of course as Others provide more of the public good. In effect, each transformation curve in these figures is a lower portion of the curve to its left). If the good is lumpy, the transformation function will be a step function, of which one plausible form is shown in figure 9. Here, the public good cannot be provided at all

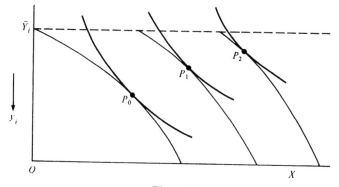

Figure 7

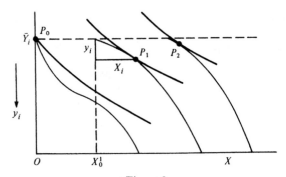

Figure 8

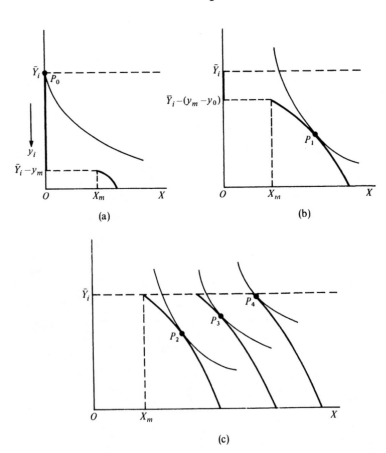

(a)

(b)

(c)

Figure 9

if total contributions are less than some threshold (y_m, say), at which the minimum 'lump' of the public good (an amount X_m) can be provided, and beyond which increasing contributions yield diminishing returns of public good. (Another possibility is that the public good can be provided at only one level – a one-step pure lumpy good – in which case the curvilinear parts of the transformation functions in figure 9 are vertical lines.)

Figure 9 assumes that $y_m < Y_i$, that is, the minimum that must be contributed if any of the public good is to be provided is less than player i's endowment (the most he can contribute). This ensures that $\overline{Y}_i - y_m$ is positive, so that if i contributes enough he alone can cause some of the public good to be provided. In figure 9(a) the Others' contribution (X_o) is zero. So if i contributes less than y_m, none of the public good is provided, and therefore part of the transformation function is the segment of the Y_i axis as shown. When i contributes y_m or more, some amount of the public good is provided, as shown by the curvilinear part of the transformation function. In figure 9(b) the Others have contributed a positive amount (y_o say) but not enough to pass the threshold, so that none of the public good is provided until i has contributed enough ($y_m - y_o$) to bring the total contributions to the threshold y_m. In figure 9(c) the Others' contributions have reached the threshold y_m exactly (the left-most transformation curve), at which point an amount X_m of the public good is provided if i contributes nothing, or they have passed it (the remaining curves). Note that the lumpy form shown in figure 9 is a limiting case of the transformation curve shown in figure 8.

The earliest phase of the sequence in figure 9 has to be modified if $y_m \geqslant \overline{Y}_i$, that is, the minimum that must be contributed if any of the public good is to be provided is at least as great as i's endowment. For as long as the Others' total contribution falls short of y_m by at least $\overline{Y}_i$, then no matter how much player i contributes, he cannot reach the threshold y_m, so cannot cause any of the public good to be provided. If the Others contribute nothing, or any amount less than or equal to $y_m - \overline{Y}_i$, the transformation function facing player i is the whole of the segment $O\overline{Y}_i$ of the Y_i axis. When the Others' contributions exceed $y_m - \overline{Y}_i$, i's transformation function is first as in figure 9(a), then as in figures 9(b) and (c) as the Others' contributions increase.

Let us look now at the pattern of i's optimal responses as the Others' contributions increase. The first point to note is that, for *any* of these transformation functions, if i's indifference curves are 'sufficiently flat' – that is, the individual's valuation of the public good is sufficiently low relative to his valuation of his private good – then his optimal response to any level of contribution by the Others is a zero contribution; so that, if this is so for every individual, the game is a Prisoners' Dilemma. (How 'flat' the indifference curves must be depends of course on the shape of the transformation function.)

If the indifference map is not like this, then the patterns of optimal response most likely to occur are of two kinds. The first, which is Chicken-like, has already been encountered in figure 6 with a linear transformation function: here, the more Others contribute, the less will i want to contribute (and if Others contribute enough, i will want to contribute nothing). This pattern is also illustrated in figure 7, and it is easy to see how it could occur (with 'steeper' indifference curves) in figure 8. For the lumpy good shown in figure 9, it could arise only if the threshold y_m was sufficiently small so that a sufficiently 'steep' in-difference curve in figure 9(a) would be tangent to the curvilinear part of the transformation function. The second pattern is shown in figure 9 and is likely to arise only where the transformation function corresponds to a step or lumpy good (of which the function in figure 9 is an example) or is of the sort shown in figure 8 (of which figure 9 is a limiting case). In this case, i's optimal response is to contribute nothing if Others contribute nothing (P_o in figure 9(a)), but to make a contribution if the Others' contributions exceed some minimum (P_1, P_2, etc. in figure 9(b) and (c)). In this respect the resulting game (if every individual has a similar response pattern) is *Assurance-like*. But when i does contribute, his contribution declines with increases in the Others' contributions. In this respect, the game is *Chicken-like*. What is happening here is that, because of the shape of the transformation function (reflecting the fact that little (figure 8) or none (figure 9) of the public good can be provided out of small contributions, but beyond some threshold a small increase in contributions yields a substantial increase in public goods provision), an individual may find that if the Others are contributing enough (but not too much), a small contribution from him yields so much more of the public good that he is more than compensated for the costs of his contribution. In figure 8, for example, if Others contribute an amount in the region of X_0^1, a small contribution (y_i) from i yields a great increase (X_i) in the public good. Similarly in figure 9(b), when Others have contributed most of the minimum necessary (y_m) to start production of the public good, a small additional contribution from i takes the group over the threshold (to the point P_1 for example).

This *Assurance/Chicken* pattern is an intuitively plausible one, and where contributions vary continuously it is likely to arise in just those situations (discussed earlier) which would be Chicken games if the individual could choose only between a zero contribution and a single fixed level of contribution. In the flood control and irrigation case, for example, if each cultivator could choose *any* level of contribution (work effort) up to some maximum, then the transformation function is likely to be of the kind shown in figures 8 or 9; so that, unless every individual values the public good (irrigation, flood control, etc.) so little as to make the resulting game a Prisoners' Dilemma, which is unlikely in this case, there are two possibilities: (a) the Chicken-like case in which each individual values the public good so much that he is able and prepared to provide some of it when Others provide none, but will contribute less as Others contribute more; or (b) the combined Assurance/Chicken case in which each individual does not value the public good highly enough to find it worthwhile to provide some of it alone, but will contribute to its provision if Others do, though contributing less as Others contribute more. In the irrigation and flood control example, the first of these possibilities is perhaps less likely than the second, because although each individual may value this public good very highly indeed he is unable alone to provide any of it (figure 9) or enough of it to make it worth his while (figure 8).

These are not the only possible response patterns, of course, though they are probably the ones most likely to occur.

In chapter 1 I suggested that *indivisibility* and *nonrivalness* should be distinguished, though they are commonly not. The difference between them can be clearly seen in terms of the diagrams we are using here. If a good is not perfectly indivisible, then as group size, N, increases, the amount available for an individual's consumption decreases. Since the transformation function represents the consumption *possibilities* for an individual, given the amounts of public good already provided by Others and by himself, its shape would change as N varied. In fact, as N increased in the case of an imperfectly indivisible good, the amount of the public good available to i (for a given total contribution of the private good) would decrease (so the transformation curve would rotate or shift in a southwesterly direction).

On the other hand, if some rivalness was present, the indifference maps should change as N varied, becoming 'flatter' with increasing N to reflect the lower value that *a given quantity of the public good* has to the individual in question as more consumers are present.

The effect of an increase in N on the individual's contribution (for a given contribution by the Others) need not be the same in the two cases.

Cournot analysis

We saw in the last section that an individual could determine his optimal level of contribution – given the total amount of public good provided by the remaining individuals and assuming that their choices in turn are not influenced by his decision, that is, that each individual behaves non-strategically (such behaviour is known as Cournot behaviour). Suppose now that there are just two individuals and that for each of them we can determine an optimal response to each level of public good provided by the other. Let $X_1^0(X_2)$ denote individual 1's optimal response for a given value of X_2, the amount of the public good provided by individual 2. Define $X_2^0(X_1)$ similarly. These *response functions* or *reaction curves* can take many forms. For the Chicken-like cases illustrated in figures 6 and 7 above, typical shapes of the reaction curves are those shown in figure 10.

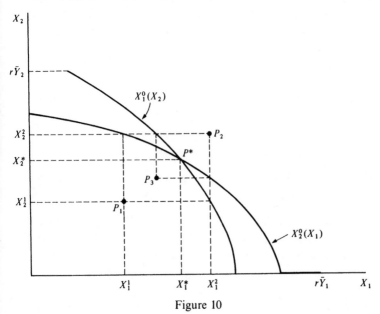

Figure 10

Assuming still that each individual behaves non-strategically, suppose that initially the two individuals choose to produce amounts X_1^1 and X_2^1 of the public good (the point P_1 in figure 10). Then each realizes that his own production is not optimal, given the other's choice. Individual 1 will increase his production to $X_1^0(X_2^1) = X_1^2$, and individual 2 will increase his to X_2^2. This brings them to P_2. But here, too, each has an incentive to alter his level of production, and they will move to P_3. This 'process' will converge to the point P^* in figure 10, the point at which the two reaction curves intersect, and P^* is the only point at which neither individual has an incentive to change his production level unilaterally. It is, in other words, an equilibrium. This equilibrium need not be Pareto-optimal.

On the assumption of non-strategic behaviour, an individual's optimal response to a given level of provision of the public good by Others – and therefore his entire reaction curve – would be the same no matter how many other individuals there were. If we also assume that all individuals have identical preferences and the same initial endowments of private good that can be devoted to production of the public good, then it is possible to examine the movement of the (Cournot) equilibrium as the size of the group increases. This has been done by John Chamberlin and Martin McGuire, who have shown that if the good exhibits pure jointness or indivisibility and there is perfect nonrivalness, then the amount contributed by each individual at the Cournot equilibrium declines with increasing group size, tending to zero as N approaches infinity, but that provided the public good is not an inferior good[13] for any individual the *total* amount of the public good provided at the equilibrium *increases* with group size.[14] (This result depends critically on the assumption that the reaction curves do not vary with N – which holds only if the good is purely indivisible and perfectly nonrival *and the total costs of providing the public good do not rise with N*. This second condition is not mentioned by Chamberlin or McGuire.)

If, on the other hand, the public good is not purely indivisible or there is some degree of rivalness (though the good is still non-excludable), then the individual's equilibrium production decreases as N increases, but the group's total production may increase *or* decrease depending on how the reaction curves vary with N.[15]

These results for the case of non-strategic or Cournot behaviour are consistent with those stated in the discussion of Olson's 'size' argument in chapter 1. But in my view we should not attach much significance to them, for three reasons. First, as it is conventional to point out, the Cournot analysis is based on the quite unacceptable assumption that each individual reacts to what others do while assuming that they do not react to what he does, that is, that in reacting to their choices he can ignore the effect of his actions on theirs. Second, the analysis is entirely static. The reactions and counter-reactions of which it speaks constitute only a sort of pseudo-dynamics; they are merely conjectural, taking place, as it were, only in the heads of the players. As I have argued already, public goods provision is generally a *process*; interaction, usually strategic, takes place *in time*. This should be modelled explicitly (as it is in the analysis in the next two chapters). Third, in many important public goods interactions, the reaction curves will not resemble those shown in figure 10 and in some (perfectly plausible) cases there will be multiple local equilibria and the Cournot analysis will provide no reason to expect that any one of them will be the outcome. For example, if in a two-person situation the transformation function and indifference maps are such as to produce the Assurance/Chicken pattern of optimal responses illustrated by figures 8 and 9 above, then the two reaction curves resemble those in figure 11. In this case, the points O and P^* are locally stable. But starting at some points, such as A and B in figure 11, the Cournot series of reactions will not converge on O or P^* or on any other point.

A summary remark

The general thrust of this chapter, with or without the Cournot analysis, has been that in public goods interaction the individuals' preferences at any point in time are not necessarily those of a Prisoners' Dilemma game. This is true of both two-person and N-person games and of cases where strategy sets are continuous as well as those where the players have only two strategies available to them. I have argued in particular that important classes of public goods provision problems are better represented by Assurance and especially Chicken games and in the continuous case by games that are Chicken-like or like a hybrid of Assurance and Chicken. In these cases, arguably, if the games are played only once, *some* cooperation is more likely to be forthcoming than in cases for which the Prisoners' Dilemma is the appropriate model.

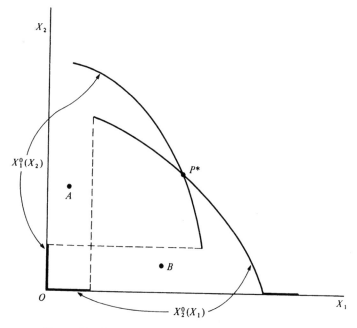

Figure 11   Reaction curves for an Assurance/Chicken Game

In the next two chapters, however, I shall assume the worst: that preferences at any point in time are indeed those of a Prisoners' Dilemma game. But then I shall go on to consider the possibility of cooperation when this game is repeated.

3. The two-person Prisoners' Dilemma supergame

The treatment of the problem of public goods provision in the last chapter was entirely static. It was concerned only with preferences at one point in time, and conclusions about public goods provision were derived solely from these static preferences. Individuals were supposed, in effect, to make only one choice, once and for all (a choice of how much to contribute to the provision of the public good). Olson's *Logic of Collective Action* and other studies referred to in the first two chapters are static in this way.

Needless to say, it is not always like this in the real world. With respect to most public goods, the choice of whether to contribute to their provision and of how much to contribute is a recurring choice; in some cases it is a choice that is permanently before the individual. This is true of the choice of how much to exploit the 'common': how many whales to take in each year, how much to treat industrial waste before discharging it into the lake and so on. It is also true of the individual's choice of whether or not to behave peaceably, to refrain from violence, robbery and fraud and so on.

I propose to treat these recurring choices in the context of a supergame.

Supergames

The remarks and definitions in this section apply both to the two-person analysis to which the remainder of this chapter is devoted and to the *N*-person analysis in the following chapter.

A *supergame* is simply a sequence of games. The games in the sequence are called the *constituent games* of the supergame. In this book I shall consider only supergames which are iterations of a single game. The constituent game will be a Prisoners' Dilemma in which two strategies are available to each player: to Cooperate (C) or to Defect (D). In each constituent game of this Prisoners' Dilemma supergame the players make their choices simultaneously (that is, in ignorance of the other players' choices in that game), but they know the strategies chosen by all the players in all previous games.

The Prisoners' Dilemma is by definition a non-cooperative game. The Prisoners' Dilemma supergame is thus also a non-cooperative game. Either agreements may not be made (perhaps because communication is impossible or because the making of agreements is prohibited) or, if agreements may be made, players are not constrained to keep them. It is the possibility of cooperation in the *absence* of such constraint that I am interested in here.

In this dynamic setting it is possible for an actor to make his choices dependent on the earlier choices of other players. In particular, cooperation could be made conditional on the cooperation of the other player or players. This idea will be central in the analysis which follows. It will emerge, as one would intuitively expect, that if cooperation is to be sustained amongst rational egoists, it must be through the use of conditionally cooperative strategies.

The constituent game of a supergame will be thought of as being played at regular discrete intervals of time, or one in each time period. Each player receives his constituent game payoff at the end of each time period. The supergame is assumed to 'begin' at $t = 0$ and the constituent game payoffs to be made at $t = 1, 2, 3, \ldots$

It is reasonable to assume that the present worth to a player of a future payoff is less the more distant in time the payoff is to be made. Specifically, I make the usual assumption that future payoffs are discounted exponentially. Thus the value at time $t = 0$ of a payoff X_t to be made at time t (at the end of the tth game) is $X_t a_i^t$. The number a_i is called the *discount factor* of player i, and its complement $1 - a_i$ is the discount *rate*.[1] It is assumed that $0 < a_i < 1$. Thus the present value of a finite payoff from a game infinitely distant in the future is zero. The discount rates, though they may differ between individuals, are assumed to remain constant through time. An important consequence of this assumption (given that the constituent games do not change over time) is that for each player the supergame in prospect looks the same at any point in time.

The processes in which I am interested are of indefinite length. They are represented here by supergames which can be interpreted either as being composed of a countably infinite number of constituent games or as having a known and fixed probability of terminating in any time period.

These two assumptions – of discounting and indefinite length – seem to me to be appropriate ones for the problems I am interested in here, and indeed for most other social and economic processes which could be modelled by supergames. Whether or not one thinks the future *should* be discounted (especially in such contexts as the conservation of non-renewable resources or the dumping of nuclear wastes), the idea that rational egoists playing supergames of indefinite length might actually place as much value on a payoff to be received far into the future as on the same payoff to be received immediately is quite implausible.[2]

If the supergame has only a *finite* number of constituent games (and the players know this), the 'dilemma' remains, in the sense that Defection in every constituent game is the only undominated strategy, no matter what the constituent game payoffs are. Consider a two-person Prisoners' Dilemma game iterated T times. At the start of this supergame, each player knows that in the final game (there being no possibility of reprisals), Defection is his only undominated strategy, so he will choose it; and he knows that for the same reason the other player will choose D. The outcome of the final game is therefore a foregone conclusion. The penultimate, or $(T-1)^{th}$ game, is now effectively the final game and the same argument applies to it. Each player will choose D and expect the other player to do likewise. Similarly for the $(T-2)^{th}$ game, and so on, back to the first game.[3]

A *supergame strategy* is a sequence of strategies, one in each constituent game. In the Prisoners' Dilemma supergame, the strategy in which C is chosen in every constituent game will be denoted by C^∞; that in which D is chosen in every constituent game will be denoted by D^∞. Other supergame strategies of special interest will be introduced below. A *strategy vector*, in either a constituent game or in a supergame, is a list (an ordered n-tuple) of strategies, one for each player.[4]

The *outcome* of a constituent game is the actual state of affairs at the end of the game. An outcome of a supergame is a sequence of outcomes, one for each constituent game. In the constituent games and supergames considered here, an outcome is uniquely determined by the strategies actually chosen by the players.

Associated with each strategy vector in a constituent game is a *payoff vector*, which is a list (an ordered n-tuple) of payoffs, one for each player. A payoff is to be thought of as a quantity of some basic private good, such as money, or amounts of several private goods reduced to a single quantity of some *numeraire*, such as money. In this chapter and the next, each player is assumed simply to seek to maximize his own payoff, and his payoff scale is assumed to be *cardinal* (that is, it has an arbitrary zero and unit and can be replaced by any positive linear transformation of itself). Here the payoffs may be identified with 'utilities', in the sense that a player (strictly) prefers one outcome to another if and only if the first yields a greater payoff (utility) than does the second and he is indifferent between them if and only if they yield equal payoffs. But in a later chapter on altruism this identification is not made, for here a player's utility is assumed to be a function of the payoffs of other players as well as his own.

A *supergame payoff* to a player is the sum of an infinite series whose terms are his payoffs in the ordinary games. The discounted value of this payoff at $t = 0$ is thus $\Sigma_{t=1}^{\infty} X_t a_i^t$, where X_t is i's payoff at time t (his payoff from the game in period t). Since $0 < a_i < 1$, this infinite series converges (that is, the supergame payoff is finite) for any sequence of payoffs $\{X_t\}$, just as long as each X_t is finite (as it always will be here). In the two-person case, the supergame payoffs can be exhibited in a payoff matrix, as in the ordinary game.

The concepts of dominance and Pareto-optimality have already been introduced (in chapter 1). The definitions given there also apply, *mutatis mutandis*, to supergames, but a few more terms are needed. The definitions which follow apply to both ordinary games and supergames.

An outcome is said to be *Pareto-preferred* to another if and only if at least one player (strictly) prefers the first to the second and no player (strictly) prefers the second to the first.

An *equilibrium* is defined as a strategy vector such that no player can obtain a larger payoff using a different strategy while the other players' strategies remain the same. An equilibrium, then, is such that, if each player *expects* it to be the outcome, he has no incentive to use a different strategy. Thus, if indeed every player expects a certain equilibrium to be the outcome, then it is reasonable to suppose that this equilibrium will in fact be the outcome. But a player may have reasons for expecting that a certain equilibrium will not be the outcome. Then he might not use his equilibrium strategy and the equilibrium will not be the outcome.

This possibility is important, as we shall see, in the study of supergames. For whereas in the Prisoners' Dilemma ordinary game there is only one equilibrium and there is no reason for a player not to expect it to be the outcome, in Prisoners' Dilemma supergames there are generally several equilibria and the question arises whether some of them may be eliminated as possible outcomes because at least one of the players does not expect them to occur.

For convenience, the following expressions are sometimes used in this chapter and the next. A strategy vector is said to be *always* an equilibrium if and only if it is an equilibrium no matter what the ordinary game payoffs are (as long as they satisfy the inequality which makes the ordinary game a Prisoners' Dilemma) and no matter what values the discount factors assume (as long as each a_i satisfies $0 < a_i < 1$). A strategy vector is *sometimes* an equilibrium if and only if it is an equilibrium for some but not all values of the ordinary game payoffs and the discount factors. If a strategy vector is neither always nor sometimes an equilibrium, then it is said to be *never* an equilibrium.

The general purpose of the remainder of this chapter is to study the conditions under which cooperation of various kinds will occur in Prisoners' Dilemma supergames. The approach will be to determine which strategy vectors are equilibria and under what conditions, and, where there are multiple equilibria, which of them is likely to be the outcome of the game. The remainder of this chapter[5] will be concerned with the two-person supergame, and the N-person game will be tackled in the following chapter.

Unconditional Cooperation and Defection

Consider then the supergame consisting of iterations of the two-person Prisoners' Dilemma game whose payoff matrix is:[6]

	C	D
C	x, x	z, y
D	y, z	w, w

where $y > x > w > z$. Rows are chosen by player 1, columns by player 2.

The first, and depressing, thing to note about this supergame is that it never pays either player to change his strategy unilaterally if both players are playing D^∞, the strategy of choosing D in every constituent game regardless of the other player's previous choices; that is, *mutual unconditional Defection is always an equilibrium*. This is easily demonstrated. Any strategy *other* than D^∞ must either result in D being played on every move (in which case switching to it unilaterally from D^∞ yields the same payoff) or in C being played in one or more constituent games. Such a switch has no effect on the other player, since he Defects unconditionally. So, in these C-moves, the player who switches gets less (z rather than w) than he would have done if he'd stuck to D^∞, while in all the remaining moves he gets the same (w). This is so regardless of the values of the constituent game payoffs and of the discount rates. So (D^∞, D^∞) is always an equilibrium. It is therefore a candidate for the outcome of the supergame. The conditions under which this disastrous result would occur are examined below.

We note next that (C^∞, C^∞) is *never* an equilibrium, for either player can obtain a greater payoff by switching unilaterally to D^∞.

In fact, any strategy pair in which *either* player chooses C^∞ is never an equilibrium. Against C^∞, another player can always gain by changing his strategy to D^∞, since whatever he changes to will have no effect on the first player, whose choices are unconditional. And if one player is already using D^∞, then the C^∞ player can gain by switching to D^∞. More generally, *any* strategy which results in C being played in any constituent game is never an equilibrium when paired with D^∞. This will include any of the conditionally cooperative strategies to be defined below. In any constituent game in which the strategy specifies a C move, the player could do better by switching to D when playing against D^∞. In other words, *it doesn't pay to Cooperate against D^∞*.

The possibility of conditional Cooperation

Both C and D are *unconditional* strategies. Since a C^∞ player persists in playing C regardless of the other player's moves, he can be taken advantage of. Suppose he instead adopts a *conditionally* cooperative approach, playing C only if the other player does too. More precisely, suppose he chooses C in the first constituent game, and in successive games chooses C if and only if the other player chose C in the preceding game. Call this strategy B. It has often been referred to as the 'Tit-for-Tat' strategy. Of course, against a player who Defects unconditionally, playing B produces a worse outcome than would playing D^∞. But if both players use B, then mutual Cooperation is the outcome in every constituent game. Can this be sustained; that is, is (B, B) an equilibrium?

Let us first see whether it pays either player to defect unilaterally from B to D^∞, given that the other player is using B. The result of such a switch is that the other player, after playing C in the first constituent game, observes that the first player chose D in that game and therefore chooses D in the second game, and similarly in every succeeding game. His conditional Cooperation, in other words, 'collapses' immediately. Now whether such a switch yields any gain depends on his *discount rate*, since in making this switch the player *gains* in the first time period (the one in which he switches) but *loses* in every period thereafter – relative, that is, to the payoffs he would have received had he stuck to strategy B. This would only produce a net gain if he valued later payoffs so much less than earlier ones that the gain in the first period outweighed the losses in all later periods. Let us derive the precise form of this condition.

If, against a player using B, player i (with discount factor a_i) also uses B, his payoff in each constituent game is x, so that his discounted supergame payoff is the sum of the infinite series $x(a_i + a_i^2 + a_i^3 + \ldots)$, which is $xa_i/(1 - a_i)$. If he switches unilaterally to D^∞, his payoff in the first game is y and in every succeeding game w, so that his supergame payoff is $ya_i + wa_i^2/(1 - a_i)$. So the switch does *not* yield a gain if and only if this second payoff is no greater than the first. When this inequality is rearranged, we find that we must have:

$$a_i \geqslant \frac{y - x}{y - w} \tag{3.1}$$

or, in terms of the discount *rate*,

$$1 - a_i \leqslant \frac{x - w}{y - w}$$

So: if unilateral defection from (B, B) to D^∞ is not to pay, the discount rate must not be too great. How great depends on the constituent game payoffs. In particular, it is intuitively obvious, and condition (3.1) shows formally, that the smaller the 'instant' gain from defection – the difference $y - x$, which we could call the player's *temptation* – the less likely, other things being equal, will unilateral defection to D^∞ yield a gain in the supergame.

An Assurance game

Suppose for the moment that B and D^∞ are the only strategies available to each player or the only ones they consider, and suppose that condition (3.1) is satisfied for both players, so that (B, B) is an equilibrium. More strongly, suppose that the inequality in (3.1) is strict, so that (B, B) is *strictly* preferred by player 1 to (D^∞, B) and by player 2 to (B, D^∞). Then it is easily verified that the ordinal preferences among the four possible outcomes are:

	B	D^∞
B	4, 4	1, 3
D^∞	3, 1	2, 2

(where as usual a higher number represents a more preferred outcome). This makes the supergame an *Assurance* game (as defined in chapter 2). There are then two equilibria, (D^∞, D^∞) and (B, B), but since one of them, (B, B), is preferred by both players to the other, neither player would expect (D^∞, D^∞) to be the outcome, so that (B, B) would be the outcome (because the point about an equilibrium of this kind is that *if* every player *expects* it to be the outcome – which means that every player is expected to play the appropriate strategy – then it *will* be the outcome).

But if (B, B) is *not* an equilibrium, this reduced supergame is itself a Prisoners' Dilemma, and then of course (D^∞, D^∞) is the outcome.

Conditions for (B, B) to be an equilibrium

We have shown that under certain conditions (B, B) is robust against unilateral defections to D^∞. But the number of possible strategies in any supergame is infinite. If defection by either player from (B, B) to D^∞ does not pay, might it nevertheless pay to defect to some other strategy? Consider the supergame strategy which, like B, is a tit-for-tat strategy, but unlike B begins with D in the first constituent game. Call it B'. If one player (i) switched from B to B' while the other (j) played B, then in the sequence of moves which would result, (D, C) would *alternate* with (C, D):

$$\text{player } i \ (B'): DCDC \ldots$$
$$\text{player } j \ (B): CDCD \ldots$$

The same sequence would result, of course, if player i switched to the strategy of unconditionally alternating between D and C after playing D in the first game. Player i's discounted supergame payoff is now:

$$ya_i + za_i^2 + ya_i^3 + za_i^4 + \ldots$$

which sums to

$$\frac{ya_i}{1 - a_i^2} + \frac{za_i^2}{1 - a_i^2}$$

or $(y + za_i)a_i/(1 - a_i^2)$. Such a switch from (B, B) to B' would not yield player i a gain if and only if this sum is no greater than his payoff from (B, B), which is $xa_i/(1 - a_i)$. On rearranging, this condition becomes

$$a_i \geqslant \frac{y - x}{x - z} \tag{3.2}$$

Note that (3.2) neither entails nor is entailed by (3.1). So both conditions must be included in the necessary conditions for (B, B) to be an equilibrium. Or combining them, we can say that a *necessary* condition for (B, B) to be an equilibrium is that both players' discount factors, a_1 and a_2, must be at least as big as the larger of the two ratios specified in (3.1) and (3.2).

Is this a sufficient condition? It turns out that it is. At an equilibrium, each player's strategy is the 'best response' to the other player's strategy, in the sense that there is no strategy which it would be better to use than the equilibrium strategy, given that the other player will use *his* equilibrium strategy. Suppose that one player is using strategy B. His first move is therefore C. Now consider the other player's response to B.

Suppose that, whatever is the best response to B, it begins with C in the first constituent game. Then the B-player's move in the second game is C. So if the best response to B begins with C in the first game, then it must also play C in the second game. This is because (1) for each player the game ahead is the same at any point in time (since both the discount rates and the constituent game payoffs were assumed to remain constant), and (2), a player using strategy B is responsive to the other player's choices in the preceding game only. It follows that, if the best response to B begins with C, it must play C in every constituent game.

Suppose now that, whatever is the best response to B, it begins with D. (It follows that if in any later game the B-player chooses C, the best response will play D in that game). Then the B-player's move in the second game is D. There are now two possibilities for the best move in the second game:

(i) Suppose that whatever is the best response to B, it plays C in any game in which the B-player chooses D. Then the B-player's next move (in the third game) is C . . . so that the best response to B plays D in this game. And so on. This generates the pattern of alternation between (C, D) and (D, C) throughout the supergame.

(ii) Suppose instead that the best response to B would play D in any game in which the B-player chooses D. Then the B-player's next move (in the third game) is D. So again the best response must play D in the third game. And so on. This generates a best response in which D is chosen in every constituent game.

This exhausts the possibilities. Against B, the best response *must* be to play C in every game (as would happen if B were played) *or* to alternate between D and C beginning with D (as would happen if B' were played) *or* to play D in every game. No other response can do better against B than the best of these three. It follows that if a player cannot gain by switching unilaterally from (B, B) to B' or D^∞, then no other strategy will yield a gain. Thus, if conditions (3.1) and (3.2) – which guarantee that (B, B) is stable against defections to D^∞ and B' – are satisfied, then (B, B) is an equilibrium.

It has been shown, then, that a *necessary and sufficient condition for* (B, B) *to be an equilibrium is that each player's discount factor is no less than the larger of* $(y - x)/(y - w)$ *and* $(y - x)/(x - z)$.

Of course, this result does not imply that when this condition is satisfied, (B, B) is the outcome of the game. I return to this matter below.

Axelrod's tournaments

A similar result to the one just proved can be found in Axelrod's book *The Evolution of Cooperation*. His proof of necessity is essentially the one given above, which follows the analysis in *Anarchy and Cooperation*. Although in the earlier treatment (B, B) was shown to be stable against unilateral defections to the class of strategies A_k to be discussed below, as well as defections to D^∞ and B', I did not prove sufficiency. Axelrod's 'proof' of the sufficiency part[7] is incomplete (at least); he may have had in mind the proof I gave here but this is unclear from what he actually says.

Axelrod's result actually concerns, not the (Nash) equilibrium of the strategy pair (B, B), but the 'collective stability' of the strategy B (which he calls TIT-FOR-TAT). The notion of collective stability derives from the concept of an 'evolutionarily stable strategy' introduced into evolutionary biology by Maynard Smith, and is defined in a model which supposes that there is a population of individuals all using a certain strategy (S, say) and asks whether it can be 'invaded' by a single mutant individual using some other strategy (S'). The mutant strategy is said to *invade* the native strategy if it can do better playing repeatedly against a native than a native can do against another native. Then, a strategy is said to be *collectively stable* if no strategy can invade it.

Thus, a collectively stable strategy is, as Axelrod puts it, 'in Nash equilibrium with itself', that is, if S is a collectively stable strategy then (S, S) is an equilibrium. But of course an equilibrium need not consist of a pair (or a population) of identical strategies (and in what follows we shall see that pairs of different strategies can be equilibria under certain conditions in the two-person supergame, and in the next chapter we shall establish that there are equilibria in the N-person supergame which are composed of several different strategies). Nash equilibrium, then, is not the same thing as collective stability, and Axelrod's 'Characterization Theorem' is not very helpful in carrying out a full equilibrium analysis.

Axelrod, in fact, confines his attention to *tournaments*, in which individuals play in *pairs*. This is true both of his theoretical analysis, which is based, as we have seen, on the notion of a collectively stable strategy, and of the round-robin computer tournament he conducted. In the latter, a number of game theorists, economists, etc., submitted strategies, each of which was paired against itself and against each of the others in a Prisoners' Dilemma supergame. The strategies were then ranked according to their aggregate performance. (TIT-FOR-TAT – the strategy I have called B – won, and in a second competition, involving strategies submitted in the light of the results of the first competition, it won again.)

Axelrod comes to the same *general* conclusion we arrive at here (and which was at the heart of the analysis of the Prisoners' Dilemma supergame in *Anarchy and Cooperation*), namely that 'the two key requisites for cooperation to thrive are that the cooperation be based on reciprocity, and that the shadow of the future is important enough to make this reciprocity stable.'[8]

But is his approach, based on the idea of the tournament and the concept of a collectively stable strategy, to be preferred to an analysis using the notion of a (Nash) equilibrium? I think not. Pairwise interaction may be characteristic of non-human populations (though even this is doubted by Maynard Smith himself), but it certainly does not characterize most human interactions which give rise to collective action problems. These of course generally involve more than two individuals and, especially where the provision of public goods is at stake, an individual's behaviour typically depends on the whole aggregate pattern of behaviours of the rest of the group. For example, his decision whether or not to cooperate in the provision of a public good would generally be contingent on there being *enough others* cooperating. Situations of this kind cannot be characterized in terms of pairwise interactions. Even where, in the real world, interactions are truly pairwise, they are most unlikely to take the strange form assumed by Axelrod: his analysis hinges on the assumption that an individual will play out the whole of an infinite supergame with one other player, or each player in turn, rather than, say, ranging through the population, or part of it, playing against different players at different times in the supergame (possibly playing each of them a random number of times).[9]

Axelrod, admitting that his book 'will examine interactions between just two players at a time', suggests that 'situations that involve more than pairwise interaction can be modelled with the more complex n-person Prisoner's Dilemma',[10] but does not attempt the analysis himself. We shall take up the study of N-person Prisoners' Dilemmas in the next chapter.

Coordination equilibria

It is worth mentioning in passing that *if* (B, B) is an equilibrium in the two-person Prisoners' Dilemma supergame it is also a *coordination equilibrium*. A coordination equilibrium is a strategy pair such that either player is made no better off, not only if he himself unilaterally changes strategy, but also if the *other* player changes strategy. Consider (B, B). In the case of the other player defecting to D^∞, the effect on the non-defecting player is the same as it would have been if *he* had defected, except in the first constituent game, where now he gets even less than he would have done had he defected (z rather than y); so that if his own defection makes him no better off, the other's defection certainly will not.

Similar remarks apply to changes to other strategies (except where such a change produces the same sequence of constituent game outcomes): for example, if defection to B' by either player makes him no better off, then nor will he be made better off by the other player's defection to B', since the two resulting sequences of constituent game outcomes are identical – alternation between (C, D) and (D, C) – except that the sequence begins with (D, C) if *he* defects and (C, D), which is worse for him, if the *other* defects. Thus, if (B, B) is an equilibrium, it is a coordination equilibrium. This is not, of course, true of (D^∞, D^∞), which is always an equilibrium but never a coordination equilibrium.

Russell Hardin believes that the fact that (B, B) and other strategy vectors are *coordination* equilibria makes an important difference to the explanation of behaviour in Prisoners' Dilemma games. A coordination equilibrium, he says, is even more likely to be the outcome than a mere equilibrium because it is 'supported by a double incentive to each player', for each player has an interest in himself conforming with the equilibrium and an interest in the other player conforming as well.[11]

Actually, as we have seen, in the Prisoners' Dilemma supergame with discounting, (B, B) need not even be an equilibrium. But we have to assume that Hardin has in mind an indefinitely iterated Prisoners' Dilemma *with no discounting*, since strangely he nowhere mentions discounting, and that each player's supergame payoffs are long-run averages of the constituent game payoffs. As I have already argued, these games are of little importance in the analysis of social life. They are also much simpler analytically, since they involve none of the complex trade-offs between payoffs in different time periods that are possible in supergames with discounting. In these no-discount games, (B, B) is in fact always an equilibrium and also a coordination equilibrium.

But even if (B, B), or any other strategy vector, is a coordination equilibrium, this fact does not provide each player with a 'double incentive' to conform to it. That *I* want the *other* player to conform is of no relevance to him, for we have assumed that he, like me, is a rational egoist: *my* interest in his conforming has no effect on his actions, just as my actions are unaffected by his desire that I should conform. The possibility that my interest in his actions would lead me to do something to ensure that he acts in the right way is not one that can be considered within Hardin's framework (or mine). 'My interest in your conforming means that, if there is a way to do so at little or no net cost to me, I will want to give you further incentive to conform', says Hardin,[12] but options in *this* cost-benefit comparison are not in the model to begin with and, as always, should not be wheeled in *ad hoc.*

The existence of a coordination equilibrium, then, does not give a player *two* reasons for conforming to it, and the fact that an equilibrium is a coordination equilibrium does not make it doubly likely to be the outcome. I take up the (complicated) question of which equilibrium will be the outcome in a later section.

Other mutual Cooperation equilibria

The tit-for-tat strategy is not the only strategy which, if used by both players, will sustain mutual Cooperation throughout the supergame. Any strategy which plays C on the first move and then continues to play C *if* the other player does, will do. Any two (possibly different) strategies of this sort will sustain such cooperation regardless of what the strategies require each player to do when the other player defects. Call such a strategy *conditionally cooperative.* The *conditions* for a pair of such strategies to be an equilibrium will depend on the particular strategies chosen. Consider for example the class of strategies A_k discussed by Shubik.[13] A_k, where k is a strictly positive integer, is defined as follows:

> C is chosen in the first game, and it is chosen in each subsequent game as long as the other player chooses C in the previous game; if the other Defects in any game, D is chosen for the next k games; C is then chosen no matter what the other player's last choice is; it continues to be chosen as long as the other player chooses C in the preceding game; when the other player next Defects, D is chosen for $k + 1$ games; and so on; the number of games in which the other player is 'punished' for a Defection increases by one each time; and each time there is a return to C.

Denote the limiting case of A_k when $k \rightarrow \infty$ by A_∞: in this case, C is chosen until the other player first Defects, after which D is chosen in all succeeding constituent games.

These strategies are special cases of a class of strategies I will label $A_{k,l}$, where k is a strictly positive integer and l is a non-negative integer.

$A_{k,l}$ is the same as A_k except that the 'punishment' period (which is again of k moves duration after the other player's first Defection) is lengthened by l Defections after each succeeding Defection by the other player. When $l = 0$, the punishment periods are all of the same length. When $l = 1$, $A_{k,l}$ is equivalent to A_k.

The conditions for the strategy pair $(A_{k,l}, A_{k,l})$ to be an equilibrium are easily derived. If one player (i) defects unilaterally from this strategy pair to D^∞, then the other player (j) will choose C in game 1 $(t = 1)$, followed by D for the next k moves, then C at $t = k + 2$, followed by D for the next $k + 1$ moves, then C at $t = 2k + l + 3$, and so on. So i's total discounted payoff from the constituent games in which j plays C (and i of course plays D) is:

$$y(a_i + a_i^{k+2} + a_i^{2k+l+3} + \ldots)$$

The infinite series in parentheses is obviously convergent, since it is less than the convergent series $a_i + a_i^2 + a_i^3 + \ldots$ Call its sum $S(k, l; a_i)$ or S_i for short. We shall not need to find S_i in closed form.

Player i's discounted payoff from all the remaining moves (in which both players choose D) is then $w[a_i/(1 - a_i) - S_i]$. Hence i's total discounted payoff from the supergame is:

$$(y - w)S_i + wa_i/(1 - a_i)$$

Player i does not, therefore, gain by defecting to D^∞ from $(A_{k,l}, A_{k,l})$ if and only if this sum is not greater than the payoff from mutual Cooperation throughout the supergame, which is $xa_i/(1 - a_i)$. This condition, on rearranging, is:

$$\left(\frac{1 - a_i}{a_i}\right) S_i \leqslant \frac{x - w}{y - w} \tag{3.3}$$

Obviously, if mutual defection to D^∞ from $(A_{k,l}, A_{k,l})$ does not pay, then defection to D^∞ from (B, B) will not pay – since the former, unlike the latter, benefits from the other player's periodical return to playing C. So if condition (3.3) is satisfied, condition (3.1) should be satisfied too. This is the case, since $S_i \geqslant a_i$ regardless of the values of k and l. Note that as $k \to \infty$ (and hence the strategy $A_{k,l}$ becomes A_∞), $S_i \to a_i$, so that as $k \to \infty$ condition (3.3) becomes condition (3.1).

If player i defects unilaterally from $(A_{k,\ l},\ A_{k,\ l})$ to B', the sequence of moves is:

$$i\ (B'):\quad DCD \ldots DDCD \ldots DCD \ldots$$
$$j\ (A_{k,l}):\quad CDD \ldots DCDD \ldots CDD \ldots$$
$$\qquad\qquad\qquad\quad \uparrow \qquad\quad \uparrow$$
$$t = 123 \ldots . k+2 \ldots . 2k+l+3 \ldots .$$

Comparing this sequence of moves with that of D^{∞} against $A_{k,\ l}$ considered above, it is clear that player i's payoff gain from moving to B' is less than his payoff gain from moving to D^{∞}. Hence if (3.3) is satisfied then $(A_{k,l},\ A_{k,l})$ is also stable against unilateral defections to B'. And, more generally, against a player (j) who sticks to $A_{k,l}$, any switch by player i from $A_{k,l}$ to a strategy which includes C-moves during the punishment period (throughout which, remember, the other player chooses D regardless of i's moves, apart of course from the Defection by i which triggers the punishment) could do no better than a strategy which plays D throughout the punishment period, but is otherwise the same. The only strategy which might then improve on D^{∞}, when played against $A_{k,l}$, is one which plays C in the game in which j returns to playing C at the end of each punishment period. But if a strategy must play C at that point in order to be a better reply to $A_{k,l}$ than D^{∞}, then it must play C at the first move. Hence, against $A_{k,l}$, no strategy can do better than the better of D^{∞} and any conditionally cooperative strategy. Thus, *condition (3.3), for both players, is a necessary and sufficient condition for $(A_{k,l}, A_{k,l})$ to be an equilibrium.*

As the initial 'punishment' period or the additional 'punishment' periods lengthen, that is, as k and l increase, so S_i decreases. It follows that, for given values of x, y, w and a_i, condition (3.3) is 'increasingly likely' to be satisfied as k and/or l increases. In other words, a longer 'punishment' period (a bigger value of k or l) will succeed in deterring a player from switching to D^{∞} (and therefore from switching to any other strategy) where a shorter 'punishment' period has failed. Some economists, treating general non-cooperative supergames, have restricted their attention to the analogue of the N-person generalization of the strategy A_{∞}, in which eternal 'punishment' (D in every succeeding game) is triggered by a single Defection by the other player.[14] I agree with Shubik that this strategy contains an 'implausible' threat, and that the threats embedded in strategies A_k, for finite k, are more plausible.[15] But then, it seems to me, the strategy B (which Shubik does not mention) is even more plausible than any A_k.

Taking it in turns to Cooperate

There are many equilibria in the supergame besides those examined so far. It would be convenient if all the possible equilibria were (like those considered so far) either such as to result in mutual Cooperation throughout the supergame or such as to result in mutual Defection throughout. Unfortunately, this is not the case. One which does not fall into either category is of special interest, especially (as we shall see later) as it may be preferred by both players to mutual Cooperation throughout the supergame. This is the strategy pair in which one player uses B (tit-for-tat starting with C) and the other player uses B' (tit-for-tat starting with D). Earlier, in discussing the stability of (B, B), we saw that the pair (B, B') produces an alternation of (C, D) and (D, C) throughout the supergame. Under what conditions is it an equilibrium?

Suppose the B player is i and the B' player is j. Before either player changes strategy, i's payoff is $(z + ya_i)a_i/(1 - a_i^2)$ and j's payoff is $(y + za_j)a_j/(1 - a_j^2)$. It is easily verified that a change by i from B to C^∞ yields no gain if and only if

$$a_i \leqslant \frac{y - x}{x - z} \tag{3.4}$$

This is the reverse (not the negation) of condition (3.2).

A change by i from B to D^∞ or to B' produces mutual Defection throughout the supergame and yields i no gain if and only if

$$a_i \geqslant \frac{w - z}{y - w} \tag{3.5}$$

It also turns out that a change of strategy by player j from B' to B or C^∞ yields j no gain if and only if condition (3.4) holds, with j replacing i of course; and a change of strategy by j from B' to D^∞ yields j no gain if and only if condition (3.5) holds for j.

Thus conditions (3.4) and (3.5) are both necessary for (B, B') or (B', B) to be an equilibrium.

We can now show that these conditions are also jointly necessary and sufficient by applying the argument that was used earlier in proving the sufficiency of the condition for (B, B) to be an equilibrium. The argument there showed that, against B, the best response must be to play C in every constituent game or to play D in every game or to alternate between C and D beginning with D (as would happen if B' were played). It follows that if it does not pay to switch unilaterally from B' to C^{∞} or D^{∞}, when the other player is using B, then it does not pay to switch to any other strategy (including, for example, any strategy in the class $A_{k,l}$). A strictly *analogous* argument establishes that, against B', the best response must be to play C in every constituent game or to play D in every game or to alternate between C and D beginning with C. And from this it follows that if it does not pay to switch unilaterally from B to C^{∞} or D^{∞} or B', when the other player is using B', then it does not pay to switch to any other strategy.

Thus, *conditions* (3.4) *and* (3.5), *each holding for both players, are necessary and sufficient conditions for* (B, B') *or* (B', B) *to be an equilibrium.*

Putting the two conditions together, the necessary and sufficient condition is:

$$\frac{w - z}{y - w} \leqslant a_i \leqslant \frac{y - x}{x - z}$$

It is easily checked that this can be satisfied for some but not all permissible values of x, y, z, w and a_i.

So the pattern of alternation, in which the players take it in turns to Cooperate, can be an equilibrium. Whether it will ever actually be the outcome is another matter, which I address in the next section.

Before doing so, let us note the necessary and sufficient conditions, which the reader can easily derive, for (B', B'), (B', D^{∞}) and (D^{∞}, B') to be equilibria. Each of these results in mutual Defection throughout the supergame. For (B', B') the equilibrium conditions are: the reverse (not the negation) of condition (3.5) above (for both players) together with the condition

$$a_i \leqslant \frac{w - z}{x - z} \tag{3.6}$$

for both players. For (B', D^{∞}) the equilibrium conditions are (3.6) and the reverse of (3.5), for $i = 2$ in each case. For (D^{∞}, B') the conditions are again (3.6) and the reverse of (3.5) but now for $i = 1$ in each case.

Table 3

	B	B'	D^∞
B	(3.1) & (3.2) for $i=1, 2$	(3.5) & rev (3.2) for $i=1, 2$	Never an equilibrium
B'	(3.5) & rev (3.2) for $i=1, 2$	(3.6) & rev (3.5) for $i=1, 2$	(3.6) & rev (3.5) for $i=2$
D^∞	Never an equilibrium	(3.6) & rev (3.5) for $i=1$	Always an equilibrium

Outcomes

We have not so far considered every possible pair of strategies; nor do I intend to try. So that, even though we have established necessary and sufficient conditions for those we have considered, the following discussion, which attempts to indicate which of these equilibria is likely to be the outcome of the supergame, is incomplete. I shall confine the discussion to strategy pairs formed from B, B' and D^∞. It is unlikely that an equilibrium which is not examined here would be the outcome, since it would be equivalent to or Pareto-dominated by at least one of those that *are* considered. Table 3 assembles the relevant conditions.

The seven possible equilibria here give rise to just three distinct patterns of choices in the supergame: mutual Cooperation throughout, which occurs in the case of (B, B); the alternation pattern or 'taking it in turns to Cooperate', which results from (B, B') and (B', B); and mutual Defection thoughout, which results from (D^∞, D^∞) and the remaining three equilibria.

We noted earlier that an equilibrium is such that, if every player expects it to be the outcome, and therefore expects all the other players to choose the strategies appropriate to this equilibrium, he has no incentive to choose other than his equilibrium strategy; so the equilibrium will be the outcome. If a game has only one equilibrium, every player would expect it to be the outcome, so it would in fact be the outcome. If, for example, (D^∞, D^∞) is the *only* equilibrium in this two-person Prisoners' Dilemma supergame (i.e., none of the conditions for any of the other strategy pairs to be equilibria are satisfied), then it will be the outcome. But if two or more equilibria occurred simultaneously, then the fact that a certain strategy pair is an equilibrium is not in itself a sufficient reason for any player to expect it to be the outcome. But if, of two simultaneously occurring equilibria, one was preferred by both players to the other, then presumably no player would expect the second to be the outcome, so it would not be the outcome.

So it would be most convenient if, whenever several equilibria occur simultaneously, one of them was preferred by each player to all the remainder (or at least was Pareto-preferred to them, i.e., was no less preferred by either of the players and was strictly preferred by at least one of them). Then we could say that no player would expect any of the Pareto-dominated equilibria to be the outcome and it would not be the outcome. Suppose, for example, that (B, B) is the only equilibrium besides (D^∞, D^∞), which is always an equilibrium. (B, B) is of course strictly preferred by both players to (D^∞, D^∞), which nobody, therefore, would expect to be the outcome. So (B, B) will be the outcome. (The same conclusion, incidentally, would be reached if $A_{k,l}$ were added to table 3. Any or all of the four pairs formed from B and $A_{k,l}$ can be equilibria, but none of the pairs formed from $A_{k,l}$ and either B' or D can be. All four, of course, lead to the same outcome – mutual Cooperation throughout the supergame.) Unfortunately, such a straightforward relation of Pareto-dominance between coexisting equilibria does not always obtain.

Suppose, for example, that the two alternation pairs (B, B') and (B', B) are the only equilibria besides (D^∞, D^∞). *Then it follows that each of the alternation pairs is Pareto-preferred to the mutual Defection equilibrium.* For if (as required by equilibrium) the B player in either of the alternation equilibria does not prefer to defect unilaterally to D^∞ (which would result in mutual Defection throughout), then he must prefer the alternation equilibrium to (D^∞, D^∞) or be indifferent between them; and if the B' player does not prefer to defect unilaterally to D^∞ (as required by equilibrium), then he certainly strictly prefers the alternation pattern to (D^∞, D^∞), because the pattern resulting from such a defection is the same as the (D^∞, D^∞) pattern, except in the first game where he is better off (as unilateral Defector) in the former than in the latter. Thus, whenever (B, B') or (B', B) are equilibria, each is Pareto-preferred to (D^∞, D^∞). In this case neither player will expect (D^∞, D^∞) to be the outcome and it will not be the outcome. This still leaves two equilibria and between these, unfortunately, the two players have opposed preferences: player 1 prefers (B', B), in which *he* Defects first, to (B, B') in which player 2 Defects first, and player 2 has the opposite preference. So even if both players eliminate from consideration all strategies except B and B', they still face the 'coordination' problem of avoiding (B, B) and (B', B') as well as the problem posed by their conflicting preferences between the two equilibria. Within the formal framework we are using, there is no resolution of this problem. In a richer specification of the model, which could be made in any particular application, a solution would no doubt be indicated. The problem has features in common with the problem of Chicken, discussed in the last chapter, and some of the remarks made in the earlier discussion apply here also. But unlike Chicken players, *both* players here prefer either of the asymmetric equilibria to mutual Cooperation. One of the alternation patterns is therefore likely to be the outcome; but which one we cannot say.

So far, then, we have seen that there can be three distinct types of outcome to the supergame:

(i) mutual Defection throughout: this occurs when (D^∞, D^∞) is the only equilibrium;

(ii) mutual Cooperation throughout: this occurs when (B, B) is the only equilibrium besides (D^∞, D^∞);

(iii) alternation between (C, D) and (D, C): this occurs when (B, B') and (B', B) are the only equilibria besides (D^∞, D^∞).

This conclusion is not modified when other equilibria in table 3 coexist with these.

It is exceedingly unlikely that (B, B) is an equilibrium as well as (B, B') and (B', B). For then both condition (3.2) and its reverse must hold, which requires that each player's discount factor is *exactly* $(y - x)/(x - z)$. I think we can ignore this possibility; but if it did occur, then the B' player (in each of the alternation equilibria) would be indifferent between alternation and mutual Cooperation, and which of these outcomes prevailed would simply depend on the other player's preferences between them.[16]

The same is true when in addition to these three equilibria (B', B') is also an equilibrium. For then not only must condition (3.2) and its reverse both hold, but also condition (3.5) and its reverse. So we must have $a_i = (y - x)/(x - z)$ and $a_i = (w - z)/(y - w)$ for *both* players. But then, in any case, both players are indifferent between B and B', for both yield the same payoff no matter whether the other player chooses B or B'. An even more remote possibility is that all seven of the possible equilibria in table 3 are simultaneously equilibria, for then conditions (3.2) and (3.5) and their reverses must hold as well as conditions (3.1) and (3.6) for both players. This is possible, but very unlikely. (E.g., set $y = 3$, $x = 2$, $w = 1$, $z = 0$. Then a_i must be exactly 0.5 for both players.)

If any or all of (B', B'), (B', D^∞) and (D^∞, B') are equilibria simultaneously with (D^∞, D^∞), then if no other strategy pairs are equilibria it does not matter which of B' and D^∞ each player chooses. Mutual Defection throughout the supergame will be the upshot in any case. If these four equilibria occur simultaneously with those in the second and third cases considered above, then the conclusions in each case are unaffected: if (B, B) is also an equilibrium then it is the outcome; and if the alternation pairs are also equilibria, then one of them is the outcome.

One thing that emerges clearly from this analysis, then, is that *if each player's discount rate is sufficiently low, the outcome will be mutual Cooperation throughout the supergame.* For if the discount factors are both greater than $(y - x)/(x - z)$, then (B, B') cannot be an equilibrium (see condition (3.4)); and if both factors are *also* greater than $(y - x)/(y - w)$, then (B, B) is an equilibrium; and if (B, B) is an equilibrium then it is the outcome.

4. The N-person Prisoners' Dilemma supergame

In this chapter I take up the analysis of supergames whose constituent games are Prisoners' Dilemmas with *any* finite number (N) of players. It should hardly need emphasizing that in the real world most of the interesting problems of public goods provision, and of cooperation more generally, involve more than two actors, so that much more attention should be directed at the analysis of N-person supergames than of two-person supergames. Yet very little has been written about such games. Most of what has been done establishes only the existence of equilibrium in general classes of supergames (and, as we have seen, Axelrod's analysis is confined to 'tournaments', in which the interactions are all pairwise). In some respects, results from the two-person analysis generalize in a relatively straightforward way to the N-person games. But new and thorny problems emerge. In particular, as we shall see, in those cases where *subsets* of the players find it collectively worthwhile to provide the public good, there arises a quite different strategic problem, which results from some players having an incentive to ensure that the subset which provides the public good does not include themselves. In this way, a Chicken-like game is generated by the Prisoners' Dilemma.[1]

The analysis will be far from exhaustive. I shall, however, take the discussion far enough to show how Cooperation can arise in the N-person Prisoners' Dilemma, no matter how many players there are, and furthermore can be sustained amongst a *subset* of the players in the face of unconditional Defection throughout the supergame by the remaining players.

The penultimate section will give an informal summary and commentary on the main results and will look at what the formal analysis tells us about the empirical conditions under which cooperation is likely to occur. The reader who does not stay with the necessarily involved (though hardly at all mathematical) analysis which follows can turn to this section directly.

Payoffs in the constituent game

As in the two-person analysis, the supergame considered here consists of a countably infinite number of iterations of a single constituent game. The payoffs associated with a given outcome of the constituent game, then, do not change from game to game. This rules out the possibility that the payoffs in the constituent game are functions not only of the players' choices in that game but also of their choices in previous games. (I comment briefly in the final section on the effect of relaxing this assumption.) As before, the constituent games will be thought of as being played at regular discrete intervals of time, or one in each time period. The supergame is assumed to 'begin' at time $t = 0$ and the constituent game payoffs to be made at $t = 1, 2, 3, \ldots$

I assume that a player's payoffs in each constituent game depend upon two things only: his own strategy (C or D) in that constituent game, and *the number of other players choosing C* in that game. The second part of this assumption is in fact very weak. It is equivalent to assuming that payoffs are independent of the labelling of the players. Its relaxation entails that payoffs depend upon *which* other players choose C.

Denote by $f(v)$ the constituent game payoff to any player when he chooses C and v others choose C, and by $g(v)$ the payoff to any player when he chooses D and v others choose C. I assume that $f(v)$ and $g(v)$ are the same for all players.

The following three assumptions about the functions f and g seem appropriate for the class of problems of interest here:

(i) $g(v) > f(v)$ for each value of $v \geqslant 0$.
(ii) $f(N-1) > g(0)$.
(iii) $g(v) > g(0)$ for all $v > 0$.

The first assumption is true if and only if D dominates C for each player: no matter what strategies the other players use each player prefers D to C. The second assumption is true if and only if each player prefers the outcome which occurs when all players Cooperate to that which occurs when all the players Defect. Thus (i) and (ii) are necessary and sufficient conditions for the constituent game to be an N-person Prisoners'

Dilemma (according to the definition given in chapter 1). Assumption (iii) is eminently reasonable; in fact, a much stronger assumption usually holds in practice, namely that both $f(v)$ and $g(v)$ are strictly increasing with v.[2]

Unconditional Cooperation and Defection

C^∞ and D^∞ will again be used to denote the supergame strategies of unconditional Cooperation and Defection throughout the supergame. A player using C^∞, then, chooses C in every constituent game regardless of the choices of all the other players in the preceding game.

As in the two-person case, universal unconditional Defection – the strategy vector $(D^\infty, D^\infty, \ldots, D^\infty)$ – is always an equilibrium. For any strategy vector other than D^∞ must either result in D being played on every move (so that there is no profit in switching to it unilaterally) or in C being played on at least one move. Since a change of strategy, of any kind, by any of the players, has no effect on the subsequent behaviour of any of the D^∞ players, the player who switches must get less $-f(0)$ rather than $g(0)$ – on each of these C-moves than he would have done had he stuck to D^∞. So $(D^\infty, D^\infty, \ldots, D^\infty)$ is always an equilibrium.

Clearly, universal unconditional Cooperation – the strategy vector $(C^\infty, C^\infty, \ldots, C^\infty)$ – is never an equilibrium. Any player gains by switching unilaterally to D^∞, which yields an increase in payoff from $f(N-1)$ to $g(N-1)$ in every constituent game. In the two-person case, if any player uses C^∞, or if any player when paired with a D^∞-player uses a strategy which results in C being played in any constituent game, the strategy vector cannot be an equilibrium. These propositions do not generalize to the N-person game, where, as we shall see, strategy vectors can be in equilibrium even though *some* of the players use strategies of unconditional Cooperation or Defection. But it *is* the case, of course, that any strategy vector in which some players use C^∞ and all the rest use D^∞ is never an equilibrium, for any of the C^∞ players could gain by switching unilaterally to D^∞.

Conditional Cooperation

It is intuitively clear that, as in the two-person supergame, if any cooperation is to be sustained at all, some of the players must use *conditionally* Cooperative strategies. Consider first a natural generalization of the tit-for-tat strategy B, which I will call B_n. A player using B_n chooses C in the first constituent game, and thereafter chooses C in any game if and only if *at least n other players chose C in the preceding game.* I assume henceforth that $n > 0$ (when $n = 0$, B_n degenerates into C^∞). When $n = N - 1$, a B_n-player's Cooperation is conditional on the Cooperation of *all* the other players.

If every player uses B_n, then universal Cooperation is sustained throughout the supergame. Are there conditions in which the strategy vector $(B_n, B_n, \ldots, B_n)$ is an equilibrium?

Suppose to begin with that n is the same for every player. I first show that if $n = N - 1$ the strategy vector $(B_n, B_n, \ldots, B_n)$ can be an equilibrium. In this special case, *there are exactly enough players choosing C in each constituent game to maintain Cooperation by every player in the following game.* If any player at any time chooses D, then all the remaining players cease to Cooperate in the succeeding game. We might say there is a tacit 'compact' amongst all the players which breaks down as soon as any one of them once breaks ranks. Suppose some player, i, unilaterally changes strategy to D. Then in the constituent game in which he first Defects, he is the only non-Cooperator and his payoff is therefore $g(N - 1)$; but in all succeeding games everyone Defects and i's payoff is therefore $g(0)$. It is obvious that this defection to D^∞ will only yield i a gain if the discount rate is sufficiently high, so that his (slightly discounted) immediate gain from free-riding on the Cooperation of all the other players outweighs the (increasingly discounted) losses from the subsequent string of universal Defections.

In fact, i's payoff from universal Cooperation throughout the supergame is $f(N - 1)a_i/(1 - a_i)$ and his payoff if he changes his strategy to D^∞ is $g(N - 1)a_i + g(0)a_i^2/(1 - a_i)$, so that the defection does not yield a gain if and only if the first of these is no less than the second. On rearranging, this condition becomes:

$$a_i \geqslant \frac{g(N - 1) - f(N - 1)}{g(N - 1) - g(0)} \qquad (4.1)$$

This is the N-person analogue of inequality (3.1) in the two-person analysis.

Let us now introduce the strategy B_n', which is the N-person generalization of B'. It is the same tit-for-tat strategy as B_n, except that D is chosen in the first constituent game.

It is easy to see (and here already the N-person case differs from the two-person) that if $(B_n, B_n, . . ., B_n)$ is stable against unilateral switches to D^∞, then it is stable against switches to B'_n, if n is still $N - 1$. Following such a switch, in the second constituent game each of the $N - 1$ players still using B_n will find that only $N - 2$ *others* played C in the first game, so will choose D. The player who switched to B'_n will however Cooperate in the second game since there were $N - 1$ others (the B_n players) who chose C in the first game. But thereafter everyone will choose D. So the outcomes here differ from those which resulted from one player's switch to D^∞ in the second constituent game only, where the defector (playing C while the rest play D) receives *less* than does the defector to D^∞ (who plays D while the rest play D). So if defection to D^∞ does not pay, defection to B'_n will not either.

In fact, it is easily shown that *no* strategy does better than B_n and D^∞ when all others play B_n and that therefore *inequality* (4.1), *for every player, is a necessary and sufficient condition for* $(B_n, B_n, . . ., B_n)$ *to be an equilibrium, assuming that* $n = N - 1$ *for all players.* For if a strategy is to do better than B_n when all others are playing B_n it must at some stage (and therefore at the first move) play D. But this causes all the others to Defect in the second game, and no matter what the switcher does in this (second) game, all the others will defect in the third game and therefore in all succeeding games. So in the second game (and in each of the following games) the switcher can do no better than to play D. Hence no strategy can do better than D^∞ or B_n when playing against $N - 1$ B_n-players, with $n = N - 1$.

Can the strategy vector still be an equilibrium if $n \neq N - 1$ for some or all of the players – that is, if the Cooperation of one or more players is conditional on the Cooperation of *fewer* than *all* the other players?

If the Cooperation of *all* N players is conditional on fewer than $N - 1$ others Cooperating, then universal Cooperation is sustained throughout the supergame as before, but now, if any single player changes strategy from B_n to D^∞ it has no effect on the subsequent moves of any of the other players: for each of them there are $N - 2$ other players Cooperating and their own Cooperation requires only that number of Cooperators at most. After the defection, therefore, they continue to Cooperate throughout the supergame. Hence, from the second game onwards the player switching to D^∞ receives the maximum payoff – the lone Defector's payoff $g(N-1)$. It therefore always pays him to switch, regardless of his discount rate. So $(B_n, B_n, \ldots, B_n)$ *cannot be an equilibrium if $n < N-1$ for each player.*

This is still the case when the values of n vary between the players, just as long as *all* of them (or all but one of them) are smaller than $N-1$. For, if all of them are smaller than $N-1$, then after a player defects to D^∞, all the other players continue to Cooperate (while if the values of n are less than $N-1$ for all but one of the players and *this* player switches to D, the remaining players continue to Cooperate).

If the value of n varies among these B_n players but for more than one of them $n = N-1$, then a variety of patterns of choices could follow a switch by one player to D^∞. It is possible that an immediate but once-for-all partial collapse of Cooperation would ensue, or that there would be a progressive collapse, perhaps with an additional player or a small number of players dropping out of Cooperation in successive games. It is clear that, in *some* cases of this kind, a change from B_n to D^∞ would *not* yield *any* player a gain, so that the strategy vector in question would be an equilibrium, provided (as usual) that the relevant discount rates were not too great. The conditions which the discount rates would have to satisfy would depend of course on the distribution of the values of n among the players, which determines the particular pattern of choices in the constituent games.

So far, then, we have shown that *the strategy vector $(B_n, B_n, \ldots, B_n)$, in which each player Cooperates conditionally on the Cooperation of every other player, is an equilibrium if and only if the inequality (4.1) is satisfied by every player's discount rate.* This strategy vector can still be an equilibrium if *some* of the players' conditional Cooperation does not require the Cooperation of all the other players, provided that for some of the players this *is* required.

We note in passing that if $(B_n, B_n, \ldots, B_n)$ is an equilibrium, it is also a *coordination equilibrium.* The remarks in the section on Coordination Equilibria in chapter 3 apply here also.

All these results still hold if a subset of the players use the *un*conditionally Cooperative strategy C^∞; only a change of detail in the conditions to be met by the discount factors is necessary. Thus, strategy vectors of the form $(B_n, \ldots, B_n; C^\infty, \ldots, C^\infty)$ can be equilibria. If every player Cooperates on the condition that *all* other players Cooperated in the previous game, then if any player changes strategy to D^∞, all the *conditionally* Cooperative players choose D in the second constituent game, and hence in the third, and so on. It is easily checked that, if one of the B_n players defects, the condition for such a switch to yield a gain is the same as inequality (4.1) but with $g(0)$ replaced by $g(n_C)$, where n_C is the number of unconditional Cooperators. Call this new inequality (4.2). If one of the C^∞ players defects to D^∞, $g(0)$ is replaced by $g(n_C - 1)$. Since we have assumed that $g(v) > g(0)$ for any strictly positive value of v (i.e., Defection yields a greater payoff when some others Cooperate than it does when nobody else Cooperates), we have $g(n_C) > g(0)$ and $g(n_C - 1) > g(0)$. Thus the discount rate must now satisfy stricter requirements than previously – so that, as is intuitively obvious, if $(B_n, \ldots, B_n; C^\infty, \ldots, C^\infty)$ is stable against defection to D^∞, then so also is $(B_n, \ldots, B_n)$. If we also assume, quite reasonably, that $g(v)$ is strictly increasing with v, then $g(n_C) > g(n_C - 1)$, and therefore if $(B_n, \ldots, B_n; C^\infty, \ldots, C^\infty)$ is stable against defections to D^∞ by a B_n player, it is stable against such defections by a C^∞ player, so that if (4.1) is satisfied when $g(0)$ is replaced by $g(n_C)$, it is satisfied when $g(0)$ is replaced by $g(n_C - 1)$. As before, no strategy can do better than D^∞ or B_n when all others are playing B_n or C^∞ strategies (with $n = N - 1$ for all the B_n players). Thus, *strategy vectors of the form* $(B_n, \ldots, B_n; C^\infty, \ldots, C^\infty)$, *where* $n = N - 1$ *for all the players, are equilibria if and only if condition (4.2) is satisfied.* If the values of n vary amongst the players, the remarks made earlier about $(B_n, \ldots, B_n)$ apply here *mutatis mutandis*.

Subgroups of Cooperators

So far, we have merely generalized the basic result of the two-person analysis. But an interesting new question arises in the N-person case: is it ever rational for a *subset* of the players to sustain Cooperation throughout the supergame? Consider, then, strategy vectors of the form:

$$(B_n, \ldots, B_n; C^\infty, \ldots, C^\infty; D^\infty, \ldots, D^\infty).$$

I will also write this as $(B_n/C^\infty/D^\infty)$ for short. Can such a strategy vector be an equilibrium?

Let the number of players in these three groups be n_B, n_C and n_D, with $n_B + n_C + n_D = N$, and let $n_B + n_C$, the total number of Cooperators, be m. If a strategy vector of this kind is ever to be an equilibrium, n_B must not be zero, because a strategy vector in which there are only C^∞ and D^∞ is never an equilibrium. The following analysis covers as a special case strategy vectors in which there are only B_n and D^∞ players (i.e., $n_C = 0$).

As before, the values of n are crucial. Consider first the case when $n < m - 1$ for *every* player. All the first m players choose C in every constituent game, for at each stage their Cooperation is conditional upon at least n other players Cooperating, and since there are sufficient Cooperators in the first game, so there are in the second, and therefore also in the third, and so on. Now, since the Cooperation of each of the B_n players is conditional upon *fewer* than all the remaining Cooperators, if any member of the B_n and C^∞ subgroups unilaterally defects to D^∞, the remaining $m - 1$ conditional Cooperators continue to choose C in every constituent game. The defector's payoff will therefore increase, for $g(m - 1) > f(m - 1)$, that is, a player is better off if he Defects while everyone else Cooperates than if he Cooperates. This is true, of course, regardless of the values of the players' discount factors and of the shapes of the payoff functions $f(v)$ and $g(v)$. Thus, strategy vectors of the form $(B_n/C^\infty/D^\infty)$ are *never* equilibria if $n < m - 1$ for every B_n player, whether or not the values of n vary between the players.

With strategy vectors of this form we must also consider the possibility that $n > m - 1$. Suppose $n > m - 1$ for *every* B_n player. In this case, even before any of the Cooperators defects to D^∞, the 'compact' amongst the B_n players collapses immediately. All of the first m players choose C in the first constituent game; thereafter all conditional Cooperation collapses, for the total number of Cooperators in the first game (m) is too small. Thus, a B_n or C^∞ player who defects to D^∞ will necessarily gain, since his payoff in the first game is greater, while in every succeeding game his payoffs are the same. Thus, strategy vectors of the form $(B_n/C^\infty/D^\infty)$ are *never* equilibria if $n > m - 1$ for every player.

The point about these two cases – in which $n < m - 1$ for every B_n player or $n > m - 1$ for every B_n player – is that a defection to D^∞ by one of the Cooperators makes no difference to the subsequent actions of any of the other Cooperators. This is not so in the remaining cases, and we shall now show that under certain conditions strategy vectors of the form $(B_n/C^\infty/D^\infty)$ *can* be equilibria.

The first of these cases is where $n = m - 1$ for *all* the B_n players, that is, each B_n player chooses C as long as *all* the other Cooperators, conditional and unconditional, chose C in the preceding game. Before any player changes strategy, there are exactly enough players choosing C in each game to maintain throughout the supergame the 'compact' amongst the conditional Cooperators. The first m players (which we will index $i = 1, \ldots, m$) choose C in every constituent game and the remaining $N - m$ players (indexed $j = m + 1, m + 2, \ldots, N$) choose D in every game.

But if any one of the B_n or C^∞ players ($i = 1$, say) changes strategy to D^∞, then the 'compact' amongst the rest of these players collapses: after choosing C in the first game, all these players choose D in the second game, because in the first game the total number of *other* Cooperators was $m - 2$; they therefore also choose D in the third game; and so on. The defector, then, receives a greater payoff in the first game (in which he is the lone Defector) than he did before changing strategy, but receives less in every succeeding game. Whether his total discounted payoff from the supergame is greater depends as usual on his discount rate and on the constituent game payoffs. A B_n player who defects to D^∞ does *not* gain if and only if

$$f(m-1)\frac{a_i}{1-a_i} \geq g(m-1)a_i + g(n_C)\frac{a_i^2}{1-a_i^2}$$

that is,

$$a_i \geq \frac{g(m-1) - f(m-1)}{g(m-1) - g(n_C)} \tag{4.3}$$

(Condition (4.1) is a special case of this: if there are no C^∞ or D^∞ players, then $n_C = 0$ and $m - 1 = N - 1$, and (4.3) becomes (4.1)).

A change of strategy by a B_n player to C^∞, or by a C^∞ player to B_n, makes no difference, of course, to anyone's choices throughout the supergame.

If one of the C^∞ players defects to D^∞, then as before the cooperation amongst the B_n players collapses after the first game; the number of players choosing D in the first game is the same as before (when a B_n player switched to D^∞) but there is one less C-chooser from the second game onwards. So the condition for a C^∞ player to make no gain from defecting to D^∞ is (4.3) but with $n_C - 1$ rather than n_C. Assuming that $g(n_C) > g(n_C - 1)$, this modified condition is satisfied if (4.3) is. So *a strategy vector of the form* $(B_n/C^\infty/D^\infty)$ *is an equilibrium only if condition (4.3) is satisfied for all the B_n and C^∞ players.*

As in the case of $(B_n, \ldots, B_n)$, if it does not pay a B_n player to defect to

D^∞, it will not pay him to defect to B_n' (with $n = m - 1$ again). In fact, it is easily verified that there is *no* other strategy which it would be better for a B_n player to defect to than D^∞.

A defection by a C^∞ player to B_n' (with $n = m - 1$) results in the same pattern of choices and yields the defecting player the same payoff as in the case of a defection by a B_n player to B_n'.

And finally, it is clear that no change of strategy by a D^∞ player would yield him a gain. Whatever he did, it would have no effect on the choices of any of the other players throughout the supergame. If his new strategy was such that in any constituent game he played C, he would therefore obtain a lower payoff in that game than he did before switching $-f(m)$ instead of $g(m)$ – while in any constituent game in which he played D his payoff would be the same as before.

Thus, *condition* (4.3) *for all* $i = 1, 2, \ldots, m$ *(i.e., for all the Cooperators) is a necessary and sufficient condition for strategy vectors of the form* $(B_n/C^\infty/D^\infty)$, *where* $n = m - 1$ *for every* B_n *player, to be an equilibrium.*

We have established, then, that strategy vectors of this form can never be equilibria if $n > m - 1$ for every B_n player or $n < m - 1$ for every B_n player (whether the values of n vary or not), but that if every n is $m - 1$ they are equilibria if and only if (4.3) holds for all the Cooperators. There remain all those cases where the values of n are distributed between $n < m - 1$, $n = m - 1$ and $n > m - 1$, there being B_n players falling in at least two of these categories.

If there are any B_n players with $n = m - 1$, then their choices after the first game will be affected (if only in the second game) by a switch to D^∞ by one of the other B_n players. Such a switch can also affect the choices of some of the B_n players with $n < m - 1$, if there are any; this would depend on the particular values of n in this group as well as on the numbers of players using different values of n (the frequency distribution of n). Any choices thus affected would of course change from C to D. The player who switched may or may not gain, depending on the pattern of choices resulting from his defection and depending (as usual) on his discount rate.

If there are B_n players with $n < m - 1$ and some with $n > m - 1$ but none with $n = m - 1$, then whether a unilateral switch to D^∞ by any B_n player affects other players' choices depends on the values of n in the

$n < m - 1$ group (the only group whose members could be affected) and on the frequency distribution of n, and the defecting player may or may not gain, depending on the pattern of choices resulting from his defection and on his discount rate.

Similar observations can be made about defections to B'.

Establishing general conditions on the frequency distribution of n, indicating which cases in these last two groups are equilibria (if also the discount rates are not too great) is not very instructive. I have said enough to show (and the reader can easily construct examples which show) that *some* strategy vectors of this kind are equilibria, provided the relevant discount rates are not too great. The conditions which the discount rates would have to satisfy would depend on the frequency distribution of n (which determines the pattern of choices) as well as on the payoff functions f and g.

Chickens nesting in the Prisoners' Dilemma supergame

It is worth noting that (4.1) does not imply and is not implied by (4.3). So $(B_m, \ldots, B_n)$ can be an equilibrium without a strategy vector of the form $(B_n/C^\infty/D^\infty)$ being one, and conversely, or both can be equilibria simultaneously.

If *both* are equilibria, along with $(D^\infty, \ldots, D^\infty)$, and assuming for the moment that there is no other equilibrium, which would be the outcome? Any individual would prefer $(B_{N-1}, \ldots, B_{N-1})$ to $(B_{N-1}/C^\infty/D^\infty)$ if he was one of the Cooperators (conditional or unconditional) in the second strategy vector; but whether a D^∞ player has the same preference depends on whether $f(N-1) > g(m)$, which is not implied by our assumptions. This last inequality is increasingly less likely to hold as m increases, that is, as the group of D^∞ players shrinks. Again, every player prefers $(B_{N-1}, \ldots, B_{N-1})$ to $(D^\infty, \ldots, D^\infty)$, but whether any of the Cooperators prefers $(B_{N-1}/C^\infty/D^\infty)$ to $(D^\infty, \ldots, D^\infty)$ depends on whether $f(m-1) > g(0)$, which is not implied by our assumptions (except when $m = N$, i.e., there are no D^∞ players in the first strategy vector).

If $(B_{N-1}, \ldots, B_{N-1})$ is the only equilibrium besides $(D^\infty, \ldots, D^\infty)$, then it will be the outcome. But if strategy vectors of the form $(B_{m-1}/C^\infty/D^\infty)$ are also equilibria, then *even if* these vectors are unanimously preferred to $(D^\infty, \ldots, D^\infty)$ and *even if* there are no other preferred equilibria, it is far from certain that one of them will be the outcome.

The problem lies in the multiplicity of equilibria. Given that the payoff functions f and g are the same for all players, there could be as many as $\binom{N}{m}$ equilibria of the $(B_{m-1}/C^\infty/D^\infty)$ class, $\binom{N}{m}$ being the number of subsets of size m that can be drawn from the N players.[3] An individual is indifferent between them all *if* he is going to Cooperate (conditionally or unconditionally – it makes no difference) *or* if he is going to Defect (play D^∞). And each player would prefer to play B_{m-1} *if* otherwise there would be no Cooperation at all (i.e., if his Cooperation is critical to the success of the 'compact' amongst the B_{m-1} players). But if one of the equilibria in this class is going to be the outcome, then *he would rather it was one in which he played D^∞ than one in which he Cooperated.* Every player has this preference. If the public good is going to be provided by a *sub*group, he would rather it was a subgroup which did not include him.

Every player, then, has an incentive in this situation to *pre-commit* or *bind* himself to non-Cooperation, in the expectation that others will have to Cooperate and he will be a free rider on their efforts. The existence of an incentive of this kind is precisely the defining characteristic of the N-person *Chicken* game – according to the account given in chapter 2 at least. As I noted in that earlier discussion, there is little that the game theorist, or anyone operating within the framework of rational egoism assumed here, can say definitively about the game of Chicken played only once. (For some tentative suggestions, see the section in chapter 2 on 'Pre-commitment as a risky decision and the prospects for cooperation in Chicken games'.)

It has been suggested that in this situation there would be a 'chaotic' scramble in which each individual tries to ensure that he is not left behind in a subgroup whose members are obliged (by their own preferences) to provide the public good and that there is no reason to expect a subgroup of the right size to emerge from this 'stampede'.[4] But again it must be emphasized that there is no warrant (either in the model studied here or in any alternative model offered by the proponents of this view) for this conclusion; conclusive arguments of this kind could only be made if pre-commitment behaviour were explicitly incorporated into the model. In fact, a subgroup of conditional Cooperators *might* emerge if enough players are sufficiently risk averse – but arguments of this sort too must await a richer specification of the model.[5]

Other Cooperative equilibria

The generalized tit-for-tat strategy B_n is not of course the only strategy which, if used by all the players, would sustain universal Cooperation throughout the supergame. Consider, for example, the following N-person generalization of the strategy $A_{k,l}$ considered in the last chapter: C is chosen in the first game; it continues to be chosen as long as at least n other players ($N > n > 0$) chose C in the previous game; if the number of other Cooperators falls below n, then D is chosen for the next k games (where k is a strictly positive integer); C is then chosen in the next game no matter what the other players chose in the preceding game; it continues to be chosen as long as at least n other players chose C in the preceding game; when the number of other Cooperators next falls below n, D is chosen for $k + l$ games (where l is a non-negative integer); and so on; the number of games in which the other players are 'punished' for Defection is increased by l each time; and each time there is a return to C. Call this strategy $A_{k,l}^n$.

Note that when $n = 0$, both $A_{k,l}^n$ and B_n degenerate into C^∞. I assume henceforth that $n > 0$. In the limiting case when $k \to \infty$, the 'punishment' period lasts for ever. When $n = N - 1$, Cooperation is conditional upon the Cooperation of *all* the other players. Thus, in the special case $A_{\infty,\,l}^{N-1}$ (the value of l is now irrelevant), the first Defection of just one other player is enough to trigger 'eternal punishment', that is, it causes an $A_{\infty,\,l}^{N-1}$ player to Defect in every succeeding game. But although this strategy (or its analogue for general non-cooperative games) is the only one that some economists have paid attention to, it seems to me that it embodies an 'implausible' threat, or at any rate a threat that is less plausible than those of strategies $A_{k,l}^n$ when k is *finite*.[6]

It is easily shown that strategy vectors in which every player uses $A_{k,l}^n$ are never equilibria if $n < N - 1$, but are sometimes equilibria when $n = N - 1$ for every player. In the case when the values of k and l are the same for every player, the *necessary and sufficient conditions* for this strategy vector to be an equilibrium can be shown to be:

$$\frac{(1 - a_i)S_i}{a_i} \leqslant \frac{f(N-1) - g(0)}{g(N-1) - g(0)} \quad \text{for all } i,$$

where $S_i = S(k, l; a_i)$ is defined as in the last chapter. This condition is the N-person analogue of condition (3.3), which is the necessary and sufficient condition for $(A_{k,l}, A_{k,l})$ to be an equilibrium.

But let us derive this condition as a special case of the more general equilibrium conditions for strategy vectors in which B_n, C^∞ and D^∞ are present as well as $A_{k, l}^n$.

As in the earlier case of strategy vectors of the form $(B_n/C^\infty/D^\infty)$, if $n < m-1$ for all the conditional Cooperators or if all $n > m-1$, then unilateral defection to D^∞ by any of the Cooperators (conditional or unconditional) makes no difference to the choices made throughout the supergame by any other player. Such a defection must therefore necessarily pay: the defector's payoff in any constituent game either increases from $f(v)$ to $g(v)$ or stays the same at $g(v)$. Strategy vectors of this sort can therefore *never* be equilibria if all $n < m-1$ or if all $n > m-1$.

If $n = m-1$, then there are exactly enough players choosing C in each constituent game to maintain throughout the supergame the 'compact' amongst the conditional Cooperators. If nobody changes strategy, the first m players all choose C in every game, and the supergame payoff to each of them is $f(m-1)a_i/(1-a_i)$, while the payoff to each of the D^∞ players is $g(m-1)a_i/(1-a_i)$. But if one of the Cooperators changes strategy, switching to D in any constituent game, the 'compact' collapses for the rest of the supergame. If one of the Cooperators defects to D^∞, then his payoff becomes

$$g(m-1)a_i + g(n_A + n_C - \delta)\,(S_i - a_i) + g(n_C - \delta')\left(\frac{a_i}{1-a_i} - S_i\right)$$

where n_A and n_C are the numbers of players using $A_{k, l}^n$ and C^∞ respectively, m is the total number using conditionally or unconditionally Cooperative strategies, $S_i = S(k, l; a_i)$ is as defined earlier, and

$$\delta = \begin{cases} 0 \text{ if player } i \text{ is using } B_n \\ 1 \text{ if player } i \text{ is using } A_{k,l}^n \text{ or } C^\infty \end{cases}$$

and

$$\delta' = \begin{cases} 0 \text{ if player } i \text{ is using } A_{k,l}^n \text{ or } B_n \\ 1 \text{ if player is using } C^\infty \end{cases}$$

Call this payoff P. Then a unilateral change of strategy to D^∞ does not yield one of the Cooperators a gain if and only if

$$f\,(m-1)\,\frac{a_i}{1-a_i} \geqslant P \tag{4.4}$$

It is easily verified that, if it pays any player to change strategy at all, he can do no better than switch to D^{∞}. For, first, it does not pay a D^{∞} player to switch to *any* other strategy. And, second, if a change by any of the Cooperators is to yield a gain it must be such that in some constituent game (and therefore in the first) D is chosen; but this causes all the (other) conditional Cooperators to Defect in the second game, and no matter what the switcher does in this second game (even if C is chosen, as would happen if the switch was to B_n' for example) all the other conditional Cooperators will Defect in the third game, and therefore in all succeeding games; so in the second game (and in each of the following games) the switcher can do no better than to play D. Hence, *conditions (4.4), for all $i = 1, 2, \ldots, m$, are necessary and sufficient for strategy vectors of the form $(A_{k,l}^n / B_n / C^{\infty} / D^{\infty})$ to be equilibria.*

When k, l and n vary amongst the players, an enormous variety of patterns of choices is possible. In particular, there can easily arise a pattern in which Cooperation amongst *some* of the B_n players *rises and falls* throughout the supergame (as a result of the periodical return to Cooperation of the $A_{k,l}^n$ players). It turns out that some strategy vectors of this form are equilibria under certain conditions, which are stringent. The details of the analysis are messy and will not be set out here. The reader interested in an illustrative analysis will find one in *Anarchy and Cooperation* (at pp. 57-60).

An example

To illustrate some of the equilibrium results obtained so far, let us briefly reconsider Hardin's formulation of the collective action problem in terms of a (one-shot) Prisoners' Dilemma, first introduced in chapter 1. In that formulation, each of the N players is supposed to choose between contributing a unit of the cost of providing a public good (strategy C) or not contributing (strategy D). For each unit contributed, the total benefit to the group is r and the benefit to each individual is assumed to be r/N (the good having been tacitly assumed to be rival). Obviously we must have $r > 1$. All players benefit from a contribution by any player.

The payoff functions $f(v)$ and $g(v)$ can be specified as follows:

$$f(v) = \frac{(v+1)r}{N} - 1 \qquad\qquad g(v) = \frac{vr}{N}$$

This is a Prisoners' Dilemma if and only if: (i) D dominates C for each player; that is, $g(v) > f(v)$ for all $v \geqslant 0$, which is true if and only if $r < N$; and (ii) the outcome $(C, C, \ldots, C)$ is preferred by every player to $(D, D, \ldots, D)$; that is, $f(N-1) > g(0)$, which is true if and only if $r > 1$.

Thus $1 < r < N$ is a necessary and sufficient condition for the game to be a Prisoners' Dilemma, with D being each player's rational choice.

Suppose that this condition is met, and consider now the supergame consisting of an infinite number of iterations of this game. The results just obtained for the N-person Prisoners' Dilemma supergame can be applied, for the functions f and g satisfy the three assumptions on which those results depend. The first two assumptions are simply those which guarantee that the constituent game is a Prisoners' Dilemma; the third is that $g(v) > g(0)$ for all $v > 0$, which is satisfied here since $r > 1$.

Consider first the strategy vector in which everyone plays B_n. This was shown to be an equilibrium if and only if $n = N - 1$ for every player (i.e., everyone Cooperates if and only if everyone else does) and condition (4.1) holds for each player, that is:

$$a_i \geqslant \frac{g(N-1)-f(N-1)}{g(N-1)-g(0)} \quad \text{for all } i.$$

Substituting for f and g, this becomes

$$a_i \geqslant \frac{N-r}{(N-1)r}$$

From this, the required minimum discount factor can be calculated for any values of N and r. Note that if there is virtually total discounting (i.e., $a_i \to 0$), this equilibrium condition is satisfied for $r > N$, that is, N units of public good benefit must be produced out of each unit of contributions. If there is virtually *no* discounting (i.e., $a_i \to 1$), then the equilibrium condition is satisfied for $r > 1$, that is, for *any* value of r. This is just as we would expect. If very great public good benefit can be produced out of each unit contributed, it will pay conditional Cooperators to produce the public good even if their discount rates are very great, and conversely if discounting is negligible, conditional Cooperation will pay even if a unit of contributions only just produces more than a unit of public good benefit.

Now consider strategy vectors in which the four strategies $A_{k,l}^n$, B_n, C^∞ and D^∞ all appear, with $n = m - 1$ for all the conditional Cooperators.

We saw earlier that a necessary and sufficient condition for a strategy vector of this form to be an equilibrium is the inequality (4.4). Substituting for f and g, condition (4.4) reduces to:

$$n_A\left(\frac{a_i}{1-a_i}-S_i\right)+n_B\left(\frac{a_i^2}{1-a_i}\right)\geqslant\frac{N}{r}\left(\frac{a_i}{1-a_i}\right)-S_i \text{ for players using } A_{k,l}^n$$

$$\geqslant\frac{N}{r}\left(\frac{a_i}{1-a_i}\right)-a_i \text{ for players using } B_n$$

$$\geqslant\frac{N}{r}\left(\frac{a_i}{1-a_i}\right)-\frac{a_i}{1-a_i} \text{ for players using } C^\infty$$

These inequalities being independent of m, equilibrium is dependent only on the number of players using conditional strategies (subject of course to $n_A+n_B<m<N$). Notice, too, that since

$$a_i<S(k,\,l;\,a_i)<\frac{a_i}{1-a_i}$$

for non-zero finite k, the smallest values of n_A (given n_B) and n_B (given n_A) sufficient for defection to be irrational are greater for players using B_n (or $A_{\infty,l}^n$) than they are for those using $A_{k,l}^n$ (for any non-zero finite k), and greater for the latter than for those using C^∞. This is as one would expect.

To illustrate more concretely, assume that in all the strategies of the $A_{k,l}^n$ type, $k=3$ and $l=1$, and $a_i=0.9$, $N=100$ and $r=5$. With these values of k and l, we have

$$S(k,\,l;\,a_i)=a_i+a_i^5+a_i^{10}+a_i^{16}+\ldots$$

and with $a_i=0.9$ this is found to be approximately 2.17. Substituting for S_i, a_i, N and r, the three inequalities above become:

$$n_A+1.186n_B\geqslant26.04 \text{ for players using } A_{k,l}^n$$
$$\geqslant26.22 \text{ for players using } B_n$$
$$\geqslant25.04 \text{ for players using } C^\infty$$

Thus the second of these inequalities is necessary and sufficient for the strategy vector to be an equilibrium.

We see that strategy vectors of this type will not be equilibria if the total number of conditional Cooperators is too small. The general point is that, if there are too few conditional Cooperators, then it pays any of the players not using D^∞ to change to that strategy, because such defection leads to the defection of only a few other players and therefore (in view of the assumptions about the payoff functions f and g) to only a small loss of benefits, which is more than compensated by not having to pay the cost of Cooperating.

Alternation between blocs of conditional cooperators

In the analysis of the two-person Prisoners' Dilemma supergame we saw that the strategy vector (B, B'), which produces alternation between (C, D) and (D, C) throughout the supergame, was of special interest. There were good reasons to believe that it could be an equilibrium and at the same time preferred by both players to the strategy vectors producing mutual Cooperation throughout the supergame. Let us consider an analogous N-person strategy vector, in which some players use B and the rest use B'.

A typical B_n player will be labelled i and a typical B'_n player will be labelled j. Let the number of players using B_n be n_B as before. Then there are $N - n_B$ players using B'_n. It is still assumed that the same value of n is used by all N players. The addition of players using C^∞ and D^∞ would make no essential difference (as the earlier analysis of $(A^\infty_{k,\,l}/B_n/C^\infty/D^\infty)$-type strategies should make clear), although of course the actual payoffs and inequalities obtained below would be different.

Three cases have to be considered separately: (1) $n < n_B$: (2) $n > n_B$; and (3) $n = n_B$.

(1) $n < n_B$

The players using B_n choose C in the first game, while those using B'_n choose D. But there are enough players in the B_n group (since $n_B - 1 \geqslant n$) to guarantee their own continued Cooperation in the second game and also to cause the B'_n players to Cooperate in that game. From the second game onwards, all players Cooperate. We can see immediately that these cases can *never* be equilibria, because (whenever $n < n_B$) a change by one of the B'_n players to D^∞ has no effect on the choices of the other players: they still Cooperate from the second game onwards. Hence such a change yields a greater payoff for the defector, for while his payoff in the first game is unchanged, his payoff in each succeeding game is increased from $f(N-1)$ to $g(N-1)$.

(2) $n > n_B$

Here all players Defect from the second game onwards. If a player using B_n changes his strategy to D^∞, his payoff is thereby increased, for in the first game he receives $g(n_B - 1)$ whereas before he received $f(n_B - 1)$, and in all subsequent games his payoff is unchanged. Thus, strategy vectors in this category are *never* equilibria.

(3) $n = n_B$

The B_n players choose C in the first game but Defect in the second. The B_n' players choose D in the first game but Cooperate in the second. What happens in the rest of the game depends on the relation between n and the number of players using B_n'. This is examined in the following subcases.

(3.1) $n < N - n_B$ (so that $n_B < \frac{1}{2}N$)

Then there are enough B_n' players to bring back the B_n players to Cooperation in the third game and to maintain the Cooperation of the B_n' players themselves. All N players choose C from the third game onwards.

(3.1.1) $n < N - n_B - 1$

If one of the B_n' players changes his strategy to D^∞, then the choices of the other players are unaffected. He therefore gains by such a change, for although his payoff in the first game is unchanged, his payoff in the second and every succeeding game increases. Thus, strategy vectors in this category are *never* equilibria.

(3.1.2) $n = N - n_B - 1$ (thus $n_B = \frac{1}{2}(N - 1)$, so that N must be odd).

In this case a change of strategy by one of the B_n players to D^∞ or to B_n' does *not* leave the other players' choices unaffected. It results in all N players Defecting from the second game onwards. Such a change does not yield the defector a greater payoff if and only if

$$g(n_B - 1)a_i + g(0)\frac{a_i^2}{1 - a_i} \leqslant$$

$$f(n_B - 1)a_i + g(N - n_B)a_i^2 + f(N - 1)\frac{a_i^3}{1 - a_i} \qquad (4.5)$$

A change of strategy by one of the B'_n players to D^∞ results in the B_n players alternating between C and D throughout the supergame beginning with C in the third game, and the B'_n players alternating similarly but beginning with D in the third game. This does not yield a greater payoff for the defector if and only if (after simplifying)

$$g(n_B) \leqslant f(n_B)(1 - a_j) + f(N-1)a_j \qquad (4.6)$$

If one of the B'_n players changes his strategy to B_n, then this results in the B_n players choosing C in the second game but no other choices are changed. Thus, such a change does not yield a greater payoff if and only if

$$g(n_B) \geqslant f(n_B)(1 - a_j) + f(N-1)a_j$$

but this is the reverse of inequality (4.6) above.

It can be shown (using reasoning of the kind we've followed before) that a player switching unilaterally from B_n or B'_n cannot do better than to switch to the better of D^∞ and B'_n or B_n. Thus, *necessary and sufficient* conditions for strategy vectors in this category are the restrictive condition

$$g(n_B) = f(n_B)(1 - a_j) + f(N-1)\, a_j \qquad (4.7)$$

(for each of the B'_n players) together with inequality (4.5) for each of the B_n players. If $f(N-1) > f(n_B)$, the equality (4.7) can be written in the form

$$a_j = \frac{g(n_B) - f(n_B)}{f(N-1) - f(n_B)}$$

Clearly, then, strategy vectors of this form (which result in universal Cooperation from the third game onwards) are most unlikely to be equilibria, since this requires that this same equality be exactly satisfied by the discount factors of every one of the B'_n players, as well as inequality (4.5) holding for all the B_n players.

(3.2) $n > N - n_B$ (so that $n_B > \frac{1}{2}N$)

In this case, before any player changes strategy, all N players Defect from the third game onwards. If one of the B'_n players changes his strategy to D^∞, no other player's choices are affected, and the defector's payoff changes only in the second game, where it increases. Thus, strategy vectors in this category are *never* equilibria.

(3.3) $n=N-n_B$ (thus $n_B=\frac{1}{2}N$, so that N must be even)

In this case, before any player changes strategy, *each player's choices alternate between C and D throughout the supergame*, the B_n players beginning with C and the B'_n players beginning with D.

If one of the B_n players changes his strategy to D^∞ or B'_n, then all N players Defect from the second game onward. The defector's payoff is not increased if and only if

$$f(n_B-1)\,\frac{a^2_i}{1-a^2_i}+g(N-n_B)\,\frac{a^2_i}{1-a^2_i}\;\geqslant\;g(n_B-1)a_i+g(0)\,\frac{a^2_i}{1-a_i}$$

If one of the B'_n players (j) changes his strategy to B_n, then all N players Cooperate from the third game onwards, and j's payoff is not increased if and only if

$$g(n_B)\,\frac{a_j}{1-a^2_j}+f(N-n_B-1)\,\frac{a^2_j}{1-a^2_j}\;\geqslant\;f(n_B)a_j+f(N-1)\,\frac{a^2_j}{1-a_j}$$

If one of the B'_n players (j) changes his strategy to D^∞, then all N players Defect from the second game onwards, and j's payoff is not increased if and only if

$$g(n_B)\frac{a_j}{1-a^2_j}+f(N-n_B-1)\frac{a^2_j}{1-a^2_j}\;\geqslant$$

$$g(n_B)a_j+g(N-n_B-1)a^2_j+g(0)\frac{a^3_j}{1-a_j}\quad.$$

The three inequalities given above (the first to hold for each of the B_n players, the second and third for the B'_n players) are necessary and sufficient conditions for the strategy vectors in this category to be equilibria. Examples can be found to show that these three conditions can be satisfied simultaneously. (For example, when the payoff functions f and g take the form of the example discussed in the last section, there are permissible values of N (and hence n_B) and r and of the players' discount factors for which the conditions all hold.)

This completes the analysis of strategy vectors in which some players use B_n and the rest use B_n'. It shows that there are two sets of circumstances in which these strategy vectors can be equilibria: when $n = n_B$ and $N - n_B$ is either $n_B + 1$ or n_B. In the first case, N is odd and the number of B_n' players is just one more than the number of B_n players. In this case, all the players Cooperate from the third game onwards. But in addition to the requirements on the relations between n, n_B and $N - n_B$, the discount rates for the B_n' players must satisfy very exacting conditions. So equilibrium is very unlikely in this case. In the second case, N is even and there are exactly as many B_n' players as there are B_n players. These two equal blocs alternate between C and D: in one constituent game all the members of the B_n bloc play C while all those in the B_n' bloc play D; in the next game the opposite happens; and so on. If the provision of a public good were at stake here, this alternation could consist of the two blocs 'taking it in turns' to provide the public good, that is, the members of the two blocs contributing in alternate time periods. This is a perfectly plausible set-up, at least for small groups.

It is easily shown that when $(B_n, \ldots, B_n; B_n', \ldots, B_n')$ is an equilibrium, it is preferred to $(D^\infty, \ldots, D^\infty)$ under *some* conditions (which of course relate discount rates to constituent game payoffs). It is possible that $(B_n, \ldots, B_n)$ is simultaneously an equilibrium, but this is exceedingly unlikely, for then (as in the two-person case) the discount rates would have to satisfy a set of exact equalities. But even assuming that strategy vectors of the form $(B_n, \ldots, B_n; B_n', \ldots, B_n')$ are Pareto-preferred to both $(D^\infty, \ldots, D^\infty)$ and any strategy vectors, such as $(B_n, \ldots, B_n)$, which give rise to universal Cooperation throughout the supergame, there still remains a problem of the kind we encountered in the two-person case: each player would prefer an equilibrium in which he was in the B_n' bloc (and therefore Defected in the first game) to one in which he was in the B_n bloc (and therefore Cooperated in the first game). So even if all players eliminated from consideration all strategies except B_n and B_n', they would still face the 'coordination' problem of avoiding $(B_n, \ldots, B_n)$ and $(B_n', \ldots, B_n')$ as well as the problem of their conflicting preferences over the different alternation equilibria. Again, within the framework we are using here, there is no resolution of this problem.

Summary and discussion of results

The account given above of the N-person Prisoners' Dilemma supergame is far from complete but suffices, I think, to indicate the broad conclusions which a more comprehensive analysis would yield. I have carried the discussion far enough to show how Cooperation can arise in the Prisoners' Dilemma supergame, no matter how many players there are. This is the main point I set out to establish and it would not be undermined by a more general analysis.

We have seen that if Cooperation is to occur at all, then at least some of the players must be *conditional* Cooperators. More specifically, we saw in the first place that Cooperation by *every* player throughout the supergame, sustained by the use of the tit-for-tat strategy B_n by each player, is an equilibrium when each player's Cooperation is conditional on that of *all* the other players and his discount rate is not greater than a certain function of the constituent game payoffs (condition 4.1).

Secondly, however, we saw that *even when some of the players insist on unconditional Defection throughout the supergame, Cooperation may still be rational for the rest* – provided that there are *some* players who Cooperate conditionally on the Cooperation of *all* the other Cooperators, both conditional and unconditional, and that all the Cooperators' discount rates are not too great. But even when strategies of this sort are equilibria, it is difficult to say confidently what the outcome will be, because there are many such equilibria and each player prefers an outcome in which he is an unconditional Defector to one in which he is a Cooperator. This gives rise to a game of Chicken, whose outcome, as we saw in chapter 2, is ill-determined.

The third result of interest is that a pattern in which two equal blocs of players using strategies B_n and B'_n, which results in them 'taking it in turns' to Cooperate throughout the supergame, can be an equilibrium under certain conditions. The conditions, however, are rather exacting.

It plainly cannot be concluded from these results, and those of the last chapter, that the 'dilemma' in the Prisoners' Dilemma is resolved upon the introduction of time and the interdependence of choices over time: that people who would not Cooperate in the one-shot game will do so in the supergame. Nevertheless, it has been shown that *under certain conditions* the Cooperation of some or all of the players *could* emerge in the supergame *no matter how many players there are*. The question arises, whether these conditions are likely to be met in practice.

Speaking informally (which is all we can do here), it is pretty clear that Cooperation amongst a relatively large number of players is 'less likely' to occur than Cooperation amongst a small number. For a start, the more players there are, the greater is the number of conditions that have to be satisfied – the conditions specifying that the right kinds of conditionally Cooperative strategies are present and those specifying the inequalities that all the Cooperators' discount rates must satisfy. But the main reason for this new 'size' effect is that Cooperation can be sustained only if conditional Cooperators are present and conditional Cooperators must be able to monitor the behaviour of others. Clearly, such monitoring becomes increasingly difficult as the size of the group increases. (It is true that, in the supergame model we have analysed, a conditional Cooperator needs only to know that at least a certain number of others Cooperated in the preceding game; he does not need to know *which* other players Cooperated. This reduces but does not obviate the need for monitoring.) The required monitoring is more likely to be possible in a very small group, especially one with an unchanging or very slowly changing membership, or in a community.[7] On the account of 'community' I gave in chapter 1, communities tend to be small, but not necessarily very small. Monitoring and hence conditional Cooperation are made possible in communities in part by their relatively small size but also by the quality of relations between their members. As I argued in chapter 1, however, this is not always enough to guarantee the success of conditional Cooperation in the provision of public goods. In groups of intermediate size, including most communities, conditional Cooperation needs to be facilitated and supported by the deployment of (positive and negative) sanctions additional to those sanctions which may be thought to be embedded in conditional Cooperation itself. The additional sanctions need not, however, be centralized.[8]

A more realistic model

My aim in this book is to criticize what I believe is the strongest and most popular argument for the desirability of the state. I make no attempt to provide a positive theory of anarchy or even an indication of how people might best provide themselves with public goods. I am therefore not concerned with developing a detailed dynamic model of public goods provision. I have merely tried to show that, even if we accept the pessimistic assumption (an assumption unfavourable to the case I am making out) that individual preferences have the structure of a Prisoners' Dilemma at any point in time, mutual Cooperation over time may nevertheless take place. However, the scope of the application of this part of my critical argument would be increased if the broad conclusions of the analysis in this chapter and the last could be shown to apply to a more detailed, more realistic model of the dynamic process of public goods provision than the Prisoners' Dilemma supergame model (with or without some form of altruism) considered in those two chapters. In this section, I want briefly to indicate, then, some ways in which the supergame model might be extended or revised so as to provide a more realistic picture of public goods interaction. I shall not give any analysis of the alternative models or even specify them fully; to do so would require another book.

In the Prisoners' Dilemma supergame considered above, it is assumed that the time taken for a player to change from one strategy to another is zero. There is no time-lag between the decision to change and the actual change. Each player is perfectly 'flexible' in this respect, and therefore, in particular, his strategy choice in any ordinary game can be contingent upon the other player's choice in the immediately preceding game. In the real world, this sort of flexibility may exist in decisions such as those to commit or refrain from committing anti-social acts (a decision can be translated immediately into 'action', with instantaneous production of the public good or bad, social order or disorder), but with respect to many kinds of public goods, flexibility is less than perfect. People must be trained, equipment obtained, public works constructed, and so on, before there is any benefit to anybody.

Intuitively, it would seem that the presence of time-lags of this sort would tend to increase the 'likelihood' of non-Cooperation in the Prisoners' Dilemma supergame; for a player (A) contemplating Defection from mutual Cooperation knows that it will take the other player (B) several time periods to change his strategy after observing A's Defection, and can expect the unilateral Defection payoff during this interval; this will offer A a greater compensation for the mutual Defection payoffs which will be his lot after B's eventual Defection than it would in the model analyzed here, where A can 'exploit' B (receive the unilateral Defection payoff) for only one ordinary game. Thus, the conditions for Cooperation to be rational are likely to require a progressively smaller discount rate as this flexibility decreases (that is, as the time-lag between decision and effect increases).[9]

A second kind of inflexibility which may be present in individual decisions in public goods interaction is the limitation on the *frequency* with which strategy choices may be changed. If every strategy of every individual could be changed equally regularly, no matter how infrequently, the supergame models studied here would not have to be modified, since the durations of the time periods specified here are essentially arbitrary. However, if only *some* strategy changes could be made at any time (in any time period) while others could be changed less frequently (for example, a decision to contribute to the provision of a public good for the first time could perhaps be made at any time, but a decision to cease contributing – to switch from Cooperation to Defection – might be possible less often, because, for example, resources have been committed), then the model would have to be modified. Again, I suspect that the result of the modification would be to render more restrictive the conditions for mutual Cooperation to be the outcome of the supergame.

Perhaps the most important shortcoming of the Prisoners' Dilemma supergame as a model of the process of public goods provision is that it takes place in a static environment: the supergame consists of iterations of the same ordinary game. In some of the public goods problems of interest here, a more realistic description of reality would require a *changing* payoff matrix, possibly a changing set of available strategies, and even a changing set of players. These changes, especially the first, might be the result of influences external to the game or of the history of strategy choices of the players themselves. Where, for example, a 'common' (of the kind discussed in chapter 1) is being exploited, the payoffs might decrease steadily as more and more non-Cooperative ('exploitative') choices are made over time; they might radically change quite suddenly with the ecological collapse of the 'common' following a long succession of non-Cooperative choices; and, for the same reasons, the set of available strategies might become restricted and some of the players might be obliged to withdraw from the game.

The possibilities here are very numerous, and it is impossible to make any general statements about the effects of extensions of this sort on the conclusions of the analysis in this chapter and the last. These effects would very much depend on the particular manner in which the game changed over time. Perhaps the most important class of changes is the one suggested above: all payoffs decline as a result of non-Cooperative choices (the greater the number of players Defecting, the greater the decline), and all payoffs increase, or at least do not decrease, as a result of Cooperative choices. It seems very probable that an analysis of this sort of dynamic game would show that mutual Cooperation is a more likely outcome than in the 'static' supergame studied here; that is to say, a lower discount rate than in the present model would suffice to make Cooperation rational, for the gains from unilateral Defection from the mutual Cooperation position (assuming that conditional strategies are being used so that this unilateral Defection would cause other players to Defect also) would clearly be smaller, other things being equal.

5. Altruism and superiority

Up to this point, the assumption has been made that every individual is a pure egoist, concerned only to maximize his own payoff. I do in fact believe that this is a good approximation to actual behaviour in very many situations where collective action is a possibility. If it were not, there would not be the innumerable unsolved collective action problems that we can see around us in the world and there would not be as much need as there obviously is for action by states, political entrepreneurs, organizations and other 'external' agents in the solution of collective action problems for, as we shall see, most collective action problems would not arise or would be solved 'spontaneously' if there was enough altruism. (The division of solutions to collective action problems into 'external' and 'internal' or 'spontaneous' was made in chapter 1.)

Olson himself went astray here, arguing that if it was not rational for a pure egoist to contribute to the provision of a public good then it would not be rational even for a pure altruist to do so, since his contribution to the welfare of others 'would not be perceptible'. A rational altruist would still want to allocate his resources where they had some effect (on others).[1] This is nonsense. In the first place, although a contribution (e.g., work effort, or refraining from dumping rubbish) may not in fact be noticed by others, or if noticed may not have any effect on them in the sense of causing them to contribute, it is not literally 'imperceptible', nor is its effect 'infinitesimal'. Otherwise it would not be possible for a (finite!) number of people, however numerous, *collectively* to provide any of the public good – or any 'noticeable' amount of it at any rate.[2] Secondly, no inference can in any case be made from what is rational for a pure egoist to what is rational for a pure altruist or for someone who combines altruism with egoism. In a two-person situation, for example, my benefit from the public good provided out of my contribution might just be outweighed by the cost of my contribution, but *your* benefit from *my* contribution costs you nothing. If, for example, an egoist's preferences (his own benefits less his own costs) were those of a 2×2 Prisoners' Dilemma, then he would choose D, but a pure altruist – out to maximize the *other's* payoff – would choose C. And thirdly, the altruist, in contributing to a non-excludable good, augments the utilities of everyone else in the group, and it is the *sum*, or some other sort of aggregate, of *all* of these utilities which (together with his own payoff if he combines altruism with egoism) he compares with his costs. In a large group, this might very well cause him to contribute.

There are two other ways in which altruism can make a difference to the provision of public goods and the solution of collective action problems generally. If *some* individuals contribute because they are sufficiently altruistic (or for that matter for non-instrumental reasons, such as 'self-expression'), then they might thereby provide a 'starter' around which conditional cooperation by others who are rational egoists can develop. If, for example, the conditions established in chapter 4 for conditional cooperation amongst all or some players in a Prisoners' Dilemma supergame are not met, then a small number of players who would not otherwise have cooperated might be induced to do so because their cooperation is conditional on at least n others cooperating and the altruistic cooperators constitute a subgroup of at least that size. This might trigger further cooperation on the part of those whose cooperation is conditional on the cooperation of more players than the group of altruists contains. And so on. The second way, or group of ways, in which altruism can make a difference is that the core of altruists may be able to provide the wherewithal to bring about an 'external' solution of the collective action problem amongst the remainder. For example, the altruists' contributions might 'finance' a political entrepreneur, who goes to work on the non-altruists. Or the altruists might *shame* the others into cooperation or bring other informal social sanctions to bear on them.

In asserting that innumerable, important collective action problems go unsolved or need external help for their solution because people are insufficiently altruistic, I do not mean to say that people are *never* altruistic. There clearly is a great deal of altruistic behaviour. But what I would argue is that departures from egoism (and more radical departures from 'thin' rationality, for example those involving expressive rather than instrumental motivation) are, as it were, luxuries. They are less likely to occur where the courses of action available to an individual are limited and the incentives affecting him are well-defined, clearly apparent and substantial, and above all where the individual's choice situation combined with his benefits and costs are such that a lot (in his eyes) turns on his choice. In such situations of relative scarcity and constraint, substantial altruism is unlikely.[3]

In this chapter I shall consider very briefly what difference the introduction of altruism makes to collective action problems, or more specifically to behaviour in Prisoners' Dilemma and Chicken games. Of special interest will be games in which each player is concerned with the difference between his own payoff and the payoffs of other players – which I will call his *eminence*, after Hobbes, or his *superiority* – as well as with his own payoff *per se*. The pursuit of superiority involves 'negative altruism' (my utility increases as your payoff decreases) as well as egoism and is what Hobbes took people to be most concerned with, as we will see in the next chapter. It is also, I fear, of particular importance in relations between states.

The altruism considered here takes a very simple form.[4] Each player is assumed to maximize an additive function of his own payoff and the other players' payoffs. Just as long as the weight attached to any other player's payoff is non-zero, I shall say that the individual acts altruistically. I shall also consider briefly what I will call 'sophisticated altruism', where a player's utility depends upon the other players' utilities (which might incorporate some form of altruism) as well as their payoffs.

I emphasize that 'altruism' here is confined to a regard for other persons' payoffs and utilities. A player's utility is not dependent upon anything else to do with the other players – for example their strategy choices *per se*. (A conformist, for example, might value doing what others do regardless of their payoffs.)

In what follows, some simple ideas and results are introduced which will be of use in the two final chapters of the book. I have, however, gone a little further than is necessary in this respect. Nevertheless, only a brief introduction to this subject is given. It is mainly confined to the two-person game. In the N-person game, the different forms which altruism can take are almost limitless in number; of these I shall consider only one which is of special interest.

Altruism in two-person games

Consider a 2×2 one-shot Prisoners' Dilemma game in which the two players' payoffs are p_1 and p_2. The general form of the assumption of altruistic behaviour is that each player i maximizes the following *utility function*:

$$u_i = u_i(p_1, p_2)$$

More specifically, I assume that each player maximizes a *weighted sum* of p_1 and p_2:

$$u_i = \alpha_i p_i + \beta_i p_j \ (i, j = 1, 2; \ i \neq j)$$

Clearly, whereas it has sufficed up till now to assume only that each player's payoff scale is unique up to a linear transformation, now we must assume also that each player is able to compare other players' payoffs with his own. He must be able to place the origins and units of the payoff scales of the other players in a one-to-one correspondence with those of his own payoff scale. (To make such comparisons, a player must of course *know* the other players' payoffs. This is already a strong assumption, at least for some applications; but little could be said about altruism with it.)

When $\beta_i = 0$ (and $\alpha_i \neq 0$), player i is called *a pure egoist*. In this case the analysis is the same for all positive values of α_i. If $\alpha_i > 0$, then, I choose $\alpha_i = 1$. This is the case we have considered already (in the last chapter). Similarly, for $\alpha_i < 0$, I set $\alpha_i = -1$.

When $\alpha_i = 0$ (and $\beta_i \neq 0$), player i is called *a pure altruist*. When $\beta_i > 0$, the particular value of β_i is irrelevant, so I choose $\beta_i = 1$. Similarly, for $\beta_i < 0$, I choose $\beta_i = -1$.

These are polar cases. In between lie those cases in which egoism and altruism are present together. It is not assumed that an individual can be altruistic only at the expense of being egoistic: α_i and β_i need not, for example, be complements or inverses.

When $\beta_i > 0$, player i's altruism is said to be *positive*. When $\beta_i < 0$, it is called *negative*.

I am aware that 'altruism' is popularly limited to what I call 'positive altruism', but it is convenient here to use the more literal, root meaning. In particular contexts, 'positive altruism' and 'negative altruism' might alternatively be called 'benevolence' and 'malevolence' (or various other pairs of words). These expressions would, however, be quite inappropriate in other contexts, and I therefore use the more neutral terms.

Sometimes, 'egoism' is limited to the case when $\alpha_i > 0$, but again it is convenient here to use the term more literally.

When $\alpha_i < 0$, the player's behaviour might in various contexts be called 'ascetic', 'anticompetitive', 'masochistic', and so on.

In what follows (except for the section on sophisticated altruism), I will confine the discussion to symmetric games, in which the values of α_i and β_i do not differ between the players.

Suppose that the payoff matrix is:

	C	D
C	x, x	z, y
D	y, z	w, w

Then if each player's utility is a weighted sum of the two players' payoffs, the resulting *utility matrix* is:

	C	D
C	$(\alpha_1 + \beta_1)x$, $(\alpha_2 + \beta_2)x$	$\alpha_1 z + \beta_1 y$, $\alpha_2 y + \beta_2 z$
D	$\alpha_1 y + \beta_1 z$, $\alpha_2 z + \beta_2 y$	$(\alpha_1 + \beta_1)w$, $(\alpha_2 + \beta_2)w$

For emphasis, I shall speak of the resulting game as the *transformed game*.

Suppose that the untransformed game is a Prisoners' Dilemma, that is, suppose that $y > x > w > z$. What sort of game will the transformed game be?

In the transformed game whose utility matrix is shown above, D dominates C for player i if and only if

$$\alpha_i y + \beta_i z > (\alpha_i + \beta_i)x$$

and

$$(\alpha_i + \beta_i)w > \alpha_i z + \beta_i y$$

that is,

$$\alpha_i > \frac{x-z}{y-x}\beta_i \qquad (5.1)$$

and

$$\alpha_i > \frac{y-w}{w-z}\beta_i \qquad (5.2)$$

Outcome (C, C) is (strictly) preferred to (D, D) by player i if and only if

$$(\alpha_i + \beta_i)x > (\alpha_i + \beta_i)w$$

that is,

$$\alpha_i + \beta_i > 0 \qquad (5.3)$$

Thus, the transformed game is a Prisoners' Dilemma, with (D, D), the only equilibrium, being Pareto-inferior to (C, C), if and only if (5.1), (5.2) and (5.3) are true for both players.

We see that for given values of x, y, w and z, the inequalities (5.1) and (5.2) are 'more readily' satisfied as the ratio α_i/β_i increases, that is, as player i's 'egoism' increases relative to his 'altruism'.

I examine now some cases of special interest – some more so than others.

(1) $\alpha_i \geqslant 0, \beta_i > 0$ ($i = 1, 2$): each player's utility increases as his own payoff increases and as the other player's payoff increases.

(1.1) *Egoism and positive altruism* ($\alpha_i > 0$, $\beta_i > 0$, $i = 1, 2$): each player cares about both his own and the other player's payoff; his utility increases with increases in either of them, other things being equal. For given values of x, y, w and z, a transformed Prisoners' Dilemma may or not be a Prisoners' Dilemma. Inequality (5.3) is always satisfied, but (5.1) and (5.2) may not be. In fact (as the reader can verify) a Prisoners' Dilemma can be transformed into a game of Chicken, an Assurance game, or even a game in which C dominates D for both players. In the last two eventualities, mutual Cooperation is assured and, as I argued earlier, it is more likely in a Chicken game than in a Prisoners' Dilemma. So, as one would expect, a measure of positive altruism may improve the prospects for Cooperation. If there is *only* positive altruism, then, as paragraph (1.2) will show, mutual Cooperation is necessarily the outcome.

We saw in chapter 2 that individual preferences in many important collective action problems are more likely to be those of a Chicken game than those of a Prisoners' Dilemma. It is easily shown that positive altruism can transform a Chicken game into one in which C dominates D for each player; but (no matter what kind or degree of egoism it is combined with) it cannot transform *any* Chicken game into a Prisoners' Dilemma. Only positive egoism and *negative* altruism can do that.

(1.2) *Pure positive altruism* $(\alpha_i = 0, \beta_i > 1, i = 1, 2)$: each player desires only to maximize the other player's payoff (or some proportion of it – it makes no difference). Starting from a Prisoners' Dilemma *or* a Chicken game, pure positive altruism produces a game in which C dominates D for each player. So (C, C) is the outcome. Furthermore, it is preferred by both players to (D, D). But although (C, C) is the only equilibrium, each player's first preference is for the other player to Defect while he Cooperates.

(2) $\alpha_i \geqslant 0, \beta_i < 0$ $(i = 1, 2)$: each player's utility increases as his own payoff increases and as the other player's payoff decreases.

(2.1) *Pure negative altruism* $(\alpha_i = 0, \beta_i < 0, i = 1, 2)$: each player desires only to *minimize* the other player's payoff. Starting from a Prisoners' Dilemma *or* a Chicken game, pure negative altruism produces a game in which D is each player's dominant strategy, and (D, D), which must be the outcome, is Pareto-optimal.

(2.2) *Egoism and negative altruism* $(\alpha_i > 0, \beta_i < 0, i = 1, 2)$. Starting with a Prisoners' Dilemma, the addition of negative altruism to each individual's egoism produces a game in which D dominates C for each player (the inequalities (5.1) and (5.2) are always satisfied if the untransformed game is a Prisoners' Dilemma). So (D, D) is the outcome. But the transformed game is not necessarily a Prisoners' Dilemma, since inequality (5.3) need not hold. A Chicken game, on the other hand, may be transformed into a game with D dominant (with or without (C, C) preferred to (D, D)) or into another Chicken game.

The following special case of egoism and negative altruism is important.

(2.2.1) *Games of Difference.* These are perhaps the most interesting of the transformed games. They are relevant to the account of Hobbes's political theory given in the next chapter. Suppose that each player's utility increases both with his own payoff and with the *difference* between his and the other player's payoff. He wants to increase his own payoff but he also wants to increase his *superiority* over the other player, other things being equal. Specifically, suppose that each player seeks to maximize a convex combination of his own payoff and the excess of his own payoff over the other player's. That is,

$$u_i = \lambda_i p_i + (1 - \lambda_i)(p_i - p_j), \quad i = 1, 2, i \neq j$$

where $0 \leqslant \lambda_i < 1$ $(i = 1, 2)$. (When $\lambda_i = 1$, we have the original untransformed game.) $\lambda_i/(1 - \lambda_i)$, then, is the weight player i attaches to his payoff relative to the excess of his own payoff over the other player's payoff.

This expression for u_i can be obtained from the general form, $u_i = \alpha_i p_i + \beta_i p_j$, by setting

$$\alpha_i = 1, \ \beta_i = \lambda_i - 1 \quad (i = 1, 2)$$

The transformed game, which I call a *Game of Difference*, is:

	C	D
C	$\lambda_1 x, \ \lambda_2 x$	$z - (1 - \lambda_1)y, \ y - (1 - \lambda_2)z$
D	$y - (1 - \lambda_1)z, \ z - (1 - \lambda_2)y$	$\lambda_1 w, \ \lambda_2 w$

If we start with a Prisoners' Dilemma game, then in the transformed game, as we have already noted in paragraph (2.2), D dominates C whenever $\alpha_i > 0$ and $\beta_i < 0$ (for $i = 1, 2$), which is the case here.

Thus (D, D) is the only equilibrium. But (C, C) is preferred to (D, D) by player i, if and only if $\lambda_i > 0$. (When $\lambda_i = 0$ he is indifferent between these two outcomes.)

Thus, if the untransformed game is a Prisoners' Dilemma, the Game of Difference is always a Prisoners' Dilemma just as long as $\lambda_i \neq 0$ $(i = 1, 2)$.

We shall see below that a similar result holds for an N-person generalization of this Game of Difference.

If we call a player's gain from defecting unilaterally from mutual Cooperation his *temptation*, then in the original Prisoners' Dilemma game it is the difference $y - x$ but in the Game of Difference it becomes

$$y - (1 - \lambda_i)z - \lambda_i x$$

and it is easily verified that this is always greater than $y - x$. So each player's temptation in the Game of Difference is always greater than in the original game. If we say that a Prisoners' Dilemma becomes 'more severe' if any player's temptation increases, other things being equal, then *the Game of Difference is a more severe Prisoners' Dilemma than the original game.*

If the untransformed game is a *Chicken* game, then it is easily shown that, provided $\lambda_i \neq 0$ ($i = 1, 2$), the Game of Difference is a Chicken game or Prisoners' Dilemma according as λ_i is greater or less than the ratio $(y - x)/(y - w)$. So the Game of Difference will be a Prisoners' Dilemma – and thus mutual Cooperation will not occur – if each λ_i is sufficiently small, that is, the players attach sufficient weight to achieving superiority over each other as against their own payoffs *per se.*

In the special case when $\lambda_i = 0$ ($i = 1, 2$), each player seeks only to maximize the difference between the two payoffs. I call this zero-sum game a *Pure Difference Game.* Whatever game we start with, in the Game of Difference D is the dominant strategy for each player. So (D, D) is the outcome. But it is no longer Pareto-inferior; for each player is indifferent between (D, D) and (C, C).[5]

(3) *Games of Anti-difference or Equality.* A player in a Game of Difference is concerned, to some extent, to raise his own payoff above that of the other player. An *opposite* concern could take several forms. The most extreme of these would presumably be a desire to maximize the excess of the other player's payoff over one's own. Less extreme would be the maximization of a convex combination of this excess and one's own payoff:

$$u_i = \lambda_i p_i - (1 - \lambda_i)(p_i - p_j)$$

with $0 \leqslant \lambda_i < 1$, but I do not think behaviour of this sort is very common.

Of more interest, I think, is a desire to minimize the difference, whether positive or negative, between the other player's payoff and one's own – a desire, that is, for *equality.* More generally, consider the game in which player i seeks to maximize the following utility function:

$$u_i = \lambda_i p_i - (1 - \lambda_i)|p_i - p_j|$$

where $0 \leqslant \lambda_i < 1$. (If $\lambda_i = 1$, we have the original Prisoners' Dilemma game.) This represents a convex combination of 'egoism' (maximizing one's own payoff) and 'equality' (minimizing the absolute value of the difference between the two payoffs). I call this game a *Game of Equality or Anti-difference*. 'Anti-difference' is not a very beautiful expression, but it is sufficiently neutral to cover a number of different interpretations of this game.

I will not waste space by setting out the details, but the reader can easily verify that, unless $\lambda_i = 0$ for either player, both Prisoners' Dilemma and Chicken games can be transformed into Games of Anti-difference which are either Prisoners' Dilemma or Chicken games depending on the values of λ_i. When $\lambda_i = 0$ for both players (i.e. in the unlikely event that both players are concerned with achieving equality regardless of their own payoffs) the transformed game is a pure coordination game, each player being indifferent between (C, C) and (D, D).

Sophisticated altruism. An altruistic player was defined earlier as one whose utility function is of the form:

$$u_i = u_i(p_1, p_2)$$

where p_1 and p_2 are the payoffs to the two players. A player's utility, however, may depend not only directly on the other's payoff but also on his utility. In this case, we have:

$$u_i = u_i(p_1, p_2, u_j), \quad j \neq i$$

Thus, I may derive pleasure directly from the contemplation of your loss of payoff, but if I believe that you derive pleasure from your loss of payoff, then I may cease to be happy (and may cease to act so as to diminish your payoff).

If a player's utility depends in any way on another player's *utility*, I call him a *sophisticated altruist*.[6]

Consider, for example, two pure altruists, one positive (A) and the other negative (B), in a Prisoners' Dilemma. If their utilities are simply of the form $u_i = u_i(p_1, p_2)$, then (C, D) would be the happy outcome (a Pareto-optimal, unique equilibrium): A would be happy because B's payoff is a maximum and B would be happy because A's payoff is a minimum. At the 'first-order of sophistication', A is very happy because B is happy (with A's minimal payoff), but B is now unhappy because A is happy (with B's maximal payoff). At the 'second-order of sophistication',

A now becomes unhappy because of B's unhappiness at the first-order level, and B is very unhappy at A's increased happiness at the first-order level. And so on.

In practice, however, the levels of sophistication will not all carry the same weight, and there will be an end to this potentially infinite regress. In particular, it is unlikely that anybody goes beyond the first-order level:

$$u_i = u_i(p_1, p_2, u_j(p_1, p_2)), \quad j \neq i$$

The implications of sophisticated altruism for behaviour in the Prisoners' Dilemma are illustrated in the following example. Consider a Prisoners' Dilemma with these payoffs:

	C	D
C	1, 1	$-1, 2$
D	2, -1	0, 0

(Matrix 1)

Suppose that player 1 is a pure positive altruist while player 2 is a pure negative altruist, with utilities.

$$u_1 = p_2, \quad u_2 = -p_1$$

Then the transformed matrix is:

	C	D
C	1, -1	2, 1
D	$-1, -2$	0, 0

(Matrix 2)

This is no longer a Prisoners' Dilemma. (C, D) is the Pareto-optimal, unique equilibrium.

If the players are 'pure, first-order-sophisticated (positive and negative) altruists', then this matrix in turn becomes:

	C	D
C	$-1, -1$	1, -2
D	$-2, 1$	0, 0

(Matrix 3)

which is a Prisoners' Dilemma, but with (C, C) as the only equilibrium and (D, D) preferred to (C, C) by both players.

If the players are 'pure, second-order-sophisticated (positive and negative) altruists', then this matrix becomes:

	C	D
C	$-1, 1$	$-2, -1$
D	$1, 2$	$0, 0$

(Matrix 4)

which is not a Prisoners' Dilemma, (D, C) being the Pareto-optimal, unique equilibrium. And so on.

More realistically, suppose that both players ignore orders of sophistication beyond the first, and that their utilities are (for the sake of illustration) simply the average of those in Matrix 2 and those at the first level in Matrix 3; that is,

$$u_1 = \tfrac{1}{2}p_2 + \tfrac{1}{2}(-p_1)$$

and

$$u_2 = \tfrac{1}{2}(-p_1) - \tfrac{1}{2}(p_2)$$

Then the game is:

	C	D
C	$0, -1$	$3/2, -1/2$
D	$3/2, -1/2$	$0, 0$

Here, C dominates D for player 1, while D dominates C for player 2 so that (C, D) is the only equilibrium. But the game is not a Prisoners' Dilemma, for this equilibrium is Pareto-optimal.

The supergame. Consider the supergame consisting of an indefinite number of iterations of the general transformed 2×2 Prisoners' Dilemma game in which the players combine egoism and unsophisticated altruism. Assume that future payoffs are discounted exponentially, as in chapters 3 and 4. Then it is a straightforward matter, using the methods of chapter 3, to derive the conditions for various supergame strategy vectors to be equilibria. It transpires that, in contrast with the supergame *without* altruism, in the transformed game *every* one of the strategy vectors considered in chapter 3 is an equilibrium for some values of y, x, w, z, a_i, α_i and β_i (where a_i is i's discount parameter and α_i and β_i are the weights attached by i to his own payoff and to the other player's payoff, as before). This is not at all surprising: after all, sufficient positive altruism can transform a *one-shot* Prisoners' Dilemma into a game with C dominant for both players; so in the *supergame* even (C^∞, C^∞) is an equilibrium under certain conditions.

In particular, since a Prisoners' Dilemma, when transformed into a (non-pure) Game of Difference, is still a Prisoners' Dilemma, the results from chapter 3 can be applied directly. Since the new Prisoners' Dilemma is 'more severe' than the original one, we should find, in particular, that the conditions for mutual conditional Cooperation to be an equilibrium are more stringent. This is easily demonstrated. Recall that (B, B) is an equilibrium in the untransformed game if and only if

$$a_i \geqslant \frac{y - x}{y - w} \tag{5.4}$$

(which is the condition for unilateral defection to D^∞ not to pay) *and*

$$a_i \geqslant \frac{y - x}{x - z} \tag{5.5}$$

(which is the condition for unilateral defection to B' not to pay). In the transformed game, the Game of Difference, the equivalent of (5.4) is easily found to be:

$$a_i \geqslant \frac{y - x + (1 - \lambda_i)(x - z)}{y - w + (1 - \lambda_i)(w - z)} \tag{5.6}$$

Since $x - z > w - z$ and $1 - \lambda_i > 0$, the right hand side of this exceeds $(y - x)/(y - w)$; that is, the discount parameter must be *greater* (the discount *rate* must be smaller) in the Game of Difference than in the original Prisoners' Dilemma if unilateral defection to D^∞ from (B, B) is not to pay. Similarly, in the transformed game the equivalent of (5.5) is:

$$a_i \geqslant \frac{y - x + (1 - \lambda_i)(x - z)}{x - z + (1 - \lambda_i)(y - x)} \tag{5.7}$$

Since $x-z > y-x$ (if it were not, the right hand side of (5.5) would be greater than one) and $1-\lambda_i > 0$, the right hand side of (5.7) exceeds $(y-x)/(x-z)$; that is, the discount parameter must be *greater* (the discount *rate* must be smaller) in the Game of Difference than in the original Prisoners' Dilemma if unilateral defection to B' from (B, B) is not to pay.

Thus, the conditions (5.6 and 5.7) for mutual conditional Cooperation to be an equilibrium in the Game of Difference are indeed more stringent than they were in the original, untransformed Prisoner' Dilemma.

An N-person Game of Difference

In the general N-person Prisoners' Dilemma game, the number of different forms which altruism can take is very large. I shall consider only one of them. It is one of many possible generalizations of the two-person Game of Difference which I discussed earlier. Of all the transformed Prisoners' Dilemma games involving egoism and some form of altruism, Games of Difference are the most important for my purposes in this book. When we come to consider in the next chapter the political theory of Hobbes, we shall see that the 'game' which Hobbes assumes people to be playing in the absence of government (in 'the state of nature') is in effect a generalized Game of Difference.

In the two-person Game of Difference, each individual's utility is a convex combination of his own payoff (p_i) and the difference $(p_i - p_j)$ between his and the other player's payoff. Let us anticipate a Hobbesian term of the next chapter and call this difference the *eminence* of the ith over the jth individual. In a game with more than two players, there are a number of ways in which an individual might be said to seek 'eminence': he might, for example, seek to maximize the number of other individuals with respect to whom he is eminent (his positive eminence); he might seek to maximize the sum of his eminences over each other individual; and so on. The definition which I shall adopt here is that an individual's eminence in the N-person game is the *average* of his eminence over each other individual. I use the same word, eminence, in both the two-person and N-person cases: eminence in the former is a special case of eminence in the latter. Thus, the ith individual's *eminence* is defined as:

$$E_i = \frac{1}{N} \sum_{\text{all } j \neq i} (p_i - p_j)$$

The untransformed game (with payoff p_i to the ith individual) is the N-person Prisoners' Dilemma specified in chapter 4; that is, the two payoff functions $f(v)$ and $g(v)$ – which are each player's payoffs when he chooses C and D, respectively, and v others choose D – satisfy the three conditions:

(i) $g(v) > f(v)$ for all $v \geqslant 0$
(ii) $f(N-1) > g(0)$
(iii) $g(v) > g(0)$ for all $v > 0$

The N-person generalization of the two-person Game of Difference which I shall now consider is the game in which each individual is assumed to seek to maximize a convex combination of his own payoff and his eminence. The ith individual's utility, then, is defined as:

$$u_i = \lambda_i p_i + (1 - \lambda_i) E_i$$

where $0 \leqslant \lambda_i \leqslant 1$. When $\lambda_i = 1$ for all i, we have of course the original, untransformed Prisoners' Dilemma in which every player is a pure egoist.

I shall do no more than establish the conditons under which this N-person Game of Difference is a Prisoners' Dilemma game satisfying the three conditions listed above. This is all I require for my purposes in chapter 6. For when these conditions are met, the general results on the N-person Prisoners' Dilemma apply to the Game of Difference.

If the ith individual and v others Cooperate, then the payoff to i and to each of the v others is $f(v)$ while the payoff to each of the $N - v - 1$ who do not Cooperate is $g(v + 1)$. Thus, individual i's utility is:

$$u_i = \lambda_i f(v) + (1 - v_i) \frac{1}{N}(N - v - 1)\{f(v) - g(v+1)\}$$
$$= F(v), \text{ say.}$$

If individual i does *not* Cooperate, while v others do, then we find that

$$u_i = \lambda_i g(v) + (1 - v_i) \frac{1}{N}(v)\{g(v) - f(v-1)\} \quad \text{if } v \neq 0$$
$$= G(v), \text{ say}$$

and

$$u_i = \lambda_i g(0) = G(0) \quad \text{if } v = 0$$

because

$$f(v-1)=f(-1) \text{ is undefined.}$$

The necessary and sufficient condition for the ith individual to choose not to Cooperate is of course $G(v) > F(v)$. This condition cannot be essentially simplified unless further assumptions are made about $f(v)$ and $g(v)$.

However, we can certainly say that $G(v) > F(v)$ if (but not only if)

$$v\{g(v)-f(v-1)\} > -(N-v-1)\{g(v+1)-f(v)\}$$

which in turn is true if $g(v)$ is strictly increasing with v (for we have already assumed that $g(v) > f(v)$ for all v).

Thus, if $g(v)$ is strictly increasing, each player prefers D to C no matter what the other players choose; and therefore the outcome is that every player chooses D. Let us see whether this outcome is Pareto-inferior.

If everybody Cooperates, each player's payoff is $f(N-1)$ and therefore the ith player's utility is $F(N-1)=\lambda_i f(N-1)$.

If nobody Cooperates, each player's payoff is $g(0)$ and therefore the ith player's utility is $G(0)=\lambda_i g(0)$.

As long as $\lambda_i \neq 0$, we have $\lambda_i f(N-1) > \lambda_i g(0)$, for we have already assumed that $f(N-1) > g(0)$. Thus, if $\lambda_i \neq 0$ for all i, every individual prefers the outcome when everybody Cooperates to the outcome when everybody Defects.

Finally, observe that $G(v) > G(0)$ if (but not only if) $g(v)$ is strictly increasing with v.

Thus, *this N-person Game of Difference is a Prisoners' Dilemma satisfying conditions (i), (ii) and (iii) if (but not only if) $\lambda_i \neq 0$, for all i, and $g(v)$ is strictly increasing with v.*

The condition $\lambda_i \neq 0$, for all i, simply requires that the game is not one of *pure* eminence; each individual must attach some weight to his own payoff *per se*. All other convex combinations of his own payoff and his eminence are permitted.

The condition that $g(v)$ is strictly increasing with v requires only that the greater the number of individuals who Cooperate, the greater is the payoff to any individual who does not Cooperate.

6. The state

At the start of this book a sketch was made of an argument for the desirability of the state. The first part of the argument is that the static preferences of individuals amongst alternative courses of action with respect to the provision of public goods (in particular, domestic peace and security and environmental public goods) are those of a Prisoners' Dilemma game, at least where relatively large numbers of individuals are involved. I examined this part of the argument in chapter 2 and found that it is not necessarily true and needs to be qualified. Accepting the first part of the argument, I considered in chapters 3 & 4 the second part of the argument: that individuals would not voluntarily cooperate in such situations. If the problem is properly specified as a one-shot Prisoners' Dilemma game, this conclusion is obviously correct: but to treat the problem, as it is usually treated (tacitly or explicitly), in terms of a *one-shot* game is clearly inadequate. I therefore treated it in terms of a Prisoners' Dilemma supergame in which the players discount future payoffs. Formulated in this way, the second part of the argument is not necessarily true: under certain conditions, it is rational to Cooperate in the supergame. It remains to examine the third part of the argument, that the failure of individuals, at least in large groups, to cooperate voluntarily (to provide themselves with certain public goods) makes the state desirable.

This part of the argument will be examined in the present chapter in the forms in which it appears in the political theories of Hobbes and Hume, and more generally in the final chapter.

In this chapter, I consider two versions, those of Hobbes and Hume, of the *whole* of the argument about the desirability of the state. My reasons for doing so, and in particular for choosing Hobbes and Hume as exemplars of the general argument, were given earlier (in chapter 1) and I shall not repeat them here. I shall give an account of the two theories in such a way that they can be compared at certain points with some of the ideas in the earlier chapters. A large part of my account of Hobbes's theory is devoted to showing (what at first sight may appear almost obvious) that men, in what Hobbes calls the 'state of nature', find themselves in a Prisoners' Dilemma game.

My treatment of Hobbes's theory is based entirely on his *Leviathan*. I have resisted the temptation to buttress my argument at any point with selective quotation from his other works. *Leviathan* contains the clearest and most coherent version of the argument which is of interest here, and I have thought it unjustified to refer to a passage from another version which, taken as a whole, is different, less coherent and generally less satisfactory than the one in *Leviathan*. My treatment of Hume's theory is based chiefly on *A Treatise of Human Nature*, which I think gives a clearer and more complete account than the one in *An Enquiry Concerning the Principles of Morals*. The second differs in places from, but is not inconsistent with, the first, and I have referred to it once or twice.

Hobbes's *Leviathan*

I begin with Hobbes's description of those parts of the structure of individual preferences on which his political theory is based. His conclusions on this subject are presented here as assumptions, whereas in *Leviathan* Hobbes claims to deduce them from more fundamental, physical premises. His political theory is unaffected by this shift in the point of logical departure.

Individual preferences

All men, says Hobbes, *desire* certain things (*Lev* 31).[1] He derives this proposition from his assumptions about 'motion' and these lead him to speak of man's *ceaseless* striving for the things he desires: 'Life it self is but Motion, and can never be without Desire' (*Lev* 48); and 'Nor can a man any more live, whose Desires are at an end, than he whose Senses and Imagination are at a stand. Felicity is a continuall progresse of the desire from one object to another; the attaining of the former, being still but the way to the later' (*Lev* 75). But this adds nothing to the original statement that all men desire certain things. For this statement, in which there is no reference to time, is to apply at each point in time. The same is true of man's 'perpetuall and restlesse desire of Power'.

Hobbes defines power as follows. 'The POWER *of a Man,* (to take it Universally), is his present means, to obtain some future apparent Good. And is either *Originall,* or *Instrumentall' (Lev* 66). Later he concludes that he puts '. . . for a general inclination of all mankind, a perpetuall and restelesse desire of Power after power, that ceaseth only in Death' (*Lev* 75). This can be viewed either as a part of the initial proposition that men desire certain things (one of them, then, being power) or, better, as derivative from it: for if a man desires something, he desires also the means to obtain it in the future ('. . . anything that is a pleasure in the sense, the same also is pleasure in the imagination' (*Lev* 76) – although Hobbes is never explicit about *how* men presently value future expected goods).

Thus power-seeking (which has been so much emphasized in discussions of Hobbes) does not play an independent role in Hobbes's theory and will not appear in my restatement of it.

Now Hobbes seems to say that men do not simply desire certain primary goods, but rather they desire to have them to an 'eminent' degree. 'Vertue generally, in all sorts of subjects, is somewhat that is valued for eminence; and consisteth in comparison. For if all things were equally in all men, nothing would be prized' (*Lev* 52). Thus '. . . man, whose Joy consisteth in comparing himself with other men, can relish nothing but what is eminent' (*Lev* 130). Power, which all men seek and which is a means to other desirable things, is divided by Hobbes into 'natural' and 'instrumental' power, the first being defined as 'the eminence of the Faculties of Body, or Mind: as extraordinary Strength, Forme, Prudence, Arts, Eloquence, Liberality, Nobility', while 'Instrumentall are those Powers, which acquired by these, or by fortune, are means and Instruments to acquire more: as Riches, Reputation, Friends, and the secret working of God, which men call Good Luck' (*Lev* 66). A desire for power, then, entails by definition a desire for 'eminence'.

In my restatement of Hobbes's main argument, there will be just one assumption about individual preferences, to the effect that each person seeks to maximize a convex combination of his own payoff and his eminence (to use the language of chapter 5). But the desire for eminence needs to be specified more carefully than Hobbes does, in the passages referred to above. No problems arise if there are only two individuals who both desire the same object and nothing else. For then the assumption is that each individual seeks to maximize the excess of his amount of the object over the other individual's amount.

Yet, in the first place, Hobbes has said that not all men desire the same things (*Lev* 40). Perhaps, in the two-person case, each man seeks to have more of the things he wants than the other man has of those same things, even though the latter has no desire for them. Or, more plausibly, he seeks to have more of the things he wants than the other man has of the things *he* wants: in this case, he must presumably have some means of comparing his and the other individual's amounts of the different objects. However, neither of these is terribly plausible unless there is an acknowledged scheme for comparing the extents to which the two men desire their different objects. Yet it can be argued that Hobbes has in mind *particular* objects of desire and assumes that *all* men desire at least these objects. For example, all men desire their own preservation. All men (he seems to say in Chapter 8) desire to be eminent in the 'intellectual virtues'. All men desire to be eminent in 'Strength, Forme, Prudence, Arts, Eloquence, Liberality, Nobility', for eminence in these things gives one 'Natural Power', which all men desire, and all men desire 'Riches, Reputation, Friends, and the secret working of God, which men call Good Luck' for these are 'Instrumentall powers', which all men desire (*Lev* 66).

It is not necessary here to resolve this problem in *Leviathan* (if it is a problem). In whatever way it is resolved, the following assumption (or something very like it) must in any case be made: corresponding to every possible state of affairs which is the outcome of individual choices, there is for each individual a *payoff*; each individual's payoff scale is unique at least up to a linear transformation, and each individual is able to compare other individuals' payoffs with his own (he is able to place any other player's payoff scale in a one-to-one correspondence with his own). Then, in the two-person case, if the payoff to the ith individual is p_i, I define the *eminence* of the ith over the jth individual as $p_i - p_j$.

In the second place, there are of course more than two people in the societies Hobbes is writing about. In this case, there are a number of ways of specifying the assumption that men seek 'eminence'. (I mentioned a few in chapter 5.) In Hobbes's theory, several of these alternative definitions of 'eminence' would suffice as part of the logical basis for the rest of his argument. For the sake of concreteness, in my restatement of his argument I shall adopt the definition given in chapter 5 ('An N-person Game of Difference'), where an individual's *eminence* is defined as the average of his eminences over each other individual. Also I shall assume that each individual seeks to maximize a convex combination (as defined in the same section) of his own payoff and his eminence. This convex combination is referred to as his *utility*. It should be noted that 'pure egoism' (that is, maximizing one's own payoff only) is a special case of maximizing this convex combination; in this case, 'utility' and 'payoff' can be viewed as the same thing.

In *Leviathan* (but not in all his earlier works), Hobbes clearly believes that 'benevolence', 'pity' and other manifestations of *positive* altruism are possible, that in some degree they are found in some individuals, and that they are not reducible to or mediated by self-interest. Nevertheless, it is true that the assumption on which his political theory is based is that in the state of nature (that is, in society without government) a man seeks only to maximize a convex combination of his own payoff and his eminence; that is to say, his preferences contain a mixture of egoism and *negative* altruism only.

A Prisoners' Dilemma

In this section I argue that in what Hobbes calls the 'state of nature' men find themselves in a Prisoners' Dilemma; that is to say, Hobbes is assuming that the choices available to each man (or 'player') and the players' preferences amongst the possible outcomes are such that the game is a Prisoners' Dilemma; and the Prisoners' Dilemma is the *only* structure of utilities (out of a very large number of possibilities) which Hobbes *must* have assumed to obtain in the state of nature.

I shall present two versions of this argument and evaluate their relative merits. The first version argues that Hobbes's theory is essentially static, being an analysis of the Prisoners' Dilemma *ordinary* game. The second version is more dynamic: although, in this version, time does not play an explicit role and there is no talk of the present valuation of future benefits, *conditional* cooperation is thought to be sometimes rational (and conditional cooperation is of course not possible in a game played only once).[2]

I assume (as Hobbes does in effect) that each individual is confronted with a number of alternative courses of action, which I call *strategies*.

The number of strategies available to each player is assumed to be just two. I shall show later that nothing essential in Hobbes's argument is affected if this assumption is relaxed. Call these two strategies C and D. (It need not be assumed that C and D denote the same two courses of action for every individual; but no confusion will arise if the same two labels are used for all individuals.) There are thus four possible states of affairs or *outcomes*. A *strategy vector* is defined as a list (an ordered N-tuple, if there are N individuals in the society) of strategies, one for each player.

One of the outcomes is called 'the state of War' or simply 'War' (*Lev* 96). This is the state of affairs which obtains when every individual seeks, in the absence of restraint, to maximize his utility (as Hobbes assumes he does). If the state of War is to be a determinate, unique outcome, then it must be assumed that 'maximizing utility' has a clear meaning and entails the choice by each individual of a single strategy. Let us suppose that this strategy is D. (For the time being, strategy C is simply 'not acting without restraint so as to maximize one's utility'.) Now, when men are under no restraint, when they 'live without a common power to keep them all in awe', they are said to be in the 'state of nature' (*Lev* Chapter 8).

When men are not in the state of War, then there is 'Peace', says Hobbes. There are of course *three* outcomes other than War (assuming that there are only two strategies available to each player), but it is clear that Hobbes means that Peace corresponds to only one of these outcomes: it obtains only when *no* individual chooses strategy D. (For he later argues that *everybody* must behave differently if society is to move out of the state of War into that of Peace.) Thus, Peace obtains when every individual chooses strategy C.

Now the state of War is Pareto-inferior: every man prefers Peace to War. For in War, 'men live without . . . security' and there is 'continuall feare, and danger of violent death; And the life of man, solitary, poore, nasty, brutish, and short' (*Lev* 96–7). Despite this rhetorical flourish, Hobbes makes it clear that 'the nature of War, consisteth not in actuall fighting; but in the known disposition thereto, during all the time there is no assurance to the contrary' (*Lev* 96). Nevertheless, in this condition, a man cannot expect to obtain what he desires; whereas in the state of Peace, life and security are guaranteed to each man and he can reasonably expect to obtain some of the things he desires; so that 'all men agree . . . that Peace is good' (*Lev* 122).

In the state of nature, then, each man will so act that the outcome is War, which is Pareto-inferior. The only way, in Hobbes's view, to prevent this outcome occurring and to ensure Peace instead is for men to erect a 'common power' which will maintain conditions in which each individual will not wish to choose D; and the only way to erect such a common power is to 'authorize', 'by covenanting' amongst themselves, one man or assembly of men to do whatever is necessary to maintain such conditions. The man or assembly of men so authorized is called the 'Sovereign' (*Lev* Chapter 17).

This needs explanation. For this, several definitions are required. The 'right of nature', says Hobbes, is 'the Liberty each man hath, to use his own power, as he will himselfe, for the preservation of his own Nature; that is to say, of his own Life; and consequently, of doing any thing, which in his own Judgement, and Reason, hee shall conceive to be the aptest means thereunto' (*Lev* 99). In the state of nature, therefore, 'every man has a Right to every thing; even to one anothers body' (*Lev* 99); so there is no security of life; 'and consequently, it is a precept, or generall rule of Reason, *That every man, ought to endeavour Peace, as farre forth as he has hope of obtaining it; and when he cannot obtain it, that he may seek, and use, all helps, and advantages of Warre*' (*Lev* 100). Notice that the second part of this statement is just the Right of Nature and that this is part of 'a precept, or generall rule of Reason'. Hobbes is saying, in effect, that it is rational for a man to choose D if he thinks he cannot obtain Peace, that is, if he thinks that some other people will choose D. Hobbes calls the first part of this statement the Fundamental or First Law of Nature, a 'law of nature' having been defined earlier as 'a Precept, or generall Rule, found out by Reason, by which a man is forbidden to do, that, which is destructive of his life, or taketh away the means of preserving the same; and to omit, that, by which he thinketh it may be best preserved' (*Lev* 99).

We may now say that strategy C is 'laying aside one's Right of Nature'. This only restates our earlier definition of C as not acting without restraint so as to maximize one's utility.

This statement of the first Law of Nature will be clarified after we have seen Hobbes's discussion of obligation and covenanting.

The definition of obligation given in *Leviathan* is straightforward. The second Law of Nature requires a man under certain conditions to lay down his right to all things. He may do this by simply 'renouncing' it ('when he care not to whom the benefit thereof redoundeth') or by 'transferring' it to another (when he does so care). 'And when a man hath in either manner abandoned, or granted away his Right, then he is said to be OBLIGED, or BOUND, not to hinder those, to whom such Right is granted, or abandoned, from the benefit of it' (*Lev* 101). A man will of course only transfer or renounce his right in exchange for some good to himself, in particular 'for some Right reciprocally transferred to himselfe' (*Lev* 101). This mutual transferring of right is called 'contract', and a contract in which at least one of the parties promises to perform his part in the future is called a '*covenant*' (*Lev* 102), a 'covenant of mutual trust' being one in which both parties so promise (*Lev* 105, 110).

Now contracts would not serve their end of securing Peace if they were not kept. Thus, the third Law of Nature is that 'men performe their Covenants made' (*Lev* 110). Yet, by performing unilaterally his part of a covenant of mutual trust, a man may expose himself, and this he is forbidden to do by all the Laws of Nature. Thus, a man should not do his part unless he is sure that the other party will do his. A covenant of mutual trust made *in the state of nature* is therefore void 'upon any reasonable suspicion': 'For he that performeth first, has no assurance that the other will performe after . . . And therefore . . . does but betray himselfe to his enemy; contrary to the Right (he can never abandon) of defending his life, and means of living'. But 'if there be a common Power set over them both, with right and force sufficient to compel perform-ance', then 'that feare is no more reasonable' and so the covenant is not void (*Lev* 105).

Thus Hobbes comes to the last stage of his main argument. The central point (leaving aside the details of 'authorization' and of acquisition of sovereignty by conquest) is that the only way for men to obtain Peace is for every man to make with every other man a covenant of mutual trust instituting a Sovereign with the power to do whatever is necessary to secure Peace (*Lev* 131–2). The Sovereign will maintain Peace by compelling men 'equally to the performance of their Covenants, by the terrour of some punishment, greater than the benefit they expect by the breach of their Covenant' (*Lev* 110); in other words, by creating appropriate laws and punishing transgressors.

I will return later to this point in Hobbes's argument to discuss his account of *why* men obey the Sovereign, and again on pp. 146–8 to present his description of the Sovereign's powers.

We are now in a position to develop the argument that in the state of nature men find themselves in a Prisoners' Dilemma game.

The 'game' which Hobbesian men in the state of nature are 'playing' is certainly *non-cooperative* (in the game theorists' sense, as I defined it in chapter 1), for although agreements are possible, they are not binding: the state of nature, by definition, is precisely the absence of any constraint which would keep men to their agreements.

It has been assumed that each man has a choice between two strategies, C and D. We have already seen that in the state of nature it is rational for each man to choose D, and thus the outcome in the state of nature is War. Since, as we have seen, the state of Peace is preferred by every individual to the state of War, we can conclude that the game is a Prisoners' Dilemma if D is the 'rational' strategy for each man, in the sense that it *dominates* all other strategies, that is, it yields a more preferred outcome than any other strategy no matter what strategies the other individuals choose. (There are of course other and more controversial ways in which a strategy can be said to be the 'rational' one to use; but dominance is required for the game to be a Prisoners' Dilemma.)

Now first, it is clear that in the state of nature no individual has an incentive *unilaterally* to change his strategy from D to C, if the other players are choosing D. For, as we have seen already, 'if other men will not lay down their Right, as well as he; then there is no Reason for any one, to devest himselfe of his: For that were to expose himselfe to Prey . . .' (*Lev* 100). If this were not the case, there would be no need for him to enter into a covenant. Thus the state of War, $(D, D, . . ., D)$, is certainly an equilibrium.

Consider next any two individuals who have made a covenant of mutual trust to lay down their Right of Nature, that is, to choose C. Hobbes says that it does not pay a man to perform his part of the covenant (to choose D) if he believes the other man will not. On each of the occasions in *Leviathan* where he argues this, there is no mention of what all the other members of the society are doing. Yet, clearly, the payoffs to the two individuals, each of whom is choosing between keeping and not keeping the agreement, depend on what the rest of the society is doing (on how many others are choosing D, for example). We must infer that Hobbes is assuming that his argument holds no matter what others are doing. It follows that, just as long as one other individual (the one with whom I am covenanting) chooses D, it pays me to choose D also.

This establishes that D dominates C for each individual in every contingency (i.e. for every combination of strategy choices by the $N - 1$

other individuals) *except* where all other individuals choose *C*. This contingency remains to be considered. And it is here that I believe Hobbes's argument is not wholly satisfactory; it is this contingency which gives rise to the two interpretations I mentioned earlier. The first interpretation is the static one, that Hobbes treats a Prisoners' Dilemma game played only once. The second interpretation is more dynamic, at least to the extent that it admits *sequences* of choices and the possibility of using *conditional* strategies (which are of course ruled out in a one-shot game).

Now if, as I believe, individual preferences in Hobbes's state of nature have the structure of a Prisoners' Dilemma game *at any point in time*, then (i) if the first interpretation is the correct one, it will never be rational (in the state of nature) for any individual to choose *C*, even if (indeed, especially if) every other individual chooses *C*; it will never be rational for a party to a covenant to keep his promise if the other party has performed his part already (and it makes no difference, in the state of nature, whether the two players make their choices simultaneously or one player's choice *follows* the other's in full knowledge of it); but (ii) if the second, dynamic interpretation is the correct one, it *may* be rational for an individual to Cooperate when the other individuals Cooperate; more precisely, we have seen (in chapters 3 and 4) that conditional Cooperation is rational under certain conditions in a (two-person or *N*-person) Prisoners' Dilemma supergame with future payoffs exponentially discounted. With this in mind, let us examine the relative merits of the two interpretations.

Hobbes does in fact assert that if one of the parties to a covenant has already performed his part, then it is rational (and obligatory) for the other to perform his, even in the state of nature: '. . . where one of the parties has performed already; or where there is a Power to make him performe; there is the question whether it be against reason, that is, against the benefit of the other to performe, or not. And I say it is not against reason' (*Lev* 112). This statement would seem to preclude the first, static interpretation, or at least to render it less plausible. In the continuation of this passage, Hobbes explains why it is 'not against Reason' to Cooperate when others do:

> First, that when a man doth a thing, which notwithstanding any thing can be foreseen, and reckoned on, tendeth to his own destruction, howsoever some accident which he could not expect, arriving may

turne it to his benefit; yet such events do not make it reasonably or wisely done. Secondly, that in a condition of Warre, wherein every man to every man, for want of a common Power to keep them all in awe, is an Enemy, there is no man can hope by his own strength, or wit, to defend himselfe from destruction, without the help of Confederates; . . . and therefore he which declares he thinks it reason to deceive those that help him, can in reason expect no other means of safety, than what can be had from his own single Power. He therefore that breaketh his Covenant, . . . cannot be received into any Society, that unite themselves for Peace and Defence, but by the errour of them that receive him; nor when he is received, be retayned in it, without seeing the danger of their errour; which errours a man cannot reasonably reckon on as the means of his security. (*Lev* 112)

In this passage, Hobbes clearly suggests that a man should perform his part of a covenant after the other has done so, out of a fear of the future consequences to himself should he not do so; in other words, it is suggested that the behaviour of each of the two parties to the covenant is conditional upon the behaviour of the other. The same idea appears in an earlier passage (*Lev* 108–9) where Hobbes mentions two other possible motives for not breaking any sort of covenant (not merely one in which the other party has already performed). These are fear of the consequences of breaking one's word and pride in appearing not to need to break it. The latter is a 'generosity too rarely found to be presumed upon'. The former is of two kinds: fear of the power of those one might offend and fear of God. The first of these is too limited to be effective, because of the approximate equality (to be discussed shortly) of men in the state of nature. This leaves only the fear of God; but Hobbes sets little store by this and clearly thinks it will not be effective enough to keep men to their covenants.

This idea of conditional cooperation is expressed more generally in the Fundamental Law of Nature, 'That every man, ought to endeavour Peace, *as farre as he has hope of obtaining it*; and *when he cannot obtain it*, that he may seek, and use, all helps, and advantages of Warre', and in the Second Law of Nature which follows from it, 'That a man be willing, *when others are so too*, as farre-forth, as for Peace, and defence of himself he shall think it necessary, to lay down this right to all things; and be contented with so much liberty against other men, as he would allow other men against himselfe' (*Lev* 100; emphasis supplied – the originals are italicized throughout). Hobbes seems to be saying here, and in the passages quoted earlier, that every man ought always to do what is conducive to Peace just as long as he can do so safely and this means that, in the state of nature, he should Cooperate *if* others do, but otherwise he should not Cooperate. This sounds like the 'tit-for-tat' strategy B or its N-person generalization B_n which were considered in chapters 3 and 4, though it obviously cannot be said that this is precisely what Hobbes had in mind.

Earlier, we saw that the Sovereign, which men institute by covenants of mutual trust, will maintain Peace by compelling men 'equally to the performance of their Covenants, by the terrour of some punishment, greater than the benefit they expect by the breach of their Covenant' (*Lev* 110). Yet it is clear that Hobbes is not simply asserting that the Sovereign will be effective in maintaining Peace because each man will obey him only from fear of his sanctions. He believes that because men want Peace (or at least prefer Peace to War), each of them will obey because the Sovereign has removed the only reason for not keeping one's covenants, which is a 'reasonable suspicion' that other men will not keep theirs.

Hobbes's position here is widely misunderstood. A standard view of Hobbes is that 'he has such a limited view of human motives that he cannot provide any other explanation for acceptance of authority than the fear of . . . sanctions'.[3] Exceptions to this distortion of what Hobbes actually said in *Leviathan* are rare. H. L. A. Hart, in his discussion of the 'minimal content of natural law', based on *Leviathan* and on Hume's *Treatise*, concludes that centrally organized sanctions are required 'not as the normal motive for obedience, but as a *guarantee* that those who would voluntarily obey should not be sacrificed to those who would not';[4] and Brian Barry writes that 'It is not so much that the Sovereign makes it pay to keep your covenant by punishing you if you don't, but that it always pays anyway to keep covenants provided you can do so without exposing yourself'.[5] The Sovereign is required, then, to ensure that nobody will expose himself.

Let us recall the results of the analysis of N-person Prisoners' Dilemma supergames in Chapter 4. It was found there that Cooperation in these games is rational only under certain conditions: in the first place, only *conditional* Cooperation is ever rational, and it must be contingent upon the Cooperation (in the previous constituent game) of *all* the other Cooperators (conditional and unconditional); in the second place, the discount rates of each of the Cooperators must not be too high, relative to a certain function of the constituent game payoffs. (The first condition does not require Cooperation to be conditional upon the Cooperation of all the $N - 1$ other players; it can be rational for each of a subset of the N players to Cooperate conditionally while the remaining players use unconditionally Cooperative or non-Cooperative strategies.) Now, we obviously cannot make a precise comparison of Hobbes's argument with these results. Hobbes does not clearly specify the form of the conditional Cooperation which he says is rational in the state of nature (is it, for example, contingent upon other players' behaviour in only the immediately preceding time period?); there is no talk of discounting of future benefits; and so on. Nevertheless, it is clear from these results that, even if the requirement concerning the discount rates is ignored, voluntary Cooperation in the N-person Prisoners' Dilemma supergame is somewhat precarious, and it can be argued that it was just this precariousness which in Hobbes's view made a Sovereign necessary: the Sovereign would provide the conditions in which it was rational for a man to Cooperate conditionally, by ensuring that he could rely on a sufficient number of other individuals to Cooperate.

This, then, is the case for the second, dynamic interpretation of what I take to be the core of Hobbes's political theory. According to this interpretation, individual preferences at any point in time are those of a Prisoners' Dilemma; nevertheless it is rational to Cooperate *conditionally*. The problem with this interpretation, however, is that, although the idea of conditional Cooperation is in *Leviathan* (and therefore Hobbes's analysis cannot be entirely static, for conditional Cooperation is not possible in a game played only once), Hobbes has virtually nothing explicit to say about any sort of dynamics. *Time* plays no explicit role in his political theory. It is true that Hobbes sometimes speaks of 'anticipation' and 'foresight' and of how men are in 'a perpetuall solicitude of the time to come', but on these occasions he is not speaking of the present valuation of future benefits and the effect of discounting on the prospects for voluntary Cooperation. Nor do his few explicit statements on the subject of discounting play an essential role in this theory. The most explicit statement of this kind is where, speaking of the unwillingness of the Sovereign's subjects to pay their taxes so that he may be enabled to defend them at any time in the future, Hobbes says: 'For all men are by nature provided of notable magnifying glasses, (that

is their Passions and Selfe-love), through which, every little payment
appeareth a great grievance; but are destitute of those prospective
glasses (namely Morall and Civill Science,) to see a farre off the miseries
that hang over them, and cannot without such payment be avoyded'
(*Lev* 141). This preference of man for a near to a remote good plays an
important role in Hume's justification of government, as we shall see
later, but nothing is made of the idea in Hobbes's *Leviathan*.

It is for this reason that it is tempting to fall back on the first, static
interpretation: that Hobbes is in effect treating only a Prisoners'
Dilemma ordinary game, with no dynamic elements at all. Yet on this
view Hobbes's theory is not entirely coherent. Most of what he says is
certainly consistent with the view that individual preferences are those of
a Prisoners' Dilemma; but, as we have seen, Hobbes argues that it is
rational for an individual to choose C if the other players do, whereas, of
course, it is not rational in a Prisoners' Dilemma game to choose C in
any contingency, if that game is played only once. It seems to me, then,
that the more dynamic interpretation, in which conditional Cooperation
is rational (*always* rational according to Hobbes, though only sometimes
rational in the supergame model of chapters 3 and 4) but precarious, is
closer to what Hobbes has to say in *Leviathan*, but at the same time it has
to be admitted that Hobbes does not give a very full account of any sort
of dynamics of interdependent individual choices.

There is a shorter route which might be taken to the conclusion that
Hobbes is talking about a Prisoners' Dilemma one-shot game than the
one taken at the start of this section, and it does not involve any
consideration of the performance of covenants. Hobbes says: 'Feare of
oppression, disposeth a man to anticipate, or to seek ayd by society: for
there is no other way by which a man can secure his life and liberty' (*Lev*
77); and again, because of the 'diffidence' which every man has, simply by
virtue of his knowledge that others, like himself, are seeking to maximize
their utility, 'there is no way for any man to secure himselfe, so
reasonable, as Anticipation . . .' (*Lev* 95). Now Hobbes could be read as
asserting here that a man should choose D because he can be fairly sure
that the others will choose D, and even if they do not, D is still his best
strategy. (And it makes no difference whether the others choose at the
same time as he does, or at a later time with or without knowledge of his
choice.) However, this is perhaps reading too much into too little. In any
case it would still have to be shown that the remainder of the core of

Hobbes's argument was consistent with the assumption that the game is a Prisoners' Dilemma played only once.

It is worth noting here that if it were accepted that in the state of nature men find themselves in a Prisoners' Dilemma one-shot game, then it would not make sense to argue that the Sovereign's sanctions are required, not so much to compel everybody to obey, but rather to provide a guarantee that those who would obey voluntarily can do so without exposing themselves. Clearly, if the 'game' in the state of nature is a Prisoners' Dilemma, then it follows that if a player is certain that the other players will choose C (because they fear the Sovereign's punishments), then he would not consider it in his interest to choose C himself – *unless he fears the Sovereign's punishments*. In other words, although his expectation that the Sovereign would punish others for their disobedience may reassure him that he will not be 'double-crossed', this alone does not give him reason to obey. Rather, it gives him a greater incentive to disobey: unless the Sovereign's presence changes *his* (subjective, perceived) utilities as well as his perception of the other players' utilities.

If it is still insisted that Hobbes is analysing a game played only once, but this game is not a Prisoners' Dilemma, then there are, I think, only two plausible alternatives. In both of them, as in the Prisoners' Dilemma game, each player prefers Peace to War and it pays each player to choose D if the other players do, for there is no question about these two items in *Leviathan*. But in the first alternative game, each player prefers to Cooperate rather than Defect as long as all other players Cooperate. In the two-person case, then, the preferences take the following form:

	C	D
C	x, x	z, y
D	y, z	w, w

with $x > y > w > z$; whereas in the two-person Prisoners' Dilemma the utilities satisfied the inequalities $y > x > w > z$. In this new game, there is not a dominating strategy for either player and there are now two equilibria, (C, C) and (D, D). Yet since (C, C) is preferred by both players to (D, D), neither player will expect (D, D) to be the outcome, so it will not be the outcome (cf. the discussion of equilibria and outcomes in chapter

3). In this game there is no need for coercion to prevent a Pareto-inferior equilibrium occurring; mutual Cooperation will occur without it.

The second alternative game is the one which Hart might have in mind if he is not thinking of a more dynamic model. Some players' preferences amongst the possible outcomes are as in the Prisoners' Dilemma game; those of the others are as in the first alternative game which I have just defined. In its simplest version, the two-person game in which there is one player with each of these types of preferences, the preferences take the following form:

	C	D
C	x, x'	z, y'
D	y, z'	w, w'

with $y > x > w > z$ and $x' > y' > w' > z'$. Player 1 (the row-chooser) is the sort of person who would Cooperate only if coerced, that is, only through fear of punishment. Player 2 is the sort of person who would Cooperate as long as the other does too; he would not take advantage of the other player. (D, D) is the only equilibrium in this game, and it will therefore be the outcome. Strategy D is of course dominant for player 1; player 2, seeing this, would also choose D. Thus, it appears that coercion is necessary to achieve (C, C); the Sovereign will protect player 2 against player 1; he will directly coerce player 1 by threatening sanctions, and he will thereby provide player 2, who would *voluntarily* Cooperate if he could only be sure that others would too, with a guarantee that he will not expose himself by choosing C.

I think that the assumptions made in this second alternative to the Prisoners' Dilemma game have some plausibility, but they do not fit very well with most of what Hobbes says in *Leviathan*, since they require that some players have a different sort of preference than the others; whereas there is very little in *Leviathan* which does not ascribe the same 'nature' to all men. Hobbes says, it is true, that some men take 'pleasure in contemplating their own power in the acts of conquests, which they pursue farther than their security requires', while others 'would be glad to be at ease within modest bounds' (*Lev* 95). But even if this and similar remarks could be interpreted as meaning that some men would choose C provided only that others would do likewise, there remains the fact that in those statements in *Leviathan* which I have used to support my contention that individual preferences at any point in time in the state of nature are those of a Prisoners' Dilemma game, Hobbes is not speaking of *some* people. And if *all* men would Cooperate as long as others do, as in the first alternative to the Prisoners' Dilemma, then Hobbes's problem disappears.

In my discussion of Hobbes's political theory I have not so far mentioned his assumption of 'equality'. This assumption is that:

> NATURE hath made men so equall, in the faculties of body and mind; as that though there bee found one man sometimes manifestly stronger in body, or of quicker mind than another; yet when all is reckoned together, the difference between man, and man, is not so considerable, as that one man can thereupon claim to himselfe any benefit, to which another may not pretend, as well as he. For as to the strength of body, the weakest has strength enough to kill the strongest, either by secret machination, or by confederacy with others, that are in the same danger with himselfe' (*Lev* 94).

If the assumption is made that the outcomes of the game and the individuals' preferences amongst them are such that the game at any point in time is a Prisoners' Dilemma, then the assumption of equality is superfluous. For it is, in effect, an assertion of strategic interdependence: that no man alone controls the outcome of the game. No man is safe in the state of nature; he must fear every other man. The outcome of the game and therefore his own payoff depend on the actions of all other men as well as his own. This is the case in a Prisoners' Dilemma game.

Hobbes is not, of course, asserting that the payoffs for each outcome are the same for all players; this can never be the case in a Prisoners' Dilemma. Nor is he asserting (as I assumed in chapters 3–5 to simplify my analysis) that the payoff matrix is necessarily symmetric. It is of course possible in a Prisoners' Dilemma that the players have very unequal payoffs for those outcomes in which they all choose C or all choose D. Hobbes himself clearly did not expect all men to be equally successful in obtaining what they wanted either in the state of nature, which is a state of War, or when at Peace under a Sovereign.[6]

It remains for me to show that nothing essential in Hobbes's argument is altered if the number of strategies available to each player is greater than two. Hobbes himself seems to assume only two strategies; he speaks only of 'laying aside one's natural right to all things' or not doing so. But of course there are *degrees* to which one may lay aside this right, or degrees of cooperation. Thus, to use an example of the kind discussed in chapter 1, if unrestricted pollution of a lake is strategy D, there are presumably numerous alternatives to D, corresponding to the possible levels of individual pollution less than D. As before, in the state of nature, every player chooses D; the resulting outcome is $(D, D, \ldots, D)$ which is Pareto-inferior. The Hobbesian problem remains the same: to get the players from this 'miserable condition' to an outcome preferred by every player. If there is only one such outcome this is presumably the only outcome which the players would covenant to have enforced. Hobbes's analysis of covenanting applies unchanged to this convenant. Usually, however, there will be a set (S, say) of outcomes preferred by every player to $(D, D, \ldots, D)$. The players would presumably only consider covenanting to enforce one of those which are Pareto-optimal with respect to the set S. A covenant to enforce any one of these would be necessary and Hobbes's argument applies to each of the possible covenants. The only new element introduced here is the problem of agreeing on one of the Pareto-optimal outcomes: of agreeing, for example, on a particular level of permissible individual pollution. Hobbes does not of course consider this; but his own analysis, as far as it goes, applies with full force to this multi-strategy case: men will not voluntarily act so as to obtain any one of the Pareto-superior outcomes; they will not keep covenants to refrain from choosing D and use some other strategy; they must erect a 'common power' with sufficient power to enforce one of the Pareto-superior outcomes.

A Game of Difference

I argued on pp. 126–9 that the *utility* which a Hobbesian man seeks to maximize is a convex combination of his own payoff and his eminence. *Eminence* was defined there as the average of his eminence with respect to each other individual, and his eminence with respect to another individual was defined as the excess of his payoff over that of the other individual's.

On pp. 129–42 I argued that in Hobbes's state of nature the individual preferences are such that at any point in time the players are in a Prisoners' Dilemma. The argument was entirely in terms of *ordinal* preferences; that is to say, it was independent of any considerations of the relative degree to which one outcome is preferred to another. In particular, it did not rest on the assumption that the *utility* of an outcome to a player takes the form assumed on pp. 126–9 (and is thus a cardinal utility).

If the game defined in terms of the basic *payoffs* (the 'basic game') is a Prisoners' Dilemma, then we know from chapter 5 that the game defined in terms of the derived utilities (the 'transformed game') is also a Prisoners' Dilemma, if two conditions are met: (i) λ_i is non-zero; that is, the game is not one of *pure* Difference; and (ii) the payoff $g(v)$ to a player who chooses D is strictly increasing with the number of other individuals (v) who choose C.

However, if the transformed game is a Prisoners' Dilemma, it does not follow that the basic game is a Prisoners' Dilemma. A simple two-person example shows this: if the payoff matrix is

$$\begin{bmatrix} 2, 2 & -2, 1 \\ 1, -2 & 1, 1 \end{bmatrix}$$

which is not a Prisoners' Dilemma, then the utility matrix for the Game of Difference (with $\lambda_i = \frac{1}{2}$ for $i = 1, 2$) is

$$\begin{bmatrix} 1, 1 & -2\frac{1}{2}, 2 \\ 2, -2\frac{1}{2} & \frac{1}{2}, \frac{1}{2} \end{bmatrix}$$

which *is* a Prisoners' Dilemma.

This reveals the possibility that the Hobbesian problem is the result of man's desire for eminence. (The above example illustrates this: there are two equilibria in the basic game, but neither player would expect (1, 1) to be the outcome, since both players prefer (2, 2) to it. Thus the outcome is (2, 2) which is Pareto-optimal, and there is no Hobbesian problem.) It would be of some interest to discover which sorts of games, not themselves Prisoners' Dilemmas, become Prisoners' Dilemmas when transformed to Games of Difference.

I shall not pursue this question, for I believe that in the problems of interest here (those of the kind discussed in chapter 1) the basic ordinary game is itself a Prisoners' Dilemma. If this is the case, then the transformed game is also a Prisoners' Dilemma, and this is true no matter how much 'eminence' relative to 'egoism' we assume (or read into Hobbes), just as long as eminence is not a man's *only* concern (that is, as long as λ_i is non-zero) and $g(v)$ is increasing with v.

The theory restated

I can now recapitulate most of the discussion so far by restating briefly Hobbes's central argument in *Leviathan*.

Only three assumptions are necessary. First, that in the state of nature, men find themselves in a Prisoners' Dilemma; that is, the choices confronting them and their preferences amongst the possible outcomes are such that the game which they are playing is *at each point in time* a Prisoners' Dilemma. The Prisoners' Dilemma is defined in the usual way; in particular, it is a non-cooperative game, so that there is nothing to keep men to any agreements they might make.

There are two versions of the second assumption, corresponding to the two interpretations of Hobbes's argument put forward on pp. 129–42 above in connection with what Hobbes has to say about the rationality of Cooperating when others do. The first version is that the Prisoners' Dilemma game mentioned in the first assumption is not iterated; the whole theory is restricted to the Prisoners' Dilemma one-shot game. The second version is that the Prisoners' Dilemma is iterated; we need not (and on the basis of what Hobbes actually says, we cannot) go further than this and say, for example, that the Prisoners' Dilemma game mentioned in the first assumption is a constituent game of a supergame with future benefits discounted.

The third assumption is that each individual seeks to obtain an outcome which is as high as possible in his preference ranking of outcomes. Equivalently, we may say that each individual seeks to maximize his utility. In particular, if (as in the Prisoners' Dilemma) he has a single dominant strategy, he uses it.

In this third assumption, it does not matter what is the basis of a man's preferences or how 'utility' is defined (as long as the resulting game is a Prisoners' Dilemma). However, I have argued that Hobbes assumes that a man's utility is some convex combination of his own payoff and his eminence.

If the first (static) version of the second assumption is accepted, then it follows from the three assumptions that the outcome of the game is $(D, D, \ldots, D)$; that is, the condition of men in the state of nature is War. This outcome is Pareto-inferior. There is one (and only one) outcome which every player prefers to it, namely $(C, C, \ldots, C)$, which is the state of Peace. But if the players agreed that each of them should choose C, there would be no incentive in the state of nature for any of them to carry out his part of the agreement. Clearly, if Peace is to be achieved, every man must be *coerced*, by which I mean simply that he must be made somehow to behave differently than he otherwise would (that is to say, than he would 'voluntarily' in the state of nature).

If the second (dynamic) version of the second assumption is accepted, then what follows from the three assumptions depends on the precise form of the dynamic model specified. Hobbes is not sufficiently specific here, but it is reasonable to conclude (on the basis of the analysis in chapters 3 and 4) that *conditional* Cooperation is *sometimes* rational (even though not all the other players Cooperate) but rather precarious, since the Cooperation of each of the conditional Cooperators must be contingent upon the Cooperation of all the other Cooperators and the discount rates of every one of the Cooperators must not be too high. It can be argued that it is this precariousness which in Hobbes's view makes coercion necessary if Peace is to be achieved, though the necessity of coercion is clearly less apparent here than in the case when the Prisoners' Dilemma is assumed not to be iterated.

But Hobbes goes further than this of course. For he specifies in some detail the particular form that the coercion must take and how it is to be created. Each man must make a covenant with every other man in which he promises, on the condition that the other party to the covenant does likewise, to relinquish the right to all things which he has in the state of nature in order that a 'Sovereign' may enjoy without restraint his natural right to all things and thereby be enabled to ensure 'Peace at home, and mutual ayd against enemies abroad' (*Lev* Chapter 17). The Sovereign must be either one man or an assembly of men, though the former is preferable (*Lev* 143-7).

Hobbes gives two accounts of how a particular man or assembly of men is to be made Sovereign. In the first, the Sovereign is specified in the covenants of each man with every other man and is thus unanimously agreed on (*Lev* 132). In the second, there is in effect a unanimous agreement, in the form of the covenants between every pair of men, to abide by a majority choice of a particular Sovereign (*Lev* 133). My argument is unaffected by this discrepancy; either version may be chosen.

This, in bare outline (for I have omitted, in particular, any reference to 'authorization') is the 'Generation of that great LEVIATHAN' (*Lev* 132).

But this Leviathan (whose powers will be described in the next part) is not the only possible form which the necessary coercion can assume. One alternative, which is in fact sufficient to maintain Peace (in Hobbes's sense) in many so-called primitive societies, is the system of controls characteristic of the small community. (See the brief discussion in chapter 1.) Hobbes did not discount such possibilities; he believed that by themselves they would be inadequate. However, if the core of Hobbes's theory is based, as I have argued, on the assumptions that men in the state of nature are players in a Prisoners' Dilemma game and that men are utility maximizers, then, whether the game is iterated or not, Hobbes cannot legitimately deduce the necessary of any *particular* form of coercion, but can only deduce the necessity of *any* form of coercion which has the ability, and is seen to have the ability, to deter men from breaking their covenants.

The Sovereign's powers

Whether Sovereignty has been instituted, in the manner I have just described, or has been acquired by force, the most important of the Sovereign's rights and powers are as follows. His subjects cannot change the form of government or transfer their allegiance to another man or assembly, without the Sovereign's permission; disagreement with the majority's choice of a particular Sovereign does not exempt a man from his obligation to obey the Sovereign; the Sovereign's subjects can neither 'justly' complain of his actions nor 'justly' punish him (this is a trivial consequence of Hobbes's definitions of justice and authority); the Sovereign has the right to do whatever he thinks is necessary to maintain Peace at home and defence against foreign enemies; he has the right to judge which opinions and doctrines are to be permitted in public speeches and publications, as being not detrimental to Peace; he has the 'whole Power of prescribing the Rules, whereby a man may know, what Goods he may enjoy, and what actions he may do, without being molested by any of his fellow subjects'; he has the 'Right of Judicature', that is to say, 'of deciding all controversies'; he has the right of making war and peace with other nations and commonwealths, when he thinks it is 'for the public good', of maintaining an army and taxing his subjects to pay for it, and (of course) of being in command of it; he has the right to choose 'all Counsellours, and Ministers, both of Peace and War'; he has the right to reward and punish his subjects according to the laws he has already made, or, in the absence of a law, as he thinks will most conduce 'to the encouraging of men to serve the Commonwealth, or deterring them from doing dis-service to the same' (*Lev* chapter 18); and finally, the Sovereign has the right to choose his successor (*Lev* 149). These rights, says Hobbes, are indivisible, for control of the judicature is of no use without control of a militia to execute the laws, and control of the militia is of no avail without the right to legislate taxes to support it, and so on (*Lev* 139).

This makes the Sovereign very powerful. Hobbes himself sometimes describes the Sovereign's power as being 'absolute' and 'unlimited' and 'as great, as possibly men can be imagined to make it' (*Lev* 160). Nevertheless, it has to be emphasized that Hobbes consistently makes it clear that the Great Leviathan exists *only* to maintain Peace amongst his subjects and to defend them against foreign enemies and that his powers are only those which are required to perform this role. Thus, in their covenants with each other to institute a Sovereign, men authorize the Sovereign to 'Act, or cause to be Acted, in those things which concern the Common Peace and Safetie' (*Lev* 131), and by this authority 'he hath the use of so much Power and Strength conferred on him, that by terror thereof, he is inabled to forme the wills of them all, to Peace at home, and mutuall ayd against their enemies abroad' (*Lev* 132). Again, 'the OFFICE of the Soveraign . . . consisteth in the end, for which he was trusted with the Soveraign Power, namely the procuration of *the safety of the people*' (*Lev* 258). To this end, he must make 'good laws', a good law being one 'which is *Needful*, for the *Good of the People* . . .'; and Hobbes adds that 'Unnecessary Lawes are not good Lawes; but trapps for Mony . . .' (*Lev* 268). In the few places where he speaks of the Sovereign's 'absolute power', he seems to be equating it only with that power which is 'necessarily required' for 'the Peace, and defence of the Commonwealth' (*Lev* 247). Above all, he asserts that obedience to the Sovereign is obligatory only as long as he is doing what he was established for, namely, maintaining Peace and defence (*Lev* 170).

I have argued in the preceding section that Hobbes may not legitimately deduce from his own assumptions the conclusion that the coercion which is necessary to get men out of the condition of War must take the particular form which he specifies. However, if the coercion must be in the form of a Sovereign which is either one man or an assembly of men, then Hobbes *is* quite correct to give the Sovereign just those powers which are required by him to maintain Peace. I have argued in this part that this is what Hobbes does.

Possessive market society

C. B. Macpherson, in his widely read book, *The Political Theory of Possessive Individualism*, has put forward a reconstruction of Hobbes's political theory which seriously restricts the scope of its application.[7] He argues that the theory can be made coherent only if Hobbes is assumed to be speaking of a society which resembles our modern, bourgeois, market societies. I believe that Hobbes's theory has a much greater range of application than this. More specifically, I have argued that the situations analysed by Hobbes are Prisoners' Dilemmas (possibly iterated). These are neither identical with, nor are they only to be found in, market societies. In this section, then, I must show how Macpherson's argument fails.

There are two steps in the argument: (i) Macpherson claims that after defining a man's 'power' as his means to obtain what he desires, Hobbes proceeds to *redefine* power and that a 'new postulate is implied in this redefinition of power, namely that the capacity of every man to get what he wants is opposed by the capacity of every other man' (Macpherson, p. 36); (ii) 'the postulate that the power of every man is opposed to the power of every other man requires the assumption of a model of society which permits and requires the continual invasion of every man by every other' (Macpherson, p. 42), and that the only such model of society is the 'possessive market society, which corresponds in essentials to modern market society' (Macpherson, p. 68).

Each of these assertions is incorrect. Consider (i): first, Macpherson believes that Hobbes speaks for the first time of the relations between men, of man in society, only when he comes to discuss power. Yet Hobbes has said earlier that all men desire eminence. Now clearly, desire for eminence brings men into opposition with one another, for they cannot all be eminent over others simultaneously. (And the greater the ratio of 'eminence' to 'own payoff' in each man's utility function, the more nearly the game approximates to a zero-sum game, or one of 'pure opposition'.) Second, given that every man seeks to obtain what he desires and given Hobbes's definition of power as the means to obtain what one desires, it follows (as we have seen) that every man desires power; given further that man desires to be eminent, it follows that he desires to have more power than others. No 'redefinition' of power, from 'absolute' to 'comparative' power, is involved here.

Macpherson seems to be aware that, if these two points are granted, this first step in his argument is unnecessary (Macpherson, p. 45), and we can pass immediately to the second and more important step.

If, as I have argued earlier, Hobbes's propositions about power seeking can be derived from his definition of power and his proposition that men seek to obtain the things they desire, so that 'power' plays no logically essential role in Hobbes's political theory, then Macpherson's assertion in the second part of his argument is clearly incorrect. But let us see how he defends it.

Possessive market society is an ideal type to which modern capitalist societies approximate. Its distinctive feature, as far as Macpherson's argument is concerned, is that every individual owns his capacity to labour and may sell it or otherwise transfer it as he wishes. The consequence of this (and other assumptions) is that there is a market in labour as well as in other commodities. It is this labour market which provides the means by which 'the continual invasion of every man by every other' is carried on. Labour markets may of course have this property, but Macpherson is asserting that *only* societies with (amongst other things) labour markets can provide such means. This is plainly false, for there are many societies (and many more that have perished or have been transformed) in which there is no market in labour (and in some cases there are no markets in anything) and yet there is 'continual invasion of every man by every other'. This 'invasion' may take several forms. The primary objects of a man's desire may be the possession of physical strength, skill in hunting, cattle and wives and good crops (if there is individual ownership of these things), peace of mind, ceremonial rank, and so on; his means to obtain these things, his 'power', may include all of these things and others besides; and he may suffer continual invasion and transfers of his power, simply because people steal his women, cattle and foodstocks, hunt more skilfully, spread rumours that he is a sorcerer, or whatever. None of this requires a market in labour (or in anything else for that matter).

Macpherson's only defence against this would be to *define* power as 'access to the means of labour' or 'control of labour'. This would make the second part of his argument about possessive market society trivial. At one point (p. 49) he seems to do just this, but then later (p. 56) he says only that power must 'by definition include access to the means of labour', which leaves room for power also to depend upon cattle and ceremonial rank and all the rest.

I have argued that *Leviathan* is about Prisoners' Dilemmas, and this means that Hobbes's argument, in the form in which I restated it, is not confined to situations of the sort that Hobbes himself was obviously most concerned about. If I am right, and if Prisoners' Dilemmas are to be found outside possessive market societies, then Macpherson's argument collapses. I believe that the problem Hobbes treats *is* to be found in one form or another in most, if not all societies, including so-called primitive societies with no markets in labour. In 'primitive' and other societies, stealing one another's cattle, stealing corn from the communally owned fields, or disturbing the tribe's tranquillity by excessive display, are simple examples of behaviour which may lead to the problem Hobbes was concerned with.

Although Macpherson's thesis is unacceptable, there is an interesting proposition about possessive market society and the argument in *Leviathan*, which I think has some plausibility. Very roughly, it is that the more a society approximates to the possessive market type, the more numerous are the sites and occasions for Prisoners' Dilemmas and the greater is the severity of the Prisoners' Dilemmas, where by 'greater severity' I mean a greater 'temptation' unilaterally to Defect from mutual Cooperation. I could not, of course, begin to prove this.

I should add finally that while I disagree with Macpherson's view that Hobbes's political theory is coherent only if society is assumed to be of the possessive market variety, I nevertheless agree with him that Hobbes seems to have been conscious of the possessive market nature of the society in which he lived and that in *Leviathan* he sometimes speaks of characteristic features of possessive market societies.

Hume's Leviathan

Hume's explanation of the necessity and desirability of government is not very different from Hobbes's. But he begins with assumptions about human nature which seem much less gloomy than those of Hobbes; his explanation of the origin of government appears to be more plausible

than Hobbes's contracterian account; and in place of the great
Leviathan that Hobbes sometimes made to sound so terrifying he
describes a government resembling the sort of governments that 'large
and civilis'd societies' in fact possess. Nevertheless, his assumptions
about human nature (which I shall discuss in the following section) are
effectively the same as those of Hobbes; his account of the origin of
government (pp. 159-60) rests on an analysis of the evolution of
property 'conventions' (pp. 154-5) which is itself not entirely plausible
(for reasons which I discuss on pp. 155-9); and as for the government
which Hume concludes to be necessary, its function is similar to that of
Hobbes's Leviathan and it must therefore be given as much power.
(Hence the title of this section.)

For all its essential similarity to Hobbes's theory, Hume's political
theory warrants a brief discussion here. First, because there are in fact
two new elements in Hume's account, which, though they have not been
given much attention by students of Hume, are important in the analysis
of voluntary cooperation and played an important role in my discussion
in chapters 3 and 4. Second, because it is Hume's version of the theory
rather than the stark account of Hobbes which was more acceptable to
later writers and to which many modern justifications of government
still largely correspond.

Individual preferences

I begin with a discussion of those elements of 'the passions' which are
incorporated in the assumptions on which Hume's political theory is
based.

(i) While Hobbes does not deny (in *Leviathan* at least) the existence in
some men of a positive altruism which is not reducible to egoism, he has
very little to say about it, and the effective assumption in his political
theory is that men's preferences reflect a combination of egoism and the
negative altruism which is involved in a desire for eminence. For Hume,
positive altruism, or 'benevolence', is more important. He distinguishes
two kinds of benevolence, 'private' and 'extensive'. Private benevolence
is a desire for the happiness of those we love, our family and friends. It is
not the same thing as love, but rather is a result of it; love is always
'follow'd by, or rather conjoin'd with benevolence . . .' (*Tr* 367).[8] This
private benevolence is an 'original instinct implanted in our nature', like

love of life, resentment, kindness to children, hunger and 'lust' (*Tr* 368, 417, 439).

Extensive benevolence or 'pity' is 'a concern for . . . others, without any friendship . . . to occasion this concern or joy. We pity even strangers, and such as are perfectly indifferent to us' (*Tr* 369). This kind of benevolence is not instinctive; it is due to *sympathy*. Hume defines 'sympathy' with others as our propensity 'to receive by communication their inclinations and sentiments, however different or even contrary to our own' (*Tr* 316); it is 'the conversion of an idea into an impression by the force of imagination' (*Tr* 427). This is not to say that sympathy is a form of altruism. Nor is it to say, for example, that we suffer for ourselves when we contemplate others suffering: we do not fear for our own lives when we see, and sympathize with, others in danger of death and fearing for their lives. Sympathy is simply the name for what makes it possible for us to experience, to have an impression of, the feelings of others.

Sympathy, then, makes extensive benevolence possible. 'Tis true, there is no human, and indeed no sensible, creature, whose happiness or misery does not, in some measure, affect us, when brought near to us, and represented in lively colours: . . . this proceeds merely from sympathy . . .' (*Tr* 481). Again: 'We have no such extensive concern for society but from sympathy' (*Tr* 579).

The important role played by sympathy in the *Treatise* is somewhat reduced in the *Enquiry*. In particular, extensive benevolence, which was due only to sympathy in the *Treatise*, now seems to be included with private benevolence as one of the instincts. This view is given in the Appendix on 'Self-Love' together with the argument (taken from Bishop Butler's *Fifteen Sermons*, especially the first) that self-love is not our only motivation – that there are 'instincts' (such as benevolence) which motivate us directly and are not reducible to a species of self-love. It is worth quoting Hume's argument at length:

> There are bodily wants or appetites acknowledged by every one, which necessarily precede all sensual enjoyment, and carry us directly to seek possession of the object. Thus, hunger and thirst have eating and drinking for their end; and from the gratification of these primary appetites arises a pleasure, which may become the object of another species of desire or inclination that is secondary and interested. In the same manner there are mental passions by which we are impelled

immediately to seek particular objects, such as fame or power, or vengeance without any regard to interest; and when these objects are attained a pleasing enjoyment ensues, as the consequence of our indulged affections. Nature must, by the internal frame and constitution of the mind, give an original propensity to fame, ere we can reap any pleasure from that acquisition, or pursue it from motives of self-love, and desire of happiness. . . . Were there no appetite of any kind antecedent to self-love, that propensity could scarcely ever exert itself; because we should, in that case, have felt few and slender pains or pleasures, and have little misery or happiness to avoid or to pursue.

Now where is the difficulty in conceiving, that this may likewise be the case with benevolence and friendship, and that, from the original frame of our temper, we may feel a desire of another's happiness or good, which, by means of that affection, becomes our own good, and is afterwards pursued, from the combined motives of benevolence and self-enjoyments? (*Enquiry*, pp. 301-2.)

(ii) The operation of sympathy and the extent of benevolence are limited by our manner of comparing ourselves with others. 'We seldom judge of objects from their intrinsic value', says Hume, 'but form our notions of them from a comparison with other objects; it follows that, according as we observe a greater or less share of happiness or misery in others, we must make an estimate of our own, and feel a consequent pain or pleasure' (*Tr* 375). 'This kind of comparison is directly contrary to sympathy in its operation . . .' (*Tr* 593), and accounts for the origin of malice and envy (*Tr* 377). It is itself limited, inasmuch as men tend to compare themselves with, and are envious of, only those who are similar to them in relevant respects (*Tr* 377-8).

Negative altruism is real enough for Hume; but in his political theory it does not assume the importance that it does in Hobbes's theory (as part of the desire for eminence). Hume shrinks from making any general statement, in the form of a simplifying assumption, about the predominance of positive or negative altruism. He allows that in some situations positive altruism may dominate negative altruism, and *vice versa* in other situations. But in the statement of his political theory, the effective assumptions about individual preferences contain no reference to negative altruism; as we shall see shortly, they refer only to egoism, limited positive altruism and 'shortsightedness'.

(iii) Although Hume argues for the existence of an independent motive of private benevolence and that extensive benevolence or pity is found in all men, since they are all capable of sympathy (*Tr* 317, 481), nevertheless it is clear that, when he comes to explaining the origins of justice, property and government, he assumes that benevolence is very limited. In one place, he suggests that each individual loves himself more than any other single person, but the aggregate of his benevolent concerns for all others exceeds his self-love (*Tr* 487). But more generally, he says that some men are concerned only for themselves, and that, as for the others, their benevolence extends only or chiefly to their family and friends, with only a very weak concern for strangers and indifferent persons (*Tr* 481, 489, 534).

Hume is not very precise about the relative weights of benevolence and self-interest. All we can say is that, in his political theory, his assumption is effectively that men are self-interested and benevolent, but that the benevolence is not so great that there is no need for 'conventions' about property (*Tr* 486, 492, 494–5). These will be explained below.

(iv) There is another element in the structure of individual preferences, to which Hume (in the *Treatise*) attaches great importance: we *discount* future benefits, their present value to us diminishing as the future time at which we expect to receive them recedes farther from the present. What is close to us in time or space, says Hume, affects our imagination with greater force than what is remote, the effect of time being greater than that of space (*Tr* 427–9). The consequence of this is that men 'are always much inclin'd to prefer present interest to distant and remote; nor is it easy for them to resist the temptation of any advantage, that they may immediately enjoy, in apprehension of an evil, that lies at a distance from them' (*Tr* 539, 535).

Property

Hume distinguishes 'three different species of goods' which we may possess: mental satisfactions, our natural bodily endowments, and 'such possessions as we have acquir'd by our industry and good fortune'. Only the third species, *external possessions*, may be transferred unaltered to others and used by them (*Tr* 487–8).

These external possessions are the source of 'the principal disturbance in society' and this is because (i) they are scarce and easily transferred between people (*Tr* 488–9); (ii) everyone wants them: 'This avidity alone, of acquiring goods and possessions for ourselves and our nearest friends, is insatiable, perpetual, universal, and directly destructive of society. There scarce is any one, who is not actuated by it; and there is no one, who has not reason to fear from it, when it acts without any restraint . . .' (*Tr* 491–2); and (iii) man's selfishness in the pursuit of them is insufficiently counteracted by his benevolence towards others to make him abstain from their possessions (*Tr* 492, 486–8).

The resulting situation is essentially the same as Hobbes's 'state of nature', though Hume has described it in less dramatic terms. The only remedy for it is a 'convention enter'd into by all the members of the society to bestow stability on the possession of those external goods, and leave every one in the peaceable enjoyment of what he may acquire by his fortune and industry' (*Tr* 489). However, a permanent 'stability' of possession would itself be 'a grand inconvenience', for 'mutual exchange and commerce' is necessary and desirable. Therefore there must also be a 'convention' facilitating the transfer of possessions by consent (*Tr* 514). This in turn would be of little use without a 'convention' to keep one's promises, since it is usually impracticable for the parties to an exchange to transfer possessions simultaneously (*Tr* 516–22).

There are thus three 'conventions' which men must make to obtain 'peace and security': 'that of the stability of possession, of its transference by consent, and of the performance of promises'. These are the 'laws of justice' or 'the three fundamental laws of nature' (*Tr* 526). 'Property' can now be defined as 'nothing but those goods, whose constant possession is establish'd . . . by the laws of justice' (*Tr* 491); and we can say that 'justice' consists in the observation of the current laws fixing the distribution of property and protecting the parties to exchanges of property.

Conventions

A convention, says Hume, is not like a promise; for promises themselves arise from human conventions (*Tr* 490). Conventions, he means to tell us, are not like the covenants which, according to Hobbes, are the only means of escape from the state of nature. A convention is rather

> a general sense of common interest; which sense all the members of the society express to one another, and which induces them to

regulate their conduct by certain rules. I observe, that it will be for my interest to leave another in the possession of his goods, *provided* he will act in the same manner with regard to me. He is sensible of a like interest in the regulation of his conduct. When this common sense of interest is mutually express'd, and is known to both, it produces a suitable resolution and behaviour. And this may properly enough be call'd a convention or agreement betwixt us, tho' without the interposition of a promise; since the actions of each of us have a reference to those of the other, and are perform'd upon the supposition, that something is to be perform'd on the other part. (*Tr* 490)

Now this is a perfectly reasonable definition of convention; it is roughly what we still typically mean by convention. But then, it seems to me, the laws of justice are not conventions. If they were, there would be no need for a government to constrain people to conform to them, as Hume goes on to argue.

Since this point is rather important, it is worth giving here a more precise definition of convention. We can use the one constructed by David Lewis in his *Convention: A Philosophical Study.*

Conventions are solutions to *coordination problems.* The most clear-cut case of a coordination problem (to which we may confine our attention) is the situation facing the players in a *game of pure coordination.* This is a game, having two or more proper coordination equilibria, and in which the players' interests coincide, so that their payoffs at each outcome are equal. A *coordination equilibrium* is a strategy vector such that no player can obtain a larger payoff if he *or any other player* unilaterally uses a different strategy (so that a coordination equilibrium is an equilibrium, as defined in chapter 3, but not conversely); and a coordination equilibrium is *proper* if each player *strictly* prefers it to any other outcome he could obtain, given the other strategy choices. Thus the two-person game with the payoffs shown in Matrix 1 below is a pure coordination game; strategy vectors (r_1, c_1) and (r_2, c_2) are proper coordination equilibria, while (r_3, c_3) is improper.

	c_1	c_2	c_3	
r_1	2, 2	0, 0	0, 0	
r_2	0, 0	2, 2	0, 0	(Matrix 1)
r_3	0, 0	1, 1	1, 1	

A simple example of a coordination problem is the situation facing two people who are not in communication and who wish to meet but are indifferent between several alternative meeting-plates. Suppose there are just three possible meeting-places. Then the payoff matrix is that shown as Matrix 2 (the payoffs there being merely ordinal).

$$\begin{bmatrix} 1,1 & 0,0 & 0,0 \\ 0,0 & 1,1 & 0,0 \\ 0,0 & 0,0 & 1,1 \end{bmatrix} \qquad \text{(Matrix 2)}$$

Another simple example is that of several drivers on the same road; nobody cares which side of the road he drives on, as long as everybody else drives on the same side as he does. This is an example of an iterated or *recurrent* coordination problem.

The definition of a coordination problem requires that there be at least two coordination equilibria. If there is only one, the problem is trivial, for the players will have no difficulty in coordinating their choices.

We are now in a position to define convention.

A regularity R in the behaviour of members of a population P when they are agents in a recurrent situation S is a *convention* if and only if, in any instance of S among members of P,

(1) everyone conforms to R;

(2) everyone expects everyone else to conform to R;

(3) everyone prefers to conform to R on condition that the others do, since S is a coordination problem and uniform conformity to R is a coordination equilibrium in S.[9]

Players in a coordination game will achieve coordination if they have what Lewis calls 'suitably concordant mutual expectations'. If a player is sufficiently confident that the others will do their parts of a particular coordination equilibrium, then he will do his part. Where communication is possible, *agreement* is the simplest means of producing concordant mutual expectations and hence coordination, but a convention need not be started by an agreement. In a recurrent coordination problem, concordant mutual expectations may be built up gradually, as more and more people conform to a regularity, until a convention is established. Thus, without an explicit agreement and without any coercion, a convention to drive on a particular side of the road could be expected to grow up: each man prefers to drive on the side of the road on which most others are driving; at some stage of the process, more or less by chance, a majority will be driving on the left, say; this produces or strengthens an expectation in each driver that a majority will in the future drive on the left; and in this way, a convention to drive on the left is very quickly established.

Lewis's definition of convention is (as he himself recognizes) essentially the same as the one given by Hume. Hume, too, recognizes that conventions will emerge 'spontaneously', without agreements or governments. Speaking of the conventions on property, he says that when a 'common sense of interest is mutually express'd, and is known to both, it produces a suitable resolution and behaviour'; and: 'Nor is the rule concerning the stability of possession the less deriv'd from human conventions that it arises gradually, and acquires force by a slow progression, and by our repeated experiences of the inconveniences of transgressing it. On the contrary, this experience assures us still more, that the sense of interest has become common to all our fellows, and gives us a confidence of the future regularity of their conduct: And 'tis only on the expectation of this, that our moderation and abstinence are founded' (*Tr* 490).

Conventions not only emerge but also *persist* spontaneously; for a convention is an equilibrium, from which no individual has an incentive unilaterally to deviate. It follows that everyone will conform to a convention without being coerced by a government or by any other agency.[10] Yet Hume goes on to argue that men will not voluntarily observe the conventions they make about property and government is necessary to constrain them to conform. The reason he gives for this, as I shall argue in the next part, is essentially that men find themselves, not in a recurrent coordination game, but in a recurrent or iterated Prisoners' Dilemma game (with future payoffs discounted). If this is the case, then the laws of justice cannot be conventions. And for precisely the same reason that men will not voluntarily observe their property conventions, these conventions would not emerge spontaneously in the first place.

It would be proper to call the laws of justice 'conventions' only if all men preferred *any* system of such laws (and therefore any distribution of possessions) to no laws at all and were indifferent (or nearly so) between all possible systems. The first condition is accepted by Hume, for, like Hobbes, he believes that 'without justice, society must immediately dissolve and fall into that savage and solitary condition, which is infinitely worse than can possibly be suppos'd in society', so that, upon the introduction of the laws of justice 'every individual person must find himself a gainer . . .' (*Tr* 497). As for the second condition, it is true that in the *Enquiry* Hume remarks that 'What possessions are assigned to particular persons; this is, generally speaking, pretty indifferent . . .' (*Enquiry*, p. 309 note). But this remark is quite contrary to the assumption, which is essential to his whole theory, that men have an 'insatiable, perpetual, universal' avidity for acquiring external possessions. Men are certainly not indifferent between different distributions of property and therefore are not indifferent between different laws of justice, which determine the distributions.

The necessity of government

According to Hume, government is necessary *in large societies* because without it men will not observe the laws of justice; and it is on the observance of these laws alone that 'the peace and security of human society entirely depend' (*Tr* 526; see also 491). His argument that men will not keep the laws of justice in large societies has two threads. The first is essentially the argument given by Olson in *The Logic of Collective Action*, which we considered in chapter 1. The second concerns the discounting of future benefits, which played such an important role in chapters 3 and 4. Hume does not maintain a clear distinction between these two elements. Nevertheless, the spirit of this part of his theory is that men will not voluntarily cooperate (abstain from each other's possessions; observe the laws of justice) because they are players in a Prisoners' Dilemma supergame and their discount rates are too great.

The 'size' argument appears clearly in the following passage:

> Two neighbours may agree to drain a meadow, which they possess in common; because 'tis easy for them to know each others mind; and each must perceive, that the immediate consequence of his failing in his part, is the abandoning the whole project. But 'tis very difficult, and indeed impossible, that a thousand persons shou'd agree in any such action; it being difficult for them to concert so complicated a design, and still more difficult for them to execute it; while each seeks a pretext to free himself of the trouble and expence, and wou'd lay the whole burden on others. (*Tr* 538)

Hume gives here both of the reasons why, according to Olson, large groups do not provide themselves with public goods, such as a drained meadow shared by the group: first, each individual member has no incentive to make his contribution because it is a *public* good which is being provided and he therefore benefits from it, if it is provided at all, whether he contributes or not; second, and less important, the larger the group the greater are the costs of organization.

Hume makes it quite clear that this part of his argument applies only to *large* societies, and several times proclaims his belief that the members of small societies may voluntarily conform to the property 'conventions' and may therefore live without government (*Tr* 499, 539–41, 543, 546, 553–4). But this is partly because small societies tend to be 'uncultivated', that is, they do not have very many possessions to quarrel about.

In the meadow-drainage example which I have quoted from the *Treatise*, Hume deals only with the 'static' part of his argument. But elsewhere, whenever he presents the 'logic of collective action', it is bound up with the proposition (which I discussed earlier) that men discount future benefits. Men '. . . prefer any trivial advantage, that is present, to the maintenance of order in society, which so much depends on the observance of justice. The consequences of every breach of equity seem to lie very remote, and are not able to counterbalance any immediate advantage, that may be reap'd from it' (*Tr* 535; see also 499, 537–9, 545).

In the continuation of this passage, Hume in effect speaks of behaviour in a sequence of Prisoners' Dilemmas: when you commit acts of injustice as well as me, 'Your example both pushes me forward in this way by imitation, and also affords me a new reason for any breach of equity, by shewing me, that I should be the cully of my integrity, if I alone should impose on myself a severe restraint amidst the licentiousness of others' (*Tr* 535).

The only remedy for this situation is to establish government. The only way men can obtain security and peace is to induce a few men, 'whom we call civil magistrates, kings and their ministers', to constrain every member of the society to observe the laws of justice (*Tr* 537).

Thus, Hume's case for government rests on the alleged inability of men to cooperate voluntarily in the provision of peace and security. However, he goes on to add that 'government extends farther its beneficial influence' by forcing men to cooperate in the provision of other public goods. Thus, he says, 'bridges are built; harbours open'd; ramparts rais'd; canals form'd; fleets equipp'd; and armies disciplin'd; every where, by the care of government . . .' (*Tr* 538–9).

Hume and Hobbes

The assumptions about the structure of static individual preferences on which Hume bases his political theory are not quite the same as those made by Hobbes. To use the language of chapter 5, Hobbes assumes that each man's preferences are a combination of egoism and negative altruism, reflecting a desire to maximize his own payoff and his eminence, whereas Hume assumes that they are a combination of egoism and positive altruism, with egoism predominant. However, the effect is the same in both cases: the resulting game at any point in time is a Prisoners' Dilemma. If in both cases the payoffs are such that the game is a Prisoners' Dilemma when only pure egoism is assumed on the part of each player, then we can say that the 'transformed game' (the game which results when altruism is introduced) is a more severe Prisoners' Dilemma under Hobbes's assumptions than under Hume's.

This assumption of Hume's about preferences applies only to men in *large* societies. Hume is aware that in sufficiently small societies the game may not be a Prisoners' Dilemma, and here he largely anticipates the ideas which form the core of Olson's argument. Hobbes, on the other hand, does not discuss these ideas; but we cannot say that he was unaware of them, for in *Leviathan* he apparently has in mind only large societies (especially the one in which he lived) and accordingly *assumes* in effect that the game is a Prisoners' Dilemma.

There is another important element in Hume's argument which is largely absent from Hobbes's, namely *time*. I have already commented on the fact that, although Hobbes's argument is not entirely static, there is no reference to intertemporal preferences in his assumptions; no account is taken of the discounting of future benefits, which, as we saw in chapters 3 and 4, plays such a crucial role in determining whether voluntary Cooperation will occur in sequences of Prisoners' Dilemma games. Hume's treatment is in this respect more realistic than Hobbes's. Time appears in his assumptions about individual preferences: future payoffs are to be discounted in calculating their present value. This fact plays an important role in his argument, for the discount rate is a principal reason why men do not voluntarily cooperate in observing the laws of justice.

Hume is not so specific in his detailed assumptions and arguments that one can make precise comparisons of his theory with that of Hobbes or with the analysis of the Prisoners' Dilemma supergame given in chapters 3 and 4. We certainly cannot say, for example, that Hume understood (what is shown in chapter 4) that Cooperation is rational throughout an N-person Prisoners' Dilemma supergame only if the players adopt conditional strategies of a certain form and a certain inequality relating the discount rate and the payoff functions is satisfied for each player. We cannot even say that the *Treatise* contains an analysis of the Prisoners' Dilemma supergame. Nevertheless, the general outline of Hume's theory is quite clear and we can say that there is an approximate similarity between his ideas and parts of the analysis in chapter 3. If this comparison is legitimate, then we can say that Hume failed to appreciate that even when the society is so large that the ordinary game is a Prisoners' Dilemma, Cooperation in the supergame may yet be rational if the individual discount rates are not too great.

Despite his more 'dynamic' treatment of the problem, Hume comes to essentially the same conclusion as Hobbes: governments, powerful enough to enforce 'justice' and maintain Peace, are necessary and desirable. The comment made earlier on Hobbes's conclusion applies to Hume also: from their assumptions (including, in Hume's case, the assumption of a 'high' discount rate), one can deduce only that *some form of coercion is necessary to establish or maintain Peace*; one cannot, strictly speaking, conclude that this coercion must take the form of government.

My final comment on Hobbes and Hume, before I turn in the next chapter to consider more fundamental criticisms of their approach, concerns the assumption, which is absolutely essential to their arguments, that 'the greatest, that in any forme of Government can possibly happen to the people in generall, is scarce sensible, in respect of the miseries, and horrible calamities, that accompany a Civill Warre; or that dissolute condition of masterlesse men . . .' (*Lev* 141; for an almost identical statement by Hume, see *Tr* 497). In other words, it is assumed that government-enforced Peace is preferred by every individual to the state of War no matter how great are the costs of government.

Now the only kinds of costs which Hobbes and Hume appear to have in mind in this connection are those which are to be merely *subtracted*, so to speak, from the benefits of mutual Cooperation (the resulting utility for the mutual Cooperation outcome being for every individual diminished but still greater than that of the mutual non-Cooperation outcome). Yet a government powerful enough to enforce Cooperation may impose costs of other kinds. In the first place, it may diminish the desirability of the state of Peace *per se* (in addition, that is, to imposing costs merely in order to ensure this outcome). This is because people tend to derive more satisfaction from doing things which are initiated and carried out spontaneously and voluntarily than from doing the same things at the suggestion and command of others, including the state.

Secondly, the state may have cumulative effects on the very conditions which, according to Hobbes and Hume, make states necessary. In particular, it may over a period of time cause a Prisoners' Dilemma to appear where none existed before, or cause an already existing Prisoners' Dilemma to become more severe. Dynamical effects of this sort are of a wholly different order from those mentioned earlier, and I believe that the entire approach to the justification of the state which has been considered in this chapter is undermined if they are taken seriously. I shall try to take them seriously in the next chapter.

7. Epilogue: cooperation, the state and anarchy

By his entry into any society the individual . . . offers up a portion of (his) liberty so that society will vouchsafe him the rest. Anybody who asks for an explanation is usually presented with a further saying: '*The liberty of each human being should have no limits other than that of every other.*' At first glance, this seems utterly fair, does it not? And yet this theory holds the germ of the whole theory of despotism.[1]

Bakunin, L'Empire Knouto-Germanique

Therefore we can only repeat what we have so often said concerning authority in general: 'To avoid a possible evil you have recourse to means which in themselves are a greater evil, and become the source of those same abuses that you wish to remedy . . .'

Kropotkin, The Conquest of Bread

The treatment of the problem of voluntary cooperation in the first four chapters and the political theories of Hobbes and Hume as I presented them in chapter 6 rest solely on assumptions about individuals. These assumptions embody a conception of the individual as being endowed with a *given* and *unchanging* structure of preferences. More specifically, it is assumed that each individual is characterized by a certain combination of egoism and some form of altruism, and it is further assumed that this characterization does not change with time. His preferences are treated as exogenous to what has to be explained (or justified) by the theories in question. They are independent of, and do not change in response to, his social situation. He is an example of what Marx called the 'abstract man'.

This means, in particular, that no account is taken of the effect on individual preferences of the activities of the state or of the activities of the individuals themselves. If the activities of the state may result in changes in individual preferences, then clearly it cannot be deduced from the structure of preferences in the absence of the state that the state is desirable. More generally, if individual preferences change (not necessarily as a result of state activity), the question of the desirability (or 'preferability') of the state becomes much more complex than it is in the static theories we have been considering; and if preferences change as a result of the state itself, then it is not even clear what is *meant* by the desirability of the state.

The effects of the state on individual preferences and the ways in which preferences may change in the absence of the state are the subjects of the main section of this final chapter ('The decay of voluntary cooperation'). I shall suggest there (rather inconclusively, it has to be admitted) that the effect of the state is to exacerbate the very conditions which are claimed to provide its justification and for which it is supposed to provide a partial remedy. In two preliminary sections I shall mention – much less controversially, it seems to me – two other ways in which states create or aggravate problems of the kind they are supposed to solve and undermine conditions for alternatives to the state to be workable.

In what follows I take the state to be (amongst other things) a complex system of interacting, partially independent components (like: police, security and military forces, an executive, legislature, judiciary, administrative service, and so on), and when I speak of the effects of state action I shall be referring to the aggregate (or outcome or resultant) of the components' actions which are in turn the aggregate of the actions of the individuals who staff them.

International anarchy

If, as the liberal theory argues, a state is an effective way of solving the two fundamental collective action problems of maintaining order internally and providing defence against external enemies and competitors, then the very process of becoming politically more centralised – of building or strengthening a state – is likely to be seen as threatening by neighbouring and competitor societies, and the response is likely to be the formation or strengthening of their own states, and in particular, of course, the building up of their own 'defensive' capabilities. The structure of preferences involved in this process, which can characterize relations between societies of any sort, not merely those which are usually called nations, is likely to be that of a Prisoners' Dilemma game. Interactions of this kind may also, however, generate other collective action problems, including some representable as Chicken games.[2]

If this is so, then we could say that states, established at one level (the national level, for example) to rescue people in a ('domestic') Prisoners' Dilemma or other collective action problem, may cause a Prisoners' Dilemma or other collective action problem to emerge at another level (the international level, for example) or exacerbate an already existing one.

Hobbes himself noted that 'Sovereigns', who alone can save people from the state of (domestic) 'War', are themselves in a 'state of nature', without a 'common power to keep them all in awe':

> But though there had never been any time, wherein particular men were in a condition of warre one against another; yet in all times, Kings, and Persons of Sovereigne authority, because of their Independency, are in continuall jealousies, and in the state and posture of Gladiators; having their weapons pointing, and their eyes fixed upon one another; that is, their Forts, Garrisons, and Guns upon the Frontiers of their Kingdoms; and continuall Spyes upon their neighbours; which is a posture of War. (*Lev* 98)

Nevertheless, neither Hobbes nor Hume applied to the international 'state of nature' the analysis which they made of the domestic one. But there is no reason in principle why such an application should not be made. Many people have of course done just this, arguing that a supranational state is necessary if international collective action problems, including that of the maintenance of international peace, are to be solved. And contrariwise, the possibility of conditional cooperation amongst states in the absence of such a supranational state has been taken more seriously in the last few years.[3]

The destruction of community

Hume argues that in large societies life without government is appalling, but that in small societies this need not be the case. Therefore, he says, people in a large society need, and will in fact establish, a government. When the argument is put this way, however, a radically different conclusion suggests itself: that large societies should be (or will be) disaggregated into smaller societies, and the enlargement of societies and the destruction of small ones should be (or will be) resisted. This conclusion does not follow logically from Hume's premises any more than does his own conclusion. Given these premises (or those of Hobbes), the most that we can assert in this connection is that the larger the society, the less likely it is that there will be voluntary cooperation in the provision of public goods and in the solution of other collective action problems, principally because of the increased difficulty of conditional cooperation. If the relations between the members of a smaller group are those characteristic of community, then the usual range of positive and negative sanctions, including informal social sanctions, that are most effective in small communities, can also help to maintain cooperation in the absence of the state (though it should not then be called 'voluntary'), both directly and (like the state in Hobbes's account) indirectly through bolstering conditional cooperation.

In view of this, it is perhaps ironical that the state should be presented as the saviour of people caught in the Prisoners' Dilemmas (and other collective action problems) of a large society; for historically the state has undoubtedly played a large part in providing the conditions in which societies could grow and indeed in systematically *building* large societies and destroying small communities. The state has in this way acted so as to make itself even more necessary.

Of course, states were not alone in causing the decline of community and it is difficult to disentangle their contributions from those of other causes such as the expansion of industrial capitalism; but that the state had an important independent effect there can be no doubt.

I am not thinking so much of the very origin of the long process of state formation, when the normal process of fissioning that is characteristic of stateless societies is inhibited. Such fissioning, whereby a part of a community breaks away and establishes a replica community elsewhere, ensures that the society continues to be composed of small communities. When this is no longer possible, communities must grow in size or become joined to others. This is part of the process that leads to the *emergence* of a state. But what I have more in mind is the 'self-building' of states through the intentional destruction or absorption or weakening of (small) communities and the concomitant construction or extension or strengthening of nations or other larger societies, which can only be communities in a much weaker sense.[4] This is as true of the growth of the earliest states and of the modern European states as it is of many nations made independent since the Second World War, where the new states have often quite consciously set about weakening loyalty to ethnic and other groups within the proto-nation in order to build a single 'national solidarity'.[5]

The state, then, has in this way tended to exacerbate the conditions which are claimed (in the liberal theory) to provide its justification and for which it is supposed to be the remedy. It has undermined the conditions which make the principal alternative to it workable and in this way has made itself more desirable.

The decay of voluntary cooperation

The arguments for the necessity of the state which I am criticizing in this book are founded on the supposed inability of individuals to cooperate voluntarily to provide themselves with public goods, and especially, in the theories of Hobbes and Hume, with security of person and property. The intervention of the state is necessary, according to these arguments, in order to secure for the people a Pareto-optimal provision of public goods, or at least to ensure that *some* provision is made of the most important public goods.

In this section I suggest that the more the state intervenes in such situations, the more 'necessary' (on this view) it becomes, because positive altruism and voluntary cooperative behaviour *atrophy* in the presence of the state and *grow* in its absence. Thus, again, the state exacerbates the conditions which are supposed to make it necessary. We might say that the state is like an addictive drug: the more of it we have, the more we 'need' it and the more we come to 'depend' on it.

Men who live for long under government and its bureaucracy, courts and police, come to rely upon them. They find it easier (and in some cases are legally bound) to use the state for the settlement of their disputes and for the provision of public goods, instead of arranging these things for themselves, even where the disputes, and the publics for which the goods are to be provided, are quite local. In this way, the state *mediates* between individuals; they come to deal with each other through the courts, through the tax collector and the bureaucracies which spend the taxes. In the presence of a strong state, the individual may cease to care for, or even think about, those in his community who need help; he may cease to have any desire to make a direct contribution to the resolution of local problems, whether or not he is affected by them; he may come to feel that his responsibility to society has been discharged as soon as he has paid his taxes (which are taken coercively from him by the state), for these taxes will be used by the state to care for the old, sick and unemployed, to keep his streets clean, to maintain order, to provide and maintain schools, libraries, parks, and so on. The state releases the individual from the responsibility or need to cooperate with others directly; it guarantees him a secure environment in which he may safely pursue his private goals, unhampered by all those collective concerns which it is supposed to take care of itself. This is a part of what Marx meant when he wrote (in 'On the Jewish Question') of state-enforced security as 'the assurance of egoism'.

The effects of government on altruism and voluntary cooperation can be seen as part of the general process of the destruction of small societies by the state which was described earlier. The state, as we have seen, weakens local communities in favour of the larger national society. In doing so, it relieves individuals of the necessity to cooperate voluntarily amongst themselves on a local basis, making them more dependent upon the state. The result is that altruism and cooperative behaviour gradually decay. The state is thereby strengthened and made more effective in its work of weakening the local community. Kropotkin has described this process in his *Mutual Aid*. All over Europe, in a period of three centuries beginning in the late fifteenth century, states or proto-states 'systematically weeded out' from village and city all the 'mutual-aid institutions', and the result, says Kropotkin, was that

> The State alone . . . must take care of matters of general interest, while the subjects must represent loose aggregations of individuals, connected by no particular bonds, bound to appeal to the Government each time that they feel a common need.
>
> The absorption of all social functions by the State necessarily favoured the development of an unbridled, narrowminded individualism. In proportion as the obligations towards the State grew in numbers the citizens were evidently relieved from their obligations towards each other.[6]

Under the state, there is no *practice* of cooperation and no growth of a sense of the interdependence on which cooperation depends; there are fewer opportunities for the spontaneous expression of direct altruism and there are therefore fewer altruistic acts to be observed, with the result that there is no growth of the feeling of assurance that others around one are altruistic or at least willing to behave cooperatively – an assurance that one will not be let down if one tries unilaterally to cooperate.

A part of this argument has recently been made by Richard Sennett. Sennett's interest is in reversing the trend towards 'purified' urban and suburban communities through the creation of cities in which people would learn to cope with diversity and 'disorder' through the necessity of having to deal with each other directly rather than relying on the police and courts and bureaucracies. The problem, he says, is 'how to plug people into each others' lives without making everyone feel the same'. This will not be achieved by merely devolving the city government's power onto local groups:

> Really decentralized power, so that the individual has to deal with those around him, in a milieu of diversity, involves a change in the essence of communal control, that is, in the refusal to regulate conflict. For example, police control of much civil disorder ought to be sharply curbed; the responsibility for making peace in neighbourhood affairs ought to fall to the people involved. Because men are now so innocent and unskilled in the expression of conflict, they can only view these disorders as spiralling into violence. Until they learn through experience that the handling of conflict is something that cannot be passed on to the police, this polarization and escalation of conflict into violence will be the only end they can frame for themselves.[7]

In his remarkable study of blood donorship, *The Gift Relationship*, Richard Titmuss has given us an example of how altruism *generates* altruism – of how a man is more likely to be altruistic if he experiences or observes the altruism of others or if he is aware that the community depends (for the provision of some public good) on altruistic acts.[8] The availability of blood for transfusion is of course a public good. In England and Wales, all donations are purely voluntary (with the partial exception of a very small amount collected under pressure from prison inmates). In the United States, only 9 per cent of donations were purely voluntary in 1967 (and the percentage was falling). Of the rest, most are paid for or are given 'contractually' (to replace blood received instead of paying for it, or as a 'premium' in a family blood insurance scheme). As Titmuss recognizes, even the donors he calls 'voluntary' (those who do not receive payment, do not give contractually, and are not threatened directly with tangible sanctions or promised tangible rewards) must have 'some sense of obligation, approval and interest'. Nevertheless, the voluntary donation of blood does seem to approximate as closely as is perhaps possible to the ideal of pure, spontaneous altruism: for it is given impersonally and sometimes with discomfort, without expectation of gratitude, reward or reciprocation (for the recipient is usually not known to the donor), and without imposing an obligation on the recipient or anyone else; and 'there are no personal, predictable penalities for not giving; no socially enforced sanctions of remorse, shame or guilt'.[9] It is, then, an example of the kind of altruism which Hume specifically declared to be very limited or absent; it is precisely not the 'private benevolence' towards family and friends which he thought was common.

Now, if there is any truth in the general argument about the growth and decay of altruism which was put forward above, we should at least expect that the *growth* of voluntary donations should be greater in a country in which non-voluntary donations are absent than in one where they are present, and even that voluntary donations should *decline* with time in a country where a very large proportion of donors were non-voluntary. This is precisely what has happened in the countries which Titmuss examines. In the developed countries the demand for blood has risen very steeply in recent years, much more steeply than the population. Yet in England and Wales, from 1948 to 1968, supply has kept pace with demand, and there have never been serious shortages. On the other hand, in the United States, in the period 1961–7 for which figures are available, supply has not kept pace with demand and there have been serious shortages; even more significantly, those blood banks which paid more than half of their suppliers collected an increasing quantity of blood in this period, while the supply to other banks *decreased*. In Japan, where the proportion of blood which is bought and sold has risen since 1951 from zero to the present 98 per cent, shortages are even more severe than in the United States.

These differences, between England and Wales on the one hand and America and Japan on the other, are consistent with the hypothesis that altruism fosters altruism (though of course they do not confirm it). Support (also inconclusive) for this explanation of the growth of blood donations in England comes from some of the responses to a question included in Titmuss's 1967 survey of blood donors in England: 'Could you say why you *first* decided to become a blood donor?'. Many people, it appears, became blood donors as a result of *experiencing* altruism: they or their friends or relatives had received transfusions. For example:

> To try and repay in some small way some unknown person whose blood helped me recover from two operations and enable me to be with my family, that's why I bring them along also as they become old enough. (Married woman, age 44, three children, farmer's wife)

> 'Some unknown person gave blood to save my wife's life. (Married man, age 43, two children, self-employed windowcleaner)

Some responses hint at an altruism resulting from an appreciation of the *dependence* of the system on altruism and of people's dependence on each other:

> You can't get blood from supermarkets and chaine stores. People themselves must come forward, sick people cant get out of bed to ask you for a pint to save thier life so I came forward in hope to help somebody who needs blood. (Married woman, aged 23, machine operator)[10]

Peter Singer, in his discussion of Titmuss's book, has drawn attention to some experiments which also support the hypothesis that altruism is encouraged by the observation of altruism.[11] He mentions an experiment in which a car with a flat tyre was parked at the side of the road with a helpless-looking woman standing beside it. Drivers who had just passed a woman in a similar plight but with a man who had stopped to change her wheel for her (this scene having of course been arranged by the experimenters) were significantly more likely to help than those who had not witnessed this altruistic behaviour.[12] Singer himself writes: 'I find it hardest to act with consideration for others when the norm in the circle of people I move in is to act egotistically. When altruism is expected of me, however, I find it much easier to be genuinely altruistic.'

The argument I have made in this section is not of course new. A similar (though not identical) argument is familiar to us from the writings of the classical liberals, and especially of John Stuart Mill. With the partial exception of Kropotkin, the only anarchist writer who makes full and explicit use of something like this argument is William Godwin. (Though Godwin is not wholly an anarchist. His case against government in the *Enquiry Concerning Political Justice* represents in most respects a more extensive and more throughgoing application of Mill's argument than Mill himself makes.)

For Godwin, government is an evil which is necessary only as long as people behave in the way in which they have come to behave as a result of living for a long time under government. If governments were dissolved, he says 'arguments and addresses' would not at first suffice to persuade people to 'cooperate for the common advantage' and 'some degree of authority and violence would be necessary. But this necessity does not appear to arise out of the nature of man, but out of the institutions by which he has been corrupted.'[13] Later, government would not be necessary at all: there would be a transition to anarchy during which people would learn to cooperate voluntarily (or, at least, to cooperate in order to avoid the disapprobation of neighbours: 'a species of coercion' which would presumably be effective in the *small* 'parishes' of Godwin's ideal social order[14]). The growth of cooperation would in part result from the growth of benevolence. Benevolence is 'a resource which is never exhausted' but becomes stronger the more it is exercised; and if there is no opportunity for its exercise, it decays. The idea permeates much of Godwin's *Enquiry*; we see it, for example, in his criticism of punishment by imprisonment:

> Shall we be most effectually formed to justice, benevolence and prudence in our intercourse with each other, in a state of solitude? Will not our selfish and unsocial dispositions be perpetually increased? What temptation has he to think of benevolence or justice, who has no opportunity to exercise it?[15]

At the same time as Godwin wrote the *Enquiry Concerning Political Justice*, Wilhelm von Humboldt was composing *The Limits of State Action*, a book which contains many of the ideas to be found in the *Enquiry*, especially those which are of interest here.[16] Humboldt was certainly not an anarchist; but he did argue that the scope of state activity should be strictly limited to the provision of 'mutual security and protection against foreign enemies', and his case against the further interference of the state rested on arguments similar to Godwin's and more fundamentally on the axiom (on which Mill's *On Liberty* was also to be based) that '. . . the chief point to be kept in view by the State is the development of the powers of its citizens in their full individuality.'[17]

By *security*, Humboldt meant 'the assurance of legal freedom':

freedom, that is, to enjoy one's legal rights of person and property undisturbed by the encroachments of others.[18] The state must therefore investigate and settle disputes about such encroachments and punish transgressions of its laws, since these threaten security.[19] Humboldt never considers the possibility that disputes could be settled and crimes punished directly by the people themselves without the help of the state. Indeed, his only argument in support of the thesis that security must be provided by the state is that 'it is a condition which man is wholly unable to realize by his own individual efforts.[20] Yet, if this is true of security, why is it not also true of other public goods (and perhaps some other goods too)? A case can of course be made for the special status of security. One can argue, with Hobbes, that it is fundamental, being a prerequisite to the attainment of other goods. Humboldt does in fact take this line: 'Now, without security', he writes, 'it is impossible for man either to develop his powers, or to enjoy the fruits of so doing.'[21] However, in the first place, it still remains to be shown that security cannot be realized without the help of the state, and secondly, it can be argued that if the state *is* required to provide security, then for the same reasons it will be required to provide other public goods; in other words, even when they enjoy state-enforced security, citizens will not necessarily be able to obtain other things which they want without the further intervention of the state, which Humboldt expressly forbids.

Nevertheless, the arguments which Godwin uses – and Humboldt refrains from using – against *any* sort of state intervention are eloquently set out by Humboldt in his case against the intervention of the state in matters not involving security or defence. Here, in particular, is Humboldt on the effects of the state on altruism and voluntary cooperation:

> As each individual abandons himself to the solicitous aid of the State, so, and still more, he abandons to it the fate of his fellow-citizens. This weakens sympathy and renders mutual assistance inactive: or, at least, the reciprocal interchange of services and benefits will be most likely to flourish at its liveliest, where the feeling is most acute that such assistance is the only thing to rely upon.[22]

In Mill's *On Liberty* we do not encounter this argument until, at the end of the essay, he considers cases in which the objections to government interference do not turn upon 'the principle of liberty'.

These include cases, he says, in which individuals should be left to act by themselves, without the help of the state, as a means to their own development and of 'accustoming them to the comprehension of their joint interests, the management of joint concerns – habituating them to act from public or semi-public motives, and guide their conduct by aims which unite instead of isolating them.'[23] The argument appears also in the *Principles of Political Economy*, as 'one of the strongest of the reasons against the extension of government agency'.[24] Nevertheless, Mill gives to state interference a considerably wider scope than does Humboldt. In addition to the maintenance of security,[25] he allows a number of other important exceptions to his general rule of non-interference.[26]

One of these exceptions is of peculiar interest here. The exception essentially concerns 'free-rider' situations. Mill gives the example of collective action by workers to reduce their working hours. In such situations, he says, no individual will find it in his interest to cooperate voluntarily, and the more numerous are those others who cooperate the more will he gain by not cooperating; so the assistance of the state is required to 'afford to every individual a guarantee that his competitors will pursue the same course, without which he cannot safely adopt it himself'.[27] Penal laws, he goes on to say, are necessary for just this reason: 'because even an unanimous opinion that a certain line of conduct is for the general interest, does not always make it people's individual interest to adhere to that line of conduct'. This is all Mill has to say on this subject. He is merely providing an argument for an *exception* to the general rule of non-interference. He does not appear to recognize that the same argument would justify state interference in a vast class of situations. Nor, at the same time, does he appear to recognize that his general case against the interference of the state could be applied in all of these situations, including all aspects of the provision of peace and security.

Rationality

In the last chapter, I criticized Hobbes for drawing the conclusion that government is the *only* means whereby men may be coerced to Cooperate and, more fundamentally, for his relatively static treatment of the problem. I went on to note that Hume's political theory, while it also suffers from the first of these failings, to some extent remedies the second:

but although his approach is more dynamical, Hume concurs with Hobbes in concluding that Cooperation will not occur voluntarily, neglecting the possibility that the voluntary Cooperation of all individuals may occur in a dynamic game because the adoption of a conditionally Cooperative strategy is rational under certain conditions for each individual. Finally, I questioned the assumption of both Hobbes and Hume that a government-enforced state of Peace is preferred by every individual to the state of War, and in this connection I drew particular attention to the way in which government might not only impose costs on the individual but *in addition* diminish the satisfaction he derives from being in the state of Peace.

This last point refers only to a *static* effect of government – to an effect which operates in the same way at each point in time without causing cumulative changes.

Even when time is explicitly brought into the analysis in the way this is done in Hume's political theory and in chapters 3 and 4, the resulting formulation is static in a further sense, namely, that 'human nature' is taken as given and assumed to be constant. More precisely, egoism or some combination of egoism and altruism is assumed once and for all to characterize each individual; it undergoes no modification at any stage during the 'game', no matter how the players have previously behaved; and it remains unaltered upon the introduction of government and by the continued presence of government.

This assumption could be modified, and a further dynamic element injected, by allowing the combination of egoism and altruism to change over time, while still assuming that at each point of time an individual can be characterized by a utility function embodying some combination of egoism and altruism. In particular, it could now be assumed that the egoism–altruism combination changes in a way which depends on the history of the players' choices in previous games and on whether these choices were made voluntarily or as a result of the presence of state sanctions.

Modification of this sort would already take us outside the 'abstract man' framework which I mentioned at the start of this chapter, for it introduces an individual whose 'human nature' is no longer given and fixed but is partly determined by his changing social situation (including the effects on him of the state) and is something which to some extent he himself creates.

The effects of the state on individual preferences were the subject of the preceding section. The arguments put forward there were not rigorously demonstrated and no conclusive evidence was given in their support (I doubt if this is possible). But even if it is conceded only that they *may* be true, it follows that it is not at all clear what can be assumed about 'human nature' at any point in time, in particular what the structure of preferences would be in the absence of the state. The assumptions made by Hobbes and Hume were supposed to characterize human behaviour in the absence of the state; but perhaps they more accurately describe what human behaviour would be like immediately after the state has been removed from a society *whose members had for a long time lived under states.* This is surely the mental experiment which Hobbes and Hume were performing.

Although Hobbes spoke in *Leviathan* of many different characteristics of individuals, the core of his political theory makes essential use of only one of these, namely the individual's egoism or some combination of egoism and negative altruism. The same is true of Hume's political theory, except that the negative altruism of Hobbes is replaced by a severely limited positive altruism. I have tentatively suggested in this chapter that these assumptions tend to be *self-fulfilling*, in the sense that, if they were not true before the introduction of the state, which they are said to make necessary, they would in time become true as a result of the state's activity, or, if individuals already lacked sufficient positive altruism to make the state unnecessary, they would 'learn', while they lived under the care of the state, to possess even less of it.

It has often been argued that the choice of the scope and form of social institutions (such as the state) must be based on 'pessimistic' assumptions, so that they will be 'robust' against the worst possible conditions (such as a society of egoistic or even negatively altruistic individuals) in which they might be required to operate. It is assumed in such arguments that if an institution can 'work' (or work better, in some sense, than the alternatives) when everyone is, for example, egoistic, then it will certainly do the same when some or all people are positively altruistic. But if the institutions themselves affect individual preferences – affect the content of the assumptions from which their relative desirability has been deduced – then this approach is inappropriate and may be dangerously misleading. If there is any truth in the arguments I have been making – if the state is in part the cause of changes in individual preferences – then we cannot deduce from the structure of these preferences that the state is desirable. Indeed, it is not even clear in this case what it *means* to say that the state is desirable. The same objection can be made to any theory which seeks to justify or prescribe or recommend an institution, rule, practice, technology, or any set of arrangements in terms of given and fixed preferences if these are changed over time by whatever it is that is being justified.

The theory I have been criticizing and the analysis of cooperation in chapters 2–4 are founded on what has been called the *thin* theory of rationality. This is the account of rationality which is almost universally taken for granted by economists (and not just neoclassical economists). On this account, first, rationality is relative to *given* preferences (or more generally attitudes) and beliefs, which are assumed to be consistent and do not change over time, and the agent's actions are *instrumental* in achieving the given aims in the light of the given beliefs. Secondly, the agent is assumed to be a pure egoist. A somewhat less thin account would admit a measure of altruism (as was done in chapter 5). If the mix of egoism and altruism, or the propensity to act altruistically, was allowed to vary over time, then one of the components of the first characteristic of the thin account would also have been relaxed, but rationality would still be of the instrumental kind. The third crucial feature of the thin conception of rationality is that the range of incentives assumed to affect the agent is limited. As I emphasized in chapter 1, Olson's theory of collective action limits them to the increase in the public good that results from the individual's contribution, the resources he expends in making this contribution and also his contribution to organizational costs, and selective incentives which themselves are limited to the 'material' and the 'social'. Without a limitation on the range of incentives, a rational choice theory is liable to become a tautology.

Now I want to emphasize that nothing I have said in this chapter implies that the thin account of rationality cannot provide a satisfactory foundation for *any* kind of theory. In fact, my view is that the explanation of states of affairs or outcomes (however unintended these may be) in terms of individual actions, and the explanation of actions in terms of attitudes and beliefs using a thin account of rationality of some sort, are indispensable parts of any *explanatory* social theory.[28] My objection is to the use of the thin account of rationality in 'evaluative' theories, such as the liberal (or, one might say, the neoclassical) justification of the state.

So it is not my view that the 'thin' theory of collective action, of which a theory of conditional cooperation such as that developed in chapters 3 and 4 above would be a part, is an unrealistic, inapplicable theory because it rests on a thin conception of rationality. (I do nevertheless believe that the thin theory has much more explanatory power in certain sorts of situations than in others. I have tried elsewhere to characterize these situations – as well as to assess the prospects of founding explanatory theories on alternative conceptions of rationality – and I will not repeat the arguments here.)[29]

Nor do the arguments I have made in this chapter require me to abandon rational choice explanation – or methodological individualism more generally – and embrace some version of structuralism instead. The fact that individual actions, preferences and beliefs are caused – by states, for example, or by any sort of structure – does not make them explanatorily irrelevant. Just as individual actions, attitudes and beliefs are in part the products of and must be partly explained by, amongst other things, structures, so also are structures – or collective action or the origin and evolution of states – in part the products of and must be partly explained by individual actions.[30]

Annex: the theory of metagames

I am aware of only one attempt to 'rationalize' Cooperation in the *one-shot* Prisoners' Dilemma game. This is the theory of metagames proposed by Nigel Howard in his *Paradoxes of Rationality*.[1] He believes the theory to be predictive: Cooperation in the Prisoners' Dilemma is 'rational' if a player reasons in a certain way, and this mode of reasoning is claimed to be characteristic of real persons.

If Cooperation is 'rational' in the ordinary game, then it should also be 'rational' in the supergame. Our efforts in chapters 3 and 4 were clearly unnecessary if Howard's argument is valid. Anatol Rapoport believes that it is. In an enthusiastic article, he has stated that Howard's theory has 'resolved' the 'paradox' of the Prisoners' Dilemma, reconciling individual and collective rationality.[2]

In this part of the annex, I state why I believe that Howard and Rapoport are mistaken. The relevant part of Howard's argument as it applies to the Prisoners' Dilemma is first briefly presented with reference to the two-person, two-strategy case which we considered in chapter 3.

Consider the game with the following payoff matrix:

	C	D
C	x, x	z, y
D	y, z	w, w

where $y > x > w > z$. Call this now the *basic game*.

Suppose now that player 2's choices are not between the *basic strategies C* and *D*, but between the *conditional strategies* (Howard calls them 'policies') consisting of all the mappings from player 1's basic strategies to his own. Let S_1/S_2 denote the conditional strategy whereby player 2 chooses S_1 if player 1 chooses C and S_2 if he chooses D. Then 2's conditional strategies are:

C/C: to choose C regardless of player 1's choice,
D/D: to choose D regardless of player 1's choice,
C/D: to choose the same strategy as player 1,
D/C: to choose the opposite of player 1's strategy.

If player 2's choices can in fact be made dependent upon player 1's choices in this way, then it is as if the two are playing in a game whose payoff matrix is:

	C/C	D/D	C/D	D/C
C	x, x	z, y	x, x	z, y
D	y, z	$\boxed{w, w}$	w, w	y, z

This is called the 2-*metagame*. Its only equilibrium is $(D, D/D)$, corresponding to the only equilibrium (D, D) in the basic game.

Suppose next that player 1's choices are not between the basic strategies C and D but are conditional upon the conditional strategies of player 2 in the 2-metagame. Let $S_1/S_2/S_3/S_4$ denote the conditional strategy whereby player 1 chooses S_1 if player 2 chooses C/C, S_2 if he chooses D/D, S_3 if he chooses C/D, and S_4 if he chooses D/C. If the players' choices can in fact be made interdependent in this way, then it is as if they are playing a game whose payoff matrix is that shown in table 4.

This game is called the 12-*metagame*. It has three equilibria, which are marked in the payoff matrix; but if the two players were indeed playing in this game, they would not expect the uncooperative equilibrium $(D/D/D/D, D/D)$ to occur, for each of them strictly prefers either of the other two equilibria. Both of these two other equilibria are outcomes of a single strategy of player 2, and since $D/D/C/D$ weakly dominates $C/D/C/D$ for player 1, both players should expect $(D/D/C/D, C/D)$ to be the outcome. It is therefore the outcome. $(D/D/C/D, C/D)$ corresponds to (C, C) in the basic game. In this way, according to Howard, mutual cooperation is rationalized even in the one-shot game.

A similar outcome occurs in the '21-metagame', where player 1's strategies are conditional upon the choices of player 2, which are in turn conditional upon the basic strategies of player 1. That is to say, the outcome is $(C/D, D/D/C/D)$, corresponding to (C, C) in the basic game.

Table 4. *Payoff matrix for the 12-metagame*

	C/C	D/D	C/D	D/C
C/C/C/C	x, x	z, y	x, x	z, y
D/D/D/D	y, z	[w, w]	w, w	y, z
D/D/D/C	y, z	w, w	w, w	z, y
D/D/C/D	y, z	w, w	[x, x]	y, z
D/D/C/C	y, z	w, w	x, x	z, y
D/C/D/D	y, z	z, y	w, w	y, z
D/C/D/C	y, z	z, y	w, w	z, y
D/C/C/D	y, z	z, y	x, x	y, z
D/C/C/C	y, z	z, y	x, x	z, y
C/D/D/D	x, x	w, w	w, w	y, z
C/D/D/C	x, x	w, w	w, w	z, y
C/D/C/D	x, x	w, w	[x, x]	y, z
C/D/C/C	x, x	w, w	x, x	z, y
C/C/D/D	x, x	z, y	w, w	y, z
C/C/D/C	x, x	z, y	w, w	z, y
C/C/C/D	x, x	z, y	x, x	y, z

Conditional strategies of a higher order could be considered. Thus player 2's strategies could be conditional upon those of player 1 in the 12-metagame, whose payoff matrix is exhibited in table 4. (The resulting game is called the '212-metagame'.) However, neither this nor any higher order metagame would yield new equilibria, for Howard shows that all equilibria corresponding to distinct outcomes in the basic game are revealed in the nth-order metagames in which each of the n players is 'named' once and only once – the 12-metagame and the 21-metagame in this two-person Prisoners' Dilemma instance.

I have two comments to make on this theory of metagames.

1. The first is for me decisive in rejecting the theory as an explanation of behaviour in the one-shot Prisoners' Dilemma in which, as I have assumed, binding agreements are not possible. In this game, the players choose their strategies *independently*; they are in effect chosen simultaneously, with no knowledge of the other's strategy. And no matter how much they may indulge in 'metagame reasoning' they must in fact ultimately choose one of their *basic* strategies.

In metagame theory, on the other hand, the player's strategies are required to be interdependent, even in this *one-shot* Prisoner's Dilemma game.

In the ordinary game, strategies could be made interdependent by use of a 'referee', not in the game theorist's usual sense, but in the sense of a third party who would be notified of the players' strategies, compare them, *and* ensure that a conditional strategy is in fact made dependent upon the specified strategies of others. However, this is equivalent to the user of a conditional strategy making his choice of a basic strategy *after* the choices of those whose strategies his depends upon.

Furthermore, the referee could in general decide a unique outcome only if the conditional strategies were of the appropriate orders of 'sophistication'. The 'resolution' of the two-person Prisoners' Dilemma takes place in the 12- or 21-metagame. Each of these games is asymmetric in the sense that one player's strategies are first-order conditional, while the other's are second-order conditional. This asymmetry is of course essential to the resolution, for if both players use conditional strategies of the same order, then some conditional strategy combinations do not yield determinate outcomes (as when, for example, each player would Cooperate if and only if the other Cooperates). This asymmetry is to some extent arbitrary; or rather, it emphasizes again that one player's choices of basic strategy must in fact follow the other's.

Of course, a player may try to ensure that other players will act Cooperatively, by announcing his intention to use a conditionally Cooperative strategy, and generally by *bargaining* with them. However, such exchanges, supposing them to be possible, would not have the effect of producing mutual Cooperation, unless agreements reached in this way were binding. Such agreements are ruled out in the specification of the game. In any case, if a mechanism for enforcing agreements existed, then the players would presumably have had little difficulty in agreeing on mutual Cooperation in the first place, and there would be no need of a theory of metagames to explain this.

Howard is neither clear nor consistent about the interpretation to be placed upon strategies in metagames. He often suggests that metagame strategies are made interdependent through *actual* bargaining (as on p. 101 of *Paradoxes of Rationality* and in applications of the theory throughout the book) and that a player's choice *follows* certain other players' choices in full knowledge of them (pp. 23, 27, 54 and 61 for example). Elsewhere, however, he seems to say that the choices are not actually sequential; the players behave *as if* they were. Thus (at the first order of sophistication), a player (k, say) 'sees' the other players choosing basic strategies, which he 'correctly predicts', while he himself plays as if he were in the k-metagame, his strategies being conditional on the other players' basic strategies. Metagames of higher order are reached ('subjectively') by similar reasoning.[3]

If the players can negotiate binding agreements or if in some other way their choices are made interdependently, then they are not playing in the Prisoners' Dilemma game which I have been discussing in this book. Yet Howard clearly assumes that they are. Part of his case for the need for a theory such as his own is based on the 'breakdown of rationality' (as this concept is used in conventional game theory) which is indicated, according to Howard, by the standard analysis of the Prisoners' Dilemma one-shot game.

The conclusions of the standard analysis of this game may be distressing; but they are unaffected by a consideration of metagames.

2. My second comment is that, if bargaining or any other dynamic process is indeed the object of study, then the one-shot game (with or without its metagames) is in any case an inappropriate model. In bargaining, there are *sequences* of choices; there are bluffs, threats and promises; there is learning and adaptation of expectations; the value of an outcome is discounted with future time; and so on. These things are not explicitly taken into account in the theory of metagames.

Notes

1. Introduction: the problem of collective action

1 This is a caricature of Hobbes's argument. In chapter 6, I give a more detailed account, making use of ideas developed in chapters 3–5.

2 Both of these are true of William J. Baumol's *Welfare Economics and the Theory of the State*, second edition (London: G. Bell, 1965). Much of this book is devoted to the failure of individuals to provide themselves voluntarily with public goods, but I think it is fair to say that 'the Theory of the State' is missing. He is careful to say that, before it is concluded that state action to ensure the supply of public goods is justified, all the *costs* of state action must also be taken into account (p. 22 in the introduction added to the second edition); nevertheless there is a *presumption* that *only* the state could ensure this supply.

3 Two examples are William Ophuls, 'Leviathan or oblivion?', in Herman E. Daly (ed.), *Toward a Steady-State Economy* (San Francisco: W. H. Freeman, 1973), and Robert L. Heilbroner, 'The human prospect', *The New York Review of Books*, 24 January 1974.

4 An approximate example is *A Blueprint for Survival*, by the editors of *The Ecologist* (Harmondsworth, Middlesex: Penguin Books, 1972; originally published as Vol. 2, No. 1 of *The Ecologist*, 1972). Their goal is not wholly anarchist, but it does include 'decentralisation of polity and economy at all levels, and the formation of communities small enough to be reasonably self-supporting and self-regulating'. For an anarchist's account of the necessity of anarchist society on ecological grounds, see Murray Bookchin, 'Ecology and Revolutionary Thought', in *Post-Scarcity Anarchism* (Berkeley, California: The Ramparts Press, 1971).

5 See, for example, Anthony Crosland, *A Social Democratic Britain* (Fabian Tract no. 404, London, 1971), and Jeremy Bray, *The Politics of the Environment* (Fabian Tract no. 412, London, 1972).

6 Garrett Hardin, 'The tragedy of the commons', *Science*, 162 (13 December 1968), 1243–8.

7 For a brief account of the overexploitation of whales and various species of fish, see Paul R. Ehrlich and Anne H. Ehrlich, *Population, Resources, Environment*, second edition (San Francisco: W. H. Freeman, 1972), pp.

125–34. See also Frances T. Christy and Anthony Scott, *The Common Wealth in Ocean Fisheries* (Baltimore: Johns Hopkins Press, 1965).

8 The word 'consumption' should perhaps be used only in connection with private goods, where it has a clear meaning. To speak of 'consuming' national defence, wilderness and radio broadcasts is somewhat strained, but for want of a suitable word to cover a variety of applications, I follow the custom of the economists and retain the word. In many cases, 'consume' means 'use'. Cf. Jean-Claude Milleron, 'Theory of value with public goods: a survey article', *Journal of Economic Theory*, 5 (1972), 419–77, at pp. 422–3.

9 This follows Samuelson's most recent usage (though I have added the requirement that a public good be also non-excludable). Samuelson had defined a *public good* as one which was consumed *equally* by every individual, so that $x^1 = x^2 = \ldots = x$, where x^i is the ith individual's consumption of the good and x is the total amount available; and he defined a *private good* as one which could be divided amongst individuals so that $x^1 + x^2 + \ldots = x$. See Paul A. Samuelson, 'The pure theory of public expenditure', *Review of Economics and Statistics*, 36 (1954), 387–9. In his 1955 paper, he admitted that these were two pure, polar cases; and most recently he has abandoned these two poles in favour of a 'knife-edge pole' of the pure private good and 'all the rest of the world in the public good domain'. Samuelson, 'Diagrammatic exposition of a theory of public expenditure', *Review of Economics and Statistics*, 37 (1955), 350–6; and 'Pure theory of public expenditure and taxation', in J. Margolis and H. Guitton (eds), *Public Economics* (London: Macmillan, 1969).

10 Cf. William Loehr and Todd Sandler (eds), *Public Goods and Public Policy* (Beverly Hills: Sage, 1978), p. 2 and ch. 6.

11 For a fuller discussion of social order as a public good, see my *Community, Anarchy and Liberty* (Cambridge: Cambridge University Press, 1982), sections 2.1 and 2.3.

12 Mancur Olson, *The Logic of Collective Action* (Cambridge, Mass.: Harvard University Press, 1965), p. 36.

13 Olson, *The Logic*, p. 48.

14 Cf. *The Logic*, p. 50, note 70.

15 Russell Hardin, *Collective Action* (Baltimore: The Johns Hopkins Press for Resources for the Future, 1982), pp. 41–2.

16 Including Olson himself, as we shall see when we come to discuss altruism in chapter 5.

17 Hardin, *Collective Action*, p. 44.

18 This qualifies the very useful treatment of this issue in *Collective Action*, ch. 3.

19 Olson, *The Logic*, p. 29, note 46.

20 *The Logic*, p. 132.

21 *The Logic*, p. 61, note 17. But see also p. 160, note 91.

22 On these non-instrumental motivations, see my 'Rationality and revolutionary collective action', in Michael Taylor (ed.), *Rationality and Revolution* (Cambridge: Cambridge University Press, 1987).

23 The story about two prisoners, which gave the game its name, can be found in

R. Duncan Luce and Howard Raiffa, *Games and Decisions* (New York: John Wiley, 1957), p. 95.

24 Russell Hardin, 'Collective action as an agreeable n-Prisoners' Dilemma', *Behavioral Science*, 16 (1971), 472–81.

25 Jon Elster, 'Rationality, morality, and collective action', *Ethics*, 96 (1985), 136–55. The weak definition, identifying collective action problems with the Prisoners' Dilemma, is adopted by Elster in 'Weakness of will and the free-rider problem', *Economics and Philosophy*, 1 (1985), 231–65 – but then again he admits that 'it does not . . . cover all the cases that intuitively we think of as collective action problems'.

26 Jon Elster, 'Some conceptual problems in political theory', in Brian Barry (ed.), *Power and Political Theory* (London: Wiley, 1976), at pp. 248–9.

27 Colin Clark, 'The economics of overexploitation', *Science*, 181 (17 August 1973), 630–4.

28 Taylor, *Community, Anarchy and Liberty*.

29 The two points in this paragraph where made by Brian Barry in *Sociologists, Economists and Democracy* (London: Collier-Macmillan, 1970) at pp. 27–39.

30 Olson, *The Logic*, Appendix added in 1971, p. 177.

31 Samuel L. Popkin, *The Rational Peasant: The Political Economy of Rural Society in Vietnam* (Berkeley: University of California Press, 1979), especially ch. 3.

32 Robert McC. Netting, *Balancing on an Alp: Ecological Change in a Swiss Mountain Community* (Cambridge: Cambridge University Press, 1981), especially ch. 3.

33 Lester Brown and Edward Wolf, *Soil Erosion: Quiet Crisis in the World Economy* (Washington, D.C.: Worldwatch Institute, 1984). According to this report, U.S. farms are losing topsoil at the rate of 1.7 billion tonnes a year. *The New York Times* (10 December 1985) reports that the U.S. Congress looks set to vote to pay farmers to stop farming up to 40 million acres of the worst affected land.

34 See, for example, Michael H. Glantz (ed.), *Desertification: Environmental Degradation In And Around Arid Lands* (Boulder, Colorado: Westview Press, 1977).

35 The following comments, which are critical of the property rights school's treatment of the 'tragedy of the commons', do not imply a wholesale rejection on my part of the property rights approach.

36 A. A. Alchian and Harold Demsetz, 'The property rights paradigm', *Journal of Economic History*, 33 (1973), 16–27.

37 See S. V. Ciriacy-Wantrup and Richard C. Bishop, '"Common property" as a concept in natural resources policy', *Natural Resources Journal*, 15 (1975), 713–27.

38 See, for example, Harold Demsetz, 'Toward a theory of property rights', *American Economic Review* (Papers and Proceedings), 57 (1967), 347–59.

39 Carl J. Dahlman, *The Open Field System and Beyond* (Cambridge: Cambridge University Press, 1980).

40 See, for example, Eirik G. Furobotn and Svetozar Pejovich, 'Property rights

and economic theory: a survey of recent literature', *Journal of Economic Literature*, 10 (1972), 1137–62.

41 Edna Ullman-Margalit, *The Emergence of Norms* (Oxford: Clarendon Press, 1977). A 'generalized PD-structured situation . . . is one in which the dilemma faced by the . . . participants is recurrent, or even continuous' (p. 24); but Ullman-Margalit gives no analysis of iterated games or takes any account of their distinctive problems (so, amongst other things, does not see that cooperation in these situations can occur *without* norms enforced by sanctions). Incidentally, very little of this book actually deals with the emergence of norms; it is mainly taken up with generally informal discussion of some very simple games.

42 *The Emergence of Norms*, pp. 22 and 28; my emphasis.

2. The Prisoner's Dilemma, Chicken and other games in the provision of public goods

1 This chapter draws on Michael Taylor and Hugh Ward, 'Chickens, whales, and lumpy goods: alternative models of public goods provision', *Political Studies*, 30 (1982), 350–70.

2 Russell Hardin, *Collective Action*, p. 25.

3 Russell Hardin, 'Collective action as an agreeable n-Prisoners' Dilemma', *Behavioral Science*, 16 (1971), 472–81; and again, virtually unchanged, in *Collective Action*, ch. 2.

4 Whether or not this is true of the Cournot analysis, to which one brief section is devoted, is not very important, since the Cournot approach is of little use anyway. In my view, what is involved is only a sort of pseudo-dynamics; no actual *process* is described.

5 See Dennis C. Mueller, *Public Choice* (Cambridge: Cambridge University Press, 1979), ch. 2.

6 An argument to this effect is made in Taylor and Ward, 'Chickens, whales and lumpy goods'.

7 c and b are here assumed to be independent of N. This is a reasonable assumption in many cases, including the voting one discussed earlier, but not in all cases.

8 This analysis is based on that given in Taylor and Ward, 'Chickens, whales, and lumpy goods'. It can also be found in Amnon Rapoport, 'Provision of public goods and the MCS paradigm', *American Political Science Review*, 79 (1985), 148–55. Rapoport also considers 'heterogeneous' cases where player i does not take the other players to be equally likely to Cooperate.

9 Compare Rapoport, 'Provision of public goods', pp. 150–1.

10 For further details, see Taylor and Ward, 'Chickens, whales, and lumpy goods', pp. 368–70.

11 See Hugh Ward, 'The risks of a reputation for toughness: strategy in public goods provision problems modelled by Chicken supergames', *British Journal of Political Science*, 17 (1987).

12 My presentation here draws on James M. Buchanan, *The Demand and Supply of Public Goods* (Chicago: Rand McNally, 1968); Buchanan, 'Cooperation and conflict in public-goods interaction', *Western Economic Journal*, 5 (1967), 109–21; Gerald H. Kramer and Joseph Hertzberg, 'Formal theory', in volume 7 of *The Handbook of Political Science*, F. Greenstein and N. Polsy, eds. (Reading, Mass.: Addison-Wesley, 1975); and Taylor and Ward, 'Chickens, whales, and lumpy goods'.

13 If the public good is *inferior*, then when the Others provide an additional unit of it the individual will reduce his provision of it by more than one unit.

14 John Chamberlin, 'Provision of collective goods as a function of group size', *American Political Science Review*, 68 (1974), 707–13; Martin C. McGuire, 'Group size, group homogeneity and the aggregate provision of a pure public good under Cournot behavior', *Public Choice*, 18 (1974), 107–26.

15 Chamberlin argues that if there is perfect rivalness (i.e., the good 'exhibits the same rivalness of consumption as does a private good') but non-excludability, then total production at equilibrium necessarily *decreases* as N increases. He correctly points out that if we abandon the assumption of perfect nonrivalness, the reaction curves vary with N. But they need not vary in the particular manner he assumes. Changes in an individual's reaction curve as N varies can come about as a result of changes in the transformation function facing the individual *or* in his indifference map. This follows from the remarks made at the end of the last section. Chamberlin, like many others, conflates indivisibility and nonrivalness, but my point that the reaction curves need not vary in the way he assumes holds whether their variation as N varies is due to changes in the transformation function or the indifference map or both. The (true) statement that when the public good is not purely indivisible or there is some degree of rivalness, the group's total production may increase or decrease, is said by Chamberlin to hold only for the cases 'intermediate' between perfect nonrivalness and perfect rivalness; but here too the two patterns of variation in the reaction curves as N varies which Chamberlin considers do not exhaust the possibilities. In any case, reaction curves will be radically different from the ones he considers in some important cases, in particular in lumpy goods cases, as discussion in the text below suggests.

3. The two-person Prisoners' Dilemma supergame

1 The number r_i such that $a_i = 1/(1 + r_i)$ is sometimes called the rate of time preference.

2 This has not deterred some economists and game theorists in recent years from studying finite supergames and infinite supergames with no discounting. On infinite games *without discounting*, see especially A. Rubinstein, 'Equilibrium in supergames with the overtaking criterion', *Journal of Economic Theory*, 21 (1979), 1–9; Steve Smale, 'The Prisoners' Dilemma and

dynamical systems associated to non-cooperative games', *Econometrica*, 48 (1980), 1617–34; and Robert J. Aumann, 'Survey of repeated games', pp. 11–42 in R. J. Aumann, *et al.*, *Essays in Game Theory and Mathematical Economics in Honor of Oskar Morgenstern* (Mannheim/Wien/Zurich: Bibliographisches Institut, 1981). For *finitely* repeated games, see especially the works cited in the next note. I think, however, that most economists believe that supergames of indefinite length with discounting are generally the most appropriate model.

3 This well-known result for the finitely repeated Prisoners' Dilemma no longer holds if a small amount of uncertainty is introduced into the game. If players are not quite certain about each other's motivations, options or payoffs, the backwards induction argument cannot be applied. See David M. Kreps, *et al.*, 'Rational cooperation in the finitely repeated Prisoners' Dilemma', *Journal of Economic Theory*, 27 (1982), 245–52; David M. Kreps and Robert Wilson, 'Reputation and imperfect information', *Journal of Economic Theory*, 27 (1982), 253–79; and Kreps and Wilson, 'Sequential equilibria', *Econometrica*, 50 (1982), 863–94.

4 Mixed strategies are ruled out, chiefly because they do not seem to correspond to any realistic course of action in the real world problems of public goods provision which are of interest in this book.

5 This chapter extends, in certain respects, earlier work on the two-person Prisoners' Dilemma supergame in Martin Shubik, *Strategy and Market Structure: Competition, Oligopoly, and the Theory of Games* (New York: Wiley, 1959); Shubik, 'Game theory, behavior, and the paradox of the Prisoners' Dilemma: three solutions', *Journal of Conflict Resolution*, 14 (1970), 181–93; and Michael Nicholson, *Oligopoly and Conflict* (Liverpool: Liverpool University Press, 1972).

6 Observe that the payoff matrix is *symmetric*: it remains unchanged when the players are interchanged (relabelled). Abandoning symmetry (while retaining the Prisoners' Dilemma ordering of the payoffs) would require modifications of detail (in the conditions below for strategy vectors to be equilibria, the payoffs would have to be subscripted as well as the discount factors); but the general argument would not be changed. In this book, I wish to isolate the Prisoners' Dilemma element.

7 Robert Axelrod, *The Evolution of Cooperation* (New York: Basic Books, 1984), pp. 208–9.

8 *The Evolution of Cooperation*, p. 173.

9 This last point is made by Norman Schofield, 'Anarchy, altruism and cooperation', *Social Choice and Welfare*, 2 (1985), 207–19.

10 *The Evolution of Cooperation*, p. 11 and p. 216 note 3.

11 Russell Hardin, *Collective Action*, p. 171.

12 *Collective Action*, p. 171.

13 Martin Shubik, 'Game theory, behavior, and the paradox of the Prisoner's Dilemma: three solutions', *Journal of Conflict Resolution*, 14 (1970), 181–93.

14 This strategy was introduced, I think, by Martin Shubik in *Strategy and*

Market Structure, at pp. 224–5. Its analogue for any noncooperative game is studied by James W. Friedman in 'A non-cooperative equilibrium for supergames', *The Review of Economic Studies*, 38 (1971), 1–12. See also John McMillan, 'Individual incentives in the supply of public inputs', *Journal of Public Economics*, 12 (1979), 87–98.

15 Shubik, 'Game theory, behavior, and the paradox of the Prisoner's Dilemma'.

16 A parenthetical comment is appropriate here on the condition $2x > y + z$, which is stipulatively required in some accounts of the Prisoners' Dilemma, on the grounds that, if it did not hold, then alternating between (C, D) and (D, C) would be preferable to mutual Cooperation. (It is required, for example, by Anatol Rapoport and Albert C. Chammah in their pioneering book, *The Prisoner's Dilemma*, Ann Arbor: The University of Michigan Press, 1965, p. 34.) The condition does indeed rule this out in a Prisoners' Dilemma supergame without discounting (and accordingly plays an important role in models of this supergame such as the one discussed in the annex); but in the present analysis, in which players discount future payoffs, it is *not* sufficient to make either of the alternation patterns Pareto-preferred to mutual Cooperation. In fact, for the B' player to prefer mutual Cooperation throughout the supergame to (B, B') or (B', B) we require $a_i > (y - x)/(x - z)$, and for the B player to prefer it we require $a_i < (x - z)/(y - x)$. These two inequalities, then, each holding for both players, are the necessary and sufficient conditions for mutual Cooperation to be preferred by both players to either of the alternation outcomes. I have preferred not to stipulate this but instead to analyse the conditions under which alternation occurs. The condition $2x > y + z$ is nevertheless a *necessary* condition for (B, B) to be preferred to (B, B') and (B', B) by the B' player (and is therefore a necessary condition for (B, B) to be an equilibrium), since one of the necessary conditions for this is $a_i > (y - x)/(x - z)$, and since $a_i < 1$ we must have $(y - x)/(x - z) < 1$, that is, $2x > y + x$.

4. The *N*-person Prisoners' Dilemma supergame

1 This was not made clear in *Anarchy and Cooperation*.

2 A different definition of the *N*-person Prisoners' Dilemma is given by Thomas C. Schelling in 'Hockey helmets, concealed weapons, and daylight saving: a study of binary choices with externalities', *Journal of Conflict Resolution*, 17 (1973), 381–428. He defines a 'uniform multiperson prisoner's dilemma' as a game such that: (1) each player has just two strategies available to him and the payoffs can be characterized (in effect) by two functions $f(v)$ and $g(v)$, which are the same for every individual; (2) every player has a dominant strategy (D); (3) $f(v)$ and $g(v)$ are monotonically increasing; (4) there is a number $\kappa > 1$, such that if κ or more players choose C and the rest do not, those who choose C are

better off than if they had all chosen D, but if they number less than κ, this is not true. Schelling's (1) and (2) are also part of my definition. His (3) is a much stronger requirement than my (iii). And his (4) is stronger than my (ii). For all I require in (ii) is that the first part of Schelling's (4) holds for $\kappa = N$; and I leave open the question of whether fewer than N individuals obtain a higher payoff when they all Cooperate (and the rest do not) than when they all Defect. Schelling's definition is therefore more restrictive than mine. His requirement (4), it seems to me, partly removes the 'dilemma' in the Prisoners' Dilemma.

Other ways of defining the N-person Prisoners' Dilemma more restrictively than I define it here can be found in Henry Hamburger, 'N-person Prisoner's Dilemma', *Journal of Mathematical Sociology*, 3 (1973), 27–48.

3 If there is some symmetry between the payoff functions of different players, the number of these equilibria might be smaller; but as long as *some* remain the problem to be discussed in the text would still arise. Only exceptionally would the asymmetry be such that there is just *one* subset of players such that $(B_n/C^\infty/D^\infty)$ is an equilibrium.

4 Michael Laver, 'Political solutions to the collective action problem', *Political Studies*, 28 (1980), 195–209; and Iain McLean, 'The social contract and the Prisoner's Dilemma supergame', *Political Studies*, 29 (1981), 339–51.

5 Early indications from simple computer simulation exercises with one such model (in unpublished work by Hugh Ward) suggest that a pre-commitment 'scramble' could occur which levelled out and stabilized at the desired subgroup size.

6 See the references in notes 14 and 15 to chapter 3.

7 A *very* small group *may* be 'privileged' in Olson's sense (i.e., there is at least one individual who is willing to provide some of the public good unilaterally), in which case, as we saw in chapter 2, preferences at any point in time are not those of a Prisoners' Dilemma, and the whole argument of this chapter is inapplicable. If there are *several* such individuals, each of whom has a very strong interest in the public good, a different problem of strategic interaction arises. See the discussion in chapter 2.

8 See the brief discussion in chapter 1 and for a fuller account see my *Community, Anarchy and Liberty* (Cambridge: Cambridge University Press, 1982), ch. 2.

9 This conclusion finds some support in Michael Nicholson's work, although his analysis cannot be compared directly with the one carried out here. See *Oligopoly and Conflict* (Liverpool: Liverpool University Press, 1972), Section 3.2. See also his discussion of this type of flexibility in chapter 6.

5. Altruism and superiority

1 Olson, *The Logic of Collective Action*, p. 64.

2 Brian Barry pointed this out in *Sociologists, Economists and Democracy*, at p. 32.

3 I have made this argument in more detail in 'Rationality and revolutionary collective action'.

4 A parenthetical comment is in order to explain why I have made no use of the model of altruistic behaviour proposed by Howard Margolis in his *Selfishness, Altruism, and Rationality* (Cambridge: Cambridge University Press, 1982), which on the face of it offers a much more realistic account of altruism than the simple one used here. Certainly, I believe that Margolis's theory is the most interesting attempt to date to incorporate altruistic motivation into a model of individual choice; but unfortunately it is radically incomplete and, as far as I can see, unusable. I have set out my reasons for reaching this conclusion elsewhere (*Ethics*, 94 (1983), 150-2) and will not repeat them here. To summarize drastically, an individual on Margolis's account allocates his resources between 'selfish' and 'group' interests in such a way as to feel that he has done his 'fair share', and the rule which yields allocations answering to this is as follows: 'the larger the share of my resources I have spent unselfishly, the more weight I give to my selfish interests in allocating marginal resources. On the other hand, the larger benefit I can confer on the group compared with the benefit from spending marginal resources on myself, the more I will tend to act unselfishly' (Margolis, p. 36). So the weight the individual gives to his selfish interests is a function of the *history* of his past (altruistic and/or egoistic) behaviour. But *how* this weight varies with the individual's history is not specified. Margolis does not in fact consider in detail any *dynamic* examples and it is not at all clear how the model can be applied to dynamic games in which there is strategic interaction over time.

5 What I have called Games of Difference have been considered by James R. Emshoff in 'A computer simulation model of the Prisoner's Dilemma', *Behavioral Science*, 15 (1970), 304-17. He refers to λ_i as the 'competitiveness parameter'. Pure Difference Games have been studied by Martin Shubik, 'Games of status', *Behavioral Science*, 16 (1971), 117-29, who calls them 'difference games'. He considers also a further transformation to what he calls 'games of status', in which there are only three different payoffs: one for winning (when the payoff difference is positive), one for losing (when the difference is negative) and one for drawing.

6 Sophisticated altruism or something like it is discussed under different names by Stefan Valavanis, 'The resolution of conflict when utilities interact', *Journal of Conflict Resolution*, 2 (1958), 156-69 and Thomas C. Schelling, 'Game theory and the study of ethical systems', *Journal of Conflict Resolution*, 12 (1968), 34-44.

6. The state

1 References to *Leviathan* (abbreviated *Lev*) are to the pages of the edition by W. G. Pogson Smith (Oxford: The Clarendon Press, 1909).

2 I must thank Brian Barry for helping me to see *Leviathan* in a more 'dynamic' light.

3 Alasdair MacIntyre, *A Short History of Ethics* (London: Routledge and Kegan Paul, 1967), p. 138.

4 H. L. A. Hart, *The Concept of Law* (Oxford: The Clarendon Press, 1961), p. 193.

5 Brian Barry, 'Warrender and his critics', *Philosophy*, 48 (1968), 117–37, at p. 125.

6 On symmetry, see chapter 3, note 6.

7 C. B. Macpherson, *The Political Theory of Possessive Individualism: Hobbes to Locke* (Oxford: The Clarendon Press, 1962).

8 The citations of Hume give the page numbers of the Selby-Bigge editions: L. A. Selby-Bigge (ed.), *A Treatise of Human Nature* (Oxford: The Clarendon Press, 1888) and *Enquiries Concerning the Understanding and Concerning the Principles of Morals* (Oxford: The Clarendon Press, second edition, 1902). The *Treatise* is abbreviated to *Tr* and *Enquiry* refers to *An Enquiry Concerning the Principles of Morals*.

9 David Lewis, *Convention: A Philosophical Study* (Cambridge, Mass.: Harvard University Press, 1969), p. 42. Lewis later refines this definition by adding the condition that it is 'common knowledge' in p that (1), (2) and (3) obtain. He also considers *degrees* of convention. But this 'first, rough definition' will suffice for my purposes.

10 Governments are in fact very active in establishing and modifying conventions and in many cases they make laws of them and punish non-conformists. If they are pure conventions, this is not necessary. For example, driving on the 'right' side of the road is almost a pure convention, and once it is established, there is almost no need for government enforcement: very few individuals will want to drive on the 'wrong' side. Of course, a central coordinating agency may be useful in *establishing* a convention more quickly and less painfully than it would establish itself 'spontaneously'. But this is not an argument in favour of government; for such an agency need have no *power*, and it need only be *ad hoc* and temporary: there is no need, in this connection, for a single agency to take charge of all conventions, and once a convention is established, the agency in question can be disbanded.

7. Epilogue: cooperation, the state and anarchy

1 Arthur Lehning (ed.), *Michael Bakunin: Selected Writings* (London: Jonathan Cape, 1973; New York: Grove Press, 1973).

2 For introductory accounts of problems of arms races and disarmament in terms of Prisoners' Dilemma games and of other international interactions in terms of Chicken games, see Anatol Rapoport, *Strategy and Conscience* (New York: Harper and Row, 1964); Glenn H. Snyder, ' "Prisoners' Dilemma" and

"Chicken" models in international politics', *International Studies Quarterly*, 15 (1971), 66–103; Glenn H. Snyder and Paul Diesing, *Conflict Among Nations: Bargaining, Decision Making, and System Structure in International Crises* (Princeton, N.J.: Princeton University Press, 1977); Robert Jervis, 'Cooperation under the security dilemma', *World Politics*, 30 (1978), 167–214.

3 See, most recently, Kenneth Oye (ed.), *Cooperation Under Anarchy* (Princeton, N.J.: Princeton University Press, 1986).

4 See the brief account of community in the penultimate section of chapter 1 above.

5 For example, Rupert Emerson, writing on the new nations of Africa in a volume on Nation-Building, has this to say: 'At the extremes, tribalism can be dealt with in two fashions – either use of the tribes as the building blocks of the nation or eradication of them by a single national solidarity. It is the latter course which is more generally followed.' And William Foltz, speaking generally of the new nations in his conclusion to this volume, writes: 'The old argument over the priority of state or nation is being resolved by these countries' leaders in favour of first building the state as an instrument to bring about the nation'. See Karl W. Deutsch and William J. Foltz (eds), *Nation-Building* (New York: Atherton Press, 1963). On European states, see for example Charles Tilly, 'Reflections on the history of European state-making', in Tilly (ed.), *The Formation of National States in Western Europe* (Princeton, N.J.: Princeton University Press, 1975), especially at pp. 21–4, 37 and 71.

6 Peter Kropotkin, *Mutual Aid: A Factor of Evolution* (London: Allen Lane The Penguin Press, 1972; reprinted from the edition of 1914), p. 197.

7 Richard Sennett, *The Uses of Disorder: Personal Identity and City Life* (London: Allen Lane The Penguin Press, New York: Alfred A. Knopf, 1971). This quotation is from the Pelican edition (Harmondsworth, Middlesex: Penguin Books, 1973), pp. 132–3, by courtesy of Penguin Books Ltd and Alfred A. Knopf Inc.

8 Richard M. Titmuss, *The Gift Relationship: From Human Blood to Social Policy* (London: George Allen and Unwin, New York: Random House, 1970). References here are to the Pelican edition (Harmondsworth, Middlesex: Penguin Books, 1973), quoted by courtesy of George Allen & Unwin Ltd and Pantheon Books, a Division of Random House, Inc.

9 *The Gift Relationship*, pp. 84–5.

10 *The Gift Relationship*, pp. 256–8.

11 Peter Singer, 'Altruism and Commerce: A defense of Titmuss against Arrow', *Philosophy and Public Affairs*, 2 (1973), 312–20.

12 This experiment is reported in J. H. Bryant and M. A. Test, 'Models and helping: naturalistic studies in aiding behavior', *Journal of Personality and Social Psychology*, 6 (1967), 400–7. The best source for reports of experiments of this kind is J. Macaulay and L. Berkowitz (eds), *Altruism and Helping Behavior* (New York: Academic Press, 1970), especially the chapters of the

first part, 'Situational determinants of helping'. Some of the experiments are also surveyed in D. L. Krebs, 'Altruism – an examination of the concept and a review of the literature', *Psychological Bulletin*, 73 (1970), 258–302, and in the chapter on altruism in Derek Wright, *The Psychology of Moral Behavior* (Harmondsworth, Middlesex: Penguin Books, 1971).

13 William Godwin, *Enquiry Concerning Political Justice* (abridged and edited by K. Codell Carter, Oxford: The Clarendon Press, 1971; first published in 1793), p. 221.

14 For Godwin on 'size', see especially pp. 249 and 216 of the *Enquiry*.

15 *Enquiry*, p. 271.

16 An English translation of *The Limits of State Action* did not appear until 1854, five years before the publication of Mill's *On Liberty*. I have used here the edition of J. W. Burrow (Cambridge: The University Press, 1969).

17 *The Limits*, p. 127.

18 *The Limits*, p. 83.

19 *The Limits*, chapters XII and XIII.

20 *The Limits*, p. 43.

21 *The Limits*, p. 43.

22 *The Limits*, p. 26.

23 *On Liberty* (Everyman edition, London: Dent, 1962), p. 164.

24 *Principles of Political Economy* (Vols II and III of *Collected Works*. Toronto: University of Toronto Press, London: Routledge and Kegan Paul, 1965), Book V, Chapter XI, Section 6.

25 In support of the necessity of government to the maintenance of security, Mill contents himself, as Humboldt does, with pointing out that 'Insecurity of person and property, is as much to say, uncertainty of the connection between all human sacrifice, and the attainment of the ends for the sake of which they are undergone' (*Principles*, Book V, Chapter VIII, Section 1. See also the final paragraph of the *Principles*). However, later, as we shall see, in treating of *other* exceptions to the rule of non-interference, Mill mentions (without reference to the general problem of security) that penal laws are necessary for 'free-rider' reasons.

26 *Principles*, Book V, Chapter XI.

27 *Principles*, Book V, Chapter XI, Section 12.

28 For the details, see Jon Elster, *Explaining Technical Change* (Cambridge: Cambridge University Press, 1983), part I.

29 See my 'Rationality and revolutionary collective action', in Michael Taylor (ed.), *Rationality and Revolution* (Cambridge: Cambridge University Press, 1987).

30 I argue this in more detail in 'Rationality and revolutionary collective action'.

Annex: the theory of metagames

1 Nigel Howard, *Paradoxes of Rationality: Theory of Metagames and Political Behavior* (Cambridge, Mass.: The M.I.T. Press, 1971).
2 Anatol Rapoport, 'Escape from paradox', *Scientific American*, July 1967, 50–6.
3 See for example pp. 55 and 62 of *Paradoxes of Rationality*.

Bibliography

Alchian A.A., and Demsetz, Harold. 'The property rights paradigm', *Journal of Economic History*, 33 (1973), 16–27.

Aumann, Robert J. 'Survey of repeated games', in R.J. Aumann, *et al.*, *Essays in Game Theory and Mathematical Economics in Honor of Oskar Morgenstern*. Mannheim/Wien/Zurich: Bibliographisches Institut, 1981.

Axelrod, Robert. *The Evolution of Cooperation*. New York: Basic Books, 1984.

Barry, Brian, 'Warrender and his critics', *Philosophy*, 48 (1968), 117–37.

Sociologists, Economists and Democracy. London: Collier-Macmillan, 1970.

Baumol, William J. *Welfare Economics and the Theory of the State*, second edition. London: G. Bell, 1965.

Bookchin, Murray. *Post-Scarcity Anarchism*. Berkeley, Calif.: The Ramparts Press, 1971.

Bray, Jeremy. *The Politics of the Environment*. Fabian Tract no. 412. London, 1972.

Brown, Lester, and Wolf, Edward. *Soil Erosion: Quiet Crisis in the World Economy*. Washington, D.C.: Worldwatch Institute, 1984.

Bryant, J.H., and Test, M.A. 'Models and helping: naturalistic studies in aiding behavior', *Journal of Personality and Social Psychology*, 6 (1967), 400–7.

Buchanan, James M. 'Cooperation and conflict in public-goods interaction', *Western Economic Journal*, 5 (1967), 109–21.

The Demand and Supply of Public Goods. Chicago: Rand McNally, 1968.

Chamberlin, John. 'Provision of collective goods as a function of group size', *American Political Science Review*, 68 (1974), 707–16.

Christy, Frances, T., and Scott, Anthony. *The Common Wealth in Ocean Fisheries*. Baltimore: Johns Hopkins Press, 1965.

Ciriacy-Wantrup, S.V., and Bishop, Richard C. '"Common property" as a concept in natural resources policy', *Natural Resources Journal*, 15 (1975), 713–27.

Clark, Colin. 'The economics of overexploitation', *Science*, 181 (August 17, 1973).

Crosland, Anthony. *A Social Democratic Britain*. Fabian Tract no. 404. London 1971.

Dahlman, Carl J. *The Open Field System and Beyond*. Cambridge: Cambridge University Press, 1980.

Demsetz, Harold. 'Toward a theory of property rights', *American Economic Review* (Papers and Proceedings), 57 (1967), 347–59.

Deutsch, Karl W., and Foltz, William J. (eds), *Nation-Building*. New York: Atherton Press, 1963.

Ecologist (editors of). *A Blueprint for Survival*. Harmondsworth, Middlesex: Penguin Books, 1972. Originally published as Vol. 2, No. 1 of *The Ecologist*, 1972.

Ehrlich, Paul R., and Ehrlich, Anne H. *Population, Resources, Environment*, second edition. San Francisco: W. H. Freeman, 1972.

Elster, Jon. 'Some conceptual problems in political theory', in Brian Barry, ed., *Power and Political Theory*. London: Wiley, 1976.

   Explaining Technical Change. Cambridge: Cambridge University Press, 1983.

   'Rationality, morality, and collective action', *Ethics*, 96 (1985), 136–55.

   'Weakness of will and the free-rider problem', *Economics and Philosophy*, 1 (1985), 231–65.

Emshoff, James R. 'A computer simulation model of the Prisoners' Dilemma', *Behavioral Science*, 15 (1970), 304–17.

Friedman, James W. 'A non-cooperative equilibrium for supergames', *The Review of Economic Studies*, 38 (1971), 1–12.

Furobotn, Eirik, and Pejovich, Svetozar. 'Property rights and economic theory: a survey of recent literature', *Journal of Economic Literature*, 10 (1972), 1137–62.

Glantz, Michael H. (ed.), *Desertification: Environmental Degradation In And Around Arid Lands*. Boulder, Colorado: Westview Press, 1977.

Godwin, William. *Enquiry Concerning Political Justice*, abridged and edited by K. Codell Carter. Oxford: The Clarendon Press, 1971.

Hamburger, Henry. 'N-person Prisoners' Dilemma', *Journal of Mathematical Sociology*, 3 (1973), 27–48.

Hardin, Garrett. 'The tragedy of the commons', *Science*, 162 (13 December 1968), 1243–8.

Hardin, Russell. 'Collective action as an agreeable n-Prisoners' Dilemma', *Behavioral Science*, 16 (1971), 472–81.

   Collective Action. Baltimore: The Johns Hopkins Press for Resources for the Future, 1982.

Hart, H.L.A. *The Concept of Law*. Oxford: The Clarendon Press, 1961.

Heilbroner, Robert L. 'The human prospect', *The New York Review of Books*, 24 January 1974.

Hobbes, Thomas. *Leviathan*, W. G. Pogson Smith (ed.), Oxford: The Clarendon Press, 1909.

Howard, Nigel. *Paradoxes of Rationality: Theory of Metagames and Political Behavior*. Cambridge, Mass.: The MIT Press, 1971.

Humboldt, Wilhelm von. *The Limits of State Action*, J. W. Burrow (ed.), Cambridge: The University Press, 1969.

Hume, David. *A Treatise of Human Nature*, L.A. Selby-Bigge (ed.), Oxford: The Clarendon Press, 1888.

Enquiries Concerning the Understanding and Concerning the Principles of Morals, L.A. Selby-Bigge, ed. Oxford: The Clarendon Press, second edition, 1902.

Jervis, Robert. 'Cooperation under the security dilemma', *World Politics*, 30 (1978), 167–214.

Kramer, Gerald H. and Hertzberg, Joseph. 'Formal Theory', in volume 7 of *The Handbook of Political Science*, F. Greenstein and N. Polsby (eds), Reading, Mass.: Addison-Wesley, 1975.

Krebs, D.L. 'Altruism – an examination of the concept and a review of the literature', *Psychological Bulletin*, 73 (1970), 258–302.

Kreps, David M., and Wilson, Robert. 'Reputation and imperfect information', *Journal of Economic Theory*, 27 (1982), 253–79.
'Sequential equilibria', *Econometrica*, 50 (1982), 863–94.

Kreps, David M., *et al.* 'Rational cooperation in the finitely repeated Prisoners' Dilemma', *Journal of Economic Theory*, 27 (1982), 245–52.

Kropotkin, Peter. *The Conquest of Bread*. London: Allen Lane The Penguin Press, 1972; reprinted from the edition of 1913.
Mutual Aid. London: Allen Lane The Penguin Press, 1972: reprinted from the edition of 1914.

Laver, Michael. 'Political solutions to the collective action problem', *Political Studies*, 28 (1980), 195–209.

Lehning, Arthur (ed.). *Michael Bakunin: Selected Writings* (in *Writings of the Left*, Ralph Miliband, ed.). London: Jonathan Cape, 1973; New York: Grove Press, 1973.

Lewis, David. *Convention: A Philosophical Study*. Cambridge, Mass.: Harvard University Press, 1969.

Loehr, William, and Sandler, Todd (eds). *Public Goods and Public Policy*. Beverly Hills, Calif.: Sage, 1978.

Luce, R. Duncan, and Raiffa, Howard. *Games and Decisions*. New York: John Wiley, 1957.

Macaulay, J., and Berkowitz, L. (eds). *Altruism and Helping Behavior*. New York: Academic Press, 1970.

McGuire, Martin C. 'Group size, group homogeneity and the aggregate provision of a pure public good under Cournot behavior', *Public Choice*, 18 (1974), 107–26.

MacIntyre, Alasdair. *A Short History of Ethics*. London: Routledge and Kegan Paul, 1967.

McLean, Iain. 'The social contract and the Prisoners' Dilemma super-game', *Political Studies*, 29 (1981), 339–51.

McMillan, John. 'Individual incentives in the supply of public inputs', *Journal of Public Economics*, 12 (1979), 87–98.

Macpherson, C.B. *The Political Theory of Possessive Individualism: Hobbes to Locke*. Oxford: The Clarendon Press, 1962.

Margolis, Howard. *Selfishness, Altruism, and Rationality*. Cambridge: Cambridge University Press, 1982.

Mill, John Stuart. *On Liberty*, Everyman edition. London: Dent, 1962.
  Principles of Political Economy (vols II and III of *Collective Works*). Toronto: University of Toronto Press; London: Routledge and Kegan Paul, 1965.
Milleron, Jean-Claude. 'Theory of value with public goods: a survey article', *Journal of Economic Theory*, 5 (1972), 419–77.
Mueller, Dennis C. *Public Choice*. Cambridge: Cambridge University Press, 1979.
Netting, Robert McC. *Balancing on an Alp: Ecological Change in a Swiss Mountain Community*. Cambridge: Cambridge University Press, 1981.
Nicholson, Michael. *Oligopoly and Conflict*. Liverpool: Liverpool University Press, 1972.
Olson, Mancur. *The Logic of Collective Action*. Cambridge, Mass.: Harvard University Press, 1965.
Ophuls, William. 'Leviathan or oblivion?', in Herman E. Daly (ed.), *Toward a Steady-State Economy*. San Francisco: W. H. Freeman, 1973.
Oye, Kenneth (ed.). *Cooperation under Anarchy*. Princeton, N.J.: Princeton University Press, 1986.
Popkin, Samuel L. *The Rational Peasant: The Political Economy of Rural Society in Vietnam*. Berkeley: University of California Press, 1979.
Rapoport, Amnon. 'Provision of public goods and the MCS paradigm', *American Political Science Review*, 79 (1985), 148–55.
Rapoport, Anatol. *Strategy and Conscience*. New York: Harper and Row, 1964.
  'Escape from paradox', *Scientific American*, July 1967, 50–6.
Rapoport, Anatol, and Chammah, Albert C. *Prisoners' Dilemma*. Ann Arbor: The University of Michigan Press, 1965.
Rubinstein, A. 'Equilibrium in supergames with the overtaking criterion', *Journal of Economic Theory*, 21 (1979), 1–9.
Samuelson, Paul A. 'The pure theory of public expenditure', *Review of Economics and Statistics*, 36 (1954), 387–9.
  'Diagrammatic exposition of a theory of public expenditure', *Review of Economics and Statistics*, 37 (1955), 350–6.
  'Pure theory of public expenditure and taxation', in J. Margolis and H. Guitton (eds), *Public Economics*. London: Macmillan, 1969.
Schelling, Thomas C. 'Game theory and the study of ethical systems', *Journal of Conflict Resolution*, 12 (1968), 34–44.
  'Hockey helmets, concealed weapons and daylight saving: a study of binary choices with externalities', *Journal of Conflict Resolution*, 17 (1973), 381–428.
Schofield, Norman. 'Anarchy, altruism and cooperation', *Social Choice and Welfare*, 2 (1985), 207–19.
Sennett, Richard. *The Uses of Disorder: Personal Identity and City Life*. London: Allen Lane The Penguin Press, 1971; New York: Alfred A. Knopf, 1970; Harmondsworth, Middlesex: Penguin Books, 1973.
Shubik, Martin. *Strategy and Market Structure: Competition, Oligopoly, and the Theory of Games*. New York: Wiley, 1959.

'Game theory, behavior, and the paradox of the Prisoners' Dilemma: three solutions', *Journal of Conflict Resolution*, 14 (1970), 181–93.

'Games of Status', *Behavioral Science*, 16 (1971), 117–29.

Singer, Peter. 'Altruism and commerce: a defence of Titmuss against Arrow', *Philosophy and Public Affairs*, 2 (1973), 312–20.

Smale, Steve. 'The Prisoners' Dilemma and dynamical systems associated to non-cooperative games', *Econometrica*, 48 (1980), 1617–34.

Snyder, Glenn H. ' "Prisoners' Dilemma" and "Chicken" models in international politics', *International Studies Quarterly*, 15 (1971), 66–103.

Snyder, Glenn H., and Diesing, Paul. *Conflict among Nations: Bargaining, Decision Making and System Structure in International Crises*. Princeton, N.J.: Princeton University Press, 1977.

Taylor, Michael. *Anarchy and Cooperation*. London: John Wiley, 1976.

Community, Anarchy and Liberty. Cambridge: Cambridge University Press, 1982.

'Rationality and revolutionary collective action', in Michael Taylor (ed.), *Rationality and Revolution*. Cambridge: Cambridge University Press, 1987.

Taylor, Michael, and Ward, Hugh. 'Chickens, whales and lumpy goods: alternative models of public goods provision', *Political Studies*, 30 (1982), 350–70.

Tilly, Charles. 'Reflections on the history of European state-making', in Charles Tilly (ed.), *The Formation of National States in Western Europe*. Princeton, N.J.: Princeton University Press, 1975.

Titmuss, Richard M. *The Gift Relationship: From Human Blood to Social Policy*. London: George Allen and Unwin; New York: Random House, 1970; Harmondsworth, Middlesex: Penguin Books, 1973.

Ullmann-Margalit, Edna. *The Emergence of Norms*. Oxford: Clarendon Press, 1977.

Valavanis, Stefan. 'The resolution of conflict when utilities interact', *Journal of Conflict Resolution*, 2 (1958), 156–69.

Ward, Hugh. 'The risks of a reputation for toughness: strategy in public goods provision problems modelled by Chicken supergames', *British Journal of Political Science*, 17 (1987).

Wright, Derek. *The Psychology of Moral Behaviour*. Harmondsworth, Middlesex: Penguin Books, 1971.

Index

Alchian, A.A., 27, 187 n.36
altruism, 13, 17, 33, 176–8, 193 n.4;
  defined, 111; effects of the state on,
  162–3, 164–5, 168–75, 177–8; in public
  goods provision, 109–10; pure, 112;
  sophisticated, 118–20; in supergames,
  120–2; *see also* eminence; Games of
  Difference; rationality
Assurance game, *see under* Games
Aumann, Robert J., 190 n.2
Axelrod, Robert, 69–71, 190 nn.7 and 8

Bakunin, Michael, 164, 194 n.1
Barry, Brian, 136, 187 n.29, 192 n.2, 194
  nn.2 and 5
Baumol, William J., 185 n.2
Berkowitz, L., 195 n.12
Bishop, Richard C., 187 n.37
blood donors, 170–2
Bookchin, Murray, 185 n.4
Bray, Jeremy, 185 n.5
Brown, Lester, 187 n.33
Bryant, J.H., 195 n.12
Buchanan, James M., 189 n.12
Butler, Bishop, 152
by-product theory, 12, 24

Chamberlin, John, 57, 189 nn.14 and 15
Chammah, Albert C., 191 n.16
Chicken game, *see under* Games
Christy, Frances T., 186 n.7
Ciriacy-Wantrup, S.V., 187 n.37
Clark, Colin, 21, 187 n.27
collective action: historical studies of,
  xii–xiii; problem of, ix, 3, 6, 13, 16,
  18–20, 21–30, 109
collective goods, *see* Goods, public
collective stability, 70
commitment, *see* pre-commitment
common property resources, 6, 20–1,
  26–8

community, 23, 28, 105, 167; effects of
  the state on, 166–75
conditional cooperation, 12, 13, 25, 31,
  65–9, 73, 84–8, 104–5, 129, 136–7, 145,
  166, 167
contract, *see* Hobbes, on convenanting
convention, 155–9, 194 n.10
coordination: equilibria, 71–3, 80, 87,
  103, 156; games of, 156–8
Cournot analysis, 56–8, 188 n.4
covenant, *see under* Hobbes
Crosland, Anthony, 185 n.5
crowding, *see* goods, rival

Dahlman, Carl J., 187 n.39
Demsetz, Harold, 27, 187 n.36, n.38
Deutsch, Karl W., 195 n.5
Diesing, Paul, 195 n.2
Difference Games, *see under* Games
discounting of future benefits, 12, 20–1,
  61, 62, 66, 68–9, 70, 81; in Hobbes's
  political theory, 139–40; in Hume's
  political theory, 154, 161

Ecologist, The, 185 n.4
egoism, 109, 111, 112–15, 164, 169,
  176–8
Ehrlich, Paul R. and Anne H., 185 n.7
Elster, Jon, 18, 19, 187 nn.25 and 26,
  196 n.28
Emerson, Rupert, 195 n.5
eminence, 111, 116–17, 122, 124, 127–9
Emshoff, James R., 193 n.5
environment: problems of, 2–3, 37, 43–4
equality, 117–18; in Hobbes's political
  theory, 141
equilibrium 39, 57, 63–4, 70, 78–9; *see
  also* coordination equilibria
experiments with Prisoners' Dilemmas,
  xii

203